(

LUCRETIA MOTT:
HER COMPLETE
SPEECHES AND SERMONS

Lucretia Mott

LUCRETIA MOTT:
HER COMPLETE
SPEECHES AND SERMONS

EDITED BY

DANA GREENE

THE EDWIN MELLEN PRESS
NEW YORK AND TORONTO

Edited, with an Introduction by

DANA GREENE

Studies in Women and Religion, Volume Four

The Edwin Mellen Press
New York and Toronto

Library of Congress Cataloging Number 80-81885

ISBN 0-88946-968-7

Studies in Women and Religion, ISBN 0-88946-549-5

Printed in the United States of America

FOR MY PARENTS

Dorothea Benson Greene
Charles Dresser Greene

in love and gratitude

*"Come my friends, 'tis not too late
to seek a newer world."*

Tennyson, Ulysses

ACKNOWLEDGEMENTS

I am greatly indebted to the following institutions: The American Philosophical Society and the American Association of University Women for their financial support of this project; St. Mary's College of Maryland for granting a sabbatical leave which enabled me to complete this anthology; Swarthmore College for permission to use both materials from The Friends Historical Library and the Peace Collection, and a photograph of the William Furness painting of Lucretia Mott.

Many friends and colleagues played a role in the completion of this work. I am especially grateful to Margaret Hope Bacon whose acumen and personal support for this project were invaluable; to J. William Frost, Albert Fowler and the Staff of the Friends Historical Library; to Herb Winnik for prodding me; to Delene Barry for her generous help in preparing the manuscript; to Lois Gibboney for all kinds of personal support services rendered; to Richard Roesel, my husband, who strengthened and encouraged me, and to all those who helped me understand Lucretia Mott's vision of a new world which even now is being born.

Dana Greene

St. Mary's College of Maryland
St. Mary's City, Maryland

January 1980

CONTENTS

Contents

NOTE TO READER

Lucretia Mott was a prolific speaker. Some of her speeches
may never have been recorded, some undoubtedly are lost, some
exist only in paraphrased form. This anthology contains her
extant speeches and sermons, all of which were recorded steno-
graphically. With only a few exceptions, Mott did not correct
her discourses. Since stenographers varied, there is no consistent form of capitalization or punctuation used throughout
these documents. Where the stenographer paraphrases rather
than quotes Mott directly, the language is enclosed, but
archaic spellings retained. In most cases changes in punctuation and grammar made by the editor have been bracketed.
Repetitions of examples, stories, and illustrations have not
been deleted since Mott obviously believed them to be potent
ways to communicate her ideas. An annotated index of proper
names is appended in order to assist the reader through the
labyrinth of persons mentioned in these documents. Bold face
titles have been added in order to expedite reference to
each discourse.

INTRODUCTION

1980 marks the centennial anniversary of the death of
Lucretia Mott. The passage of one hundred years confirms
rather than diminishes the important contributions of this
Philadelphia Quaker to the numerous social causes which
preoccupied nineteenth century American reformers. An
early abolitionist, supporter of woman's rights, partisan
of the free religious movement, she was as well a defender
of Indians and immigrants, proclaimer of temperance and
advocate of peace. Her contemporaries, admirers and adver-
saries alike, confirmed that Mott's defense of an issue
brought it respect and credibility. While some of her beliefs have been vindicated, her hopes for a world without
war, intolerance, injustice, and inequality have not been
realized. Yet her critique of society and her analysis of
social problems remain for the twentieth century reader
vivid and compelling.

Mott's pioneering role in major social reform movements in the nineteenth century has been recognized. For
example, her work on behalf of women was commemorated in
1923 when the Equal Rights Amendment was first introduced
in Congress as the "Lucretia Mott Amendment." Mott, heretofore principally considered a woman of action, is the
subject of numerous juvenile and two scholarly biographies,[1]
yet the breadth and consistency of her reformist philosophy
have not to date been explored. Although some of her pre-
vious correspondence has been published,[2] it reveals large-
ly the domestic Mrs. Mott——mother of six, emotional center

1

of a large, extended Quaker family, and gracious hostess to
abolitionists, feminists, runaway slaves, literati and beg-
gars. Other than her letters[3] and a diary of her trip to
England,[4] Mott left no written corpus.[5] In the primary materials published earlier, Mott's coherent reformist philosophy remains elusive. The principal source for the recon-
struction of this philosophy is her sermons and speeches,
all delivered extemporaneously over a period of forty-some
years at woman's rights conventions, anti-slavery and peace
meetings or religious gatherings. These powerful discourses
are buried in the proceedings of organizations, recorded in
the pages of reformist periodicals, or deposited in the manuscript collection of Friends Historical Library, Swarthmore
College.

This collection of Mott's sermons and speeches will
not only make readily available the principal source for
understanding Mott the reformer, it will hopefully do much
to counter the hagiography which has grown up around her.
In these documents Mott speaks for herself. She emerges
not as the ethereal, saintly creature portrayed by her sup-
portive contemporaries, but as a powerful and resolute
force in nineteenth century reform.

Although her constituencies were diverse, as an orator she relentlessly hammered away at the same themes. She
challenged irrationality in every form, be it exemplified
in custom, institutional stupidity, or superstition, and
called for a re-evaluation of society based on principles
of truth and righteousness. As an early feminist, she
brought with her insights won in the crusade against slavery, yet she was instrumental in establishing a woman's
rights movement which gradually gained autonomy from its
abolitionist origins.[6] What is less well known about Mott
is that she played an important role in other reform movements as well. She saw the causes of anti-sectarianism,
pacifism, temperance, and defense of Indians and the poor,
not as at odds with one another but as parts of the

general reform of society. Not only was she able to
achieve a remarkable correspondence between what she believed and what she did, she also was able to sustain her
activity and apply her principles consistently to a seem-
ingly endless array of societal problems. Her life was
integrated and her vision holistic; everything came within its purview.

Mott's sermons and speeches place her squarely within a prophetic tradition. She was above all a religious
woman who took as her mission to "proclaim liberty to the
captive." It was from her religious experience in the
Society of Friends that she fashioned her critique of society and her vision of its restructuring. Her sermons
and speeches contain the pieces of that religious world
view and the application of her religious principles to
the human reality she confronted in nineteenth century
America. They stand as testimony to the power of religious insight in the creation of a humane society.

Given Mott's active involvement in reform movements,
there has been surprisingly little attempt to reconstruct
her reformist philosophy or examine its sources.[7] Her sermons and speeches, which provide the best indication of
the nature of that philosophy, make clear that the principal influence shaping it was her religious experience as a
Quaker. Not only did that experience serve as the source
of an independent moral authority from which she could
criticize institutional power, it led her to reject all
forms of oppression and injustice. Although her life was
intimately connected with the Society of Friends, Mott always maintained that her views were not narrowly sectarian,
but reflected the universal teachings of the Spirit itself.
While it is impossible to understand her world view apart
from her Quakerism, her religious views were modified, affirmed, and clarified as a result of her intercourse with
Garrisonians, Unitarians, and transcendentalists. It was

her Quakerism, however, which opened her to the insights
of these groups.

Born Lucretia Coffin in 1793, the second daughter in
a family of seven, she was raised by Quaker parents on the
island of Nantucket. Although she left this tightly-knit
Quaker world for Boston when she was twelve, she always
considered herself a part of that former community. At
age thirteen she was sent to Nine Partners, a Quaker board-
ing school in New York State. Her experiences there were
seminal for her future development. Nine Partners was a
co-educational school which offered nearly equal education
to males and females. Although she did well there, and
was asked to stay on as an assistant teacher after com-
pleting the regular course of study, she chafed at the
fact that female instructors were not paid equally with
males. At Nine Partners she not only experienced first
hand the inequities endured by women, but also was exposed
to the horrors of the slave trade and the evils of the
slave system.[8]

It was at Nine Partners that she met James Mott, a
New York Friend whom she subsequently married. This was
the beginning of a long and tender relationship between two
Quakers committed to the reform of American society. Mott's
early married life was dominated by her involvement in
family concerns. She bore six children by the time she was
thirty-five years old. Early in those domestic years she
turned toward a re-evaluation of religion. When she was
twenty-eight she began to serve as an official minister in
the Society of Friends.

The Quakerism that Mott confronted in the early dec-
ades of the nineteenth century was very different from
that of the first Quakers of the mid-seventeenth century.
Early Friends were a despised, persecuted lot, immediately
distinguishable by their peculiar habits, customs and use
of language. Their central belief in the indwelling of the

Light or Spirit in each person, or, as George Fox, founder of the Society called it, "that of God in every one," had implications which were anathema to Puritans, Anglicans and Catholics alike. Quakers affirmed the spiritual equality of all persons, rejected a "hirely ministry" for a lay ministry, and maintained that the source of religious authority was not external, in the clergy, church or scripture, but internal, resulting from the indwelling of the Spirit in each person. Revelation, consequently, was not complete and objective, but on-going and personal. Scripture, while considered by early Friends to be Divinely inspired, was open to reinterpretation under the guidance of the Spirit.

Since the defining characteristic of a Friend was not doctrinal orthodoxy but a life lived in conformity with the experience of the Inner Light, the achievement of a moral life became the Quaker's paramount aim. In the early history of the Society, attempts to live out the dictates of such a morality resulted in regular persecution of Friends both in England and the colonies. By the eighteenth century, however, persecution had ceased and the Society's membership became more socially respectable. The prophetic character of early Quakerism was replaced by a quietism and an attempt to attain spiritual perfectionism by withdrawal from the world.

In the clash between Quaker ideals and worldly values, Friends began to withdraw from secular concerns. As pacifists they retreated from involvement in war and war-related activities. By the 1750s they had given up hope in the Holy Experiment in Pennsylvania. At the same time the incompatibility between their spiritual aims and slave-holding began to be widely recognized.

During the second half of the eighteenth century some Friends, responding to their heritage as a persecuted people, were led to an active involvement in attempts both to

protect Indians and to work for abolition. However, the
activist spirit did not permeate the Society as a whole.
While defense of the oppressed was deemed important, corruption by worldly values was a real fear. Tension over
the degree and kind of Quaker involvement in reform was
manifested as early as 1755 and remained strong through the
1850s. Friends did participate in their own philanthropic
activities, but they were admonished to be wary of the consequences of involvement with secular groups.

By the beginning of the nineteenth century the Society of Friends was in a state of spiritual decline. In an
attempt to remedy this decline, Quaker discipline was in-
flexibly applied. Although more and more members were disowned, the aridity of the Meeting continued. The strength
and the future of the Society were important questions for
all Friends. Thus, as a young minister in the Society of
Friends, Mott was confronted both with institutional rigi-
dity and spiritual sterility. This was the beginning of
her long conflict with the Society. She clung tenaciously
to Quakerism throughout her life even though there were attempts to disown her. Although she was often frustrated by
the intolerance and sectarianism she found within that community, she remained a member because she believed she
could do more good from within than from without.[9]

By the late 1820s Mott was caught up in the Great Separation which would rend the Society and further weaken it
for the rest of the century. Although the differences among
Friends had become more pronounced in the late eighteenth
century, it was not until 1828-29 that the Society in America divided into what came to be known as the Orthodox and
Hicksite branches. The bitterness and animosity engendered
by this separation seriously weakened the once cohesive
Quaker world.[10] At issue were questions of the importance
of doctrinal uniformity among Friends and the role Quakers
should play in worldly affairs.

The Great Separation had its immediate cause in
ideas promulgated by visiting English Friends during the
latter part of the eighteenth and early nineteenth centuries. These Friends, influenced by evangelical movements in
Britain, offered a new direction for Quakerism, one which
in many respects diverged from original Quaker tenets.
Placing an unprecedented importance on the authority of
Scripture as the principal source of the knowledge of God's
will, they also stressed doctrinal conformity and the authority of the elders. Their ideas found a positive reception particularly among the more urban, wealthy members of
the Society, that group which came to be called the Orthodox at the time of the Separation.

All Friends were not eager to accept this evangelical
emphasis, however. In an attempt to attain spiritual perfection, many returned to primitive Quakerism with its emphasis on seeking the truth and living righteously. In
general, these Friends were neither powerful nor the most
highly educated members of the Society. A diverse group,
they were called Hicksites because they were supporters
(although not doctrinaire followers) of the New York Friend,
Elias Hicks. Friends who rejected evangelical inroads,
who were quietists, or who, inspired by Hicks' boycott of
all slave-made products, entertained liberal social concerns, all found themselves within this camp. If there were
any one belief Hicksites accepted as central, it was that
of the indwelling of the Spirit in each person. It was
precisely this notion which had appeal for Mott and was to
have important implications for her life.

As a mature Friend, Mott chose to emphasize some aspects of that Quaker experience rather than others. At
the time of the Great Separation, both Orthodox and Hicksites vied for her support; she reluctantly followed her
husband's lead and joined the latter. She believed that
the ideals of primitive Quakerism were best expressed

in that branch and she supported Hicksite emphasis on the indwelling of the Inner Light.[11] This choice was to have important consequences both for her understanding of the role
and function of religion and for her understanding of herself as a person obedient to the Spirit. However, Mott keenly
remembered the pain of this Separation and later in life,
when other divisions occurred in the Quaker fold, refused
to lend her support lest she contribute to the further
splintering of the Society.

The Hicksite impact on Mott is most obvious in her
attack on both religious and secular authority which she
maintained were often illegitimate. Only truth gave authority, and the church as well as the state were frequently institutions of untruth, oppression and injustice. It
was in the personal experience of the indwelling of the
Spirit, a notion emphasized in early Quakerism and revital-
ized by the Hicksites, that one found truth and hence an
alternative source of authority from which to attack the
evils of society. Personal authority born of that religious experience could be constrained neither by Scripture
nor by the elders, as Orthodox Quakers maintained. Standing outside the bounds of mainline Christianity, Mott
claimed the authority of truth as the basis of her attack
against church and state, and took up a prophetic mission,
legitimated by the experience of truth, to combat injustice
and oppression wherever she encountered it.

Mott's acceptance of Hicksite notions also led her to
reaffirm the importance of righteous living and minimize
doctrinal orthodoxy. She continued this emphasis throughout her life and steadfastly resisted the tendency toward
orthodoxy that she subsequently found among Hicksites as
well. Her support in later years for the Anti-Sabbatarian
Convention and the Free Religious Association were manifestations of her hostility toward sectarianism. Her alternative emphasis on righteous living as the true mark of the

religious person led her to active involvement in reform
activities.

In the broadest sense, the Quaker tradition was also
important in forming Mott's understanding of what it was
to be female. From its inception, the Society of Friends
had always recognized the spiritual equality of women with
men as a corollary of the belief in the indwelling of the
Light in each person.[12] This notion provided the basis
for the acceptance of women ministers within the Society
of Friends. The non-sacramental Quaker ministry always
included numerous females who preached, travelled, and
gave their lives for the spread of the faith. The religious ideals of the Society oriented all female members to
hard work, plain living and a life of service, and provided them with the unique opportunity for prolonged periods of silence in which they could be in direct communion
with God. Although recognized as the spiritual equals of
men, women were not accorded equality in areas of church
governance. For example, women did not have equal power
with men to disown, that is to expel, members, or to make
discipline. They were, however, guaranteed certain opportunities for service. Since George Fox believed that wom-
en had special abilities to deal with the problems of the
widowed and orphaned, he insisted that they be organized
in a structure parallel, but distinct from, that of men.
In their business meetings Quaker women had unique opportunities not available to women outside the Society to
speak, to raise money, to create and manage their own activities.

Raised in this tradition, Mott accepted her spiritual
equality with men. She also had the opportunity as a minister to preach, travel, organize and agitate, all with
the blessing of the Society. While Quakerism obviously
did not claim secular equality for women, the opportunities
it offered its female members and the dignity it accorded

them could nurture such a claim. In the person of Mott,
the long-standing belief in female spiritual equality was
transformed into a full-blown claim for the secular equality of women.

     While Quakerism forged her world view, it also cre-
ated in her sympathies for other movements as well. Her
embrace of Garrisonian radicalism, as well as her openness
to Unitarianism and transcendentalism, all important influences in refining her views, were made possible because
of her Quaker background.

     Lucretia Mott met William Lloyd Garrison in 1830, and
until the Civil War, when his pacifism waned and his support for Lincoln increased, she remained his loyal champion. The mutual influence of each on the other was sub-
stantial: Garrison claimed that it was the Motts who liber-
ated him from the letter of the law and a narrow sectarian
attitude,[13] while they, on the other hand, embraced Garrison's views on slavery. It was he who convinced them
that the colonization of Negroes was an inappropriate response to slavery and that only unconditional and immediate
emancipation of all Negroes would end the heinous system.
Likewise, they accepted the Garrisonian notion that social
change would be achieved not through force or the ballot,
but through intellectual and moral agitation. Appeals to
reason and especially to moral principle were for the Motts
the essential motivators of reformist activity.

     The complexity of Lucretia Mott's initial negative
response to the demand for the extension of the franchise
to women is probably attributable to the influence of both
Garrison and her Quaker upbringing. Like all Quakers and
Garrisonians, Mott believed that women were the moral
equals of men. Likewise, she shared with some of the former plus all of the latter the thought that politics was essentially corrupt. Given this assumption, Mott probably
was reluctant to urge either males or females to direct

their energies towards politics. As a Quaker and Garrisonian, she saw herself working outside the political process,
agitating for its reform. When the question of the extension of the franchise to females was raised at the Seneca
Falls Convention, Mott opposed it. Her hesitancy, however,
was quickly overcome; she went on to work diligently for
the extension of the right to vote for both women and
Negroes.

Garrison's influence is also obvious in Mott's critique of American society. With him she believed that the
object of reform was not individuals but institutions,
particularly those of church and state which condoned, even
supported, many forms of injustice. Since individuals were
the medium through which these institutions were to be
changed, Mott called not for their religious conversion or
acceptance of certain doctrines, but for a correspondence
between their belief in Jesus' teachings and their personal actions. This call to righteousness and truth led
necessarily to involvement in the reformation of societal
institutions. Such reform activity became a moral
work in the process of which the individual would be per-
fected as well. Again, Mott's orientation toward social
reform, while rooted in a personal religious call, was affirmed and augmented through her interaction with Garrison.
Her strong Garrisonian commitment would subsequently cata-
pult her into another reform movement besides abolitionism,
that of woman's rights.

The Motts' opposition to slavery was long-standing.
As early as 1830, James Mott made the boycott of slave-made
products a personal issue by renouncing his cotton business
for one in wool. Eager to support more public efforts
against slavery, James participated in the founding convention of the American Anti-Slavery Society in 1833, and
Lucretia attended as one of the few female observers. Sub-
sequent to that meeting she took up the task of establish-

ing the Philadelphia Female Anti-Slavery Society in order
to enlist women in the cause of abolition.[14] Her anti-
slavery work throughout the 1830s led to her election as
a delegate of the American Society to the World Anti-
Slavery Convention in London in 1840. However, her alliance with Garrison, the hostility of the British committee
toward female delegates, and the suspicion of British
Quakers that as a Hicksite she was heretical, all contributed to her being excluded as a delegate.[15] Seated in
the gallery and supported by the presence of Garrison and
Wendell Phillips, Mott met Elizabeth Cady Stanton, the new
bride of abolitionist (but anti-Garrisonian) Henry Stanton.
This meeting provided not only the beginning of a life-
long friendship between these two feminists, but one of the
many personal links between partisans of abolitionism   and   woman's rights. In their wide-ranging discussions Mott and Stanton concurred on the degraded condition of women. By the end of the decade they would be
united in a common cause, the calling of the Seneca Falls
Convention in 1848.

    While Quakerism and Garrisonianism remain the most
important shapers of her reformist vision, Unitarianism
and transcendentalism also contributed insights which affirmed and bolstered her general philosophy. As early as
1818, Mott began reading the works of William Ellery Channing, the father of American Unitarianism. She was immediately attracted to his antipathy toward doctrine, his emphasis on this-worldly perfection, his commitment to hu-
manitarian efforts, and his belief in the innate goodness
of human nature and universal salvation. Although Mott was
sympathetic toward the Unitarian position, she never
claimed to be one. The Unitarians' exclusive emphasis on
reason as the only source of valid insight was unacceptable
to a woman who clung tenaciously to the belief in the indwelling of the Inner Light.

Among the transcendentalists, however, Mott found
like-minded believers in a superior source of knowledge.
The emphasis on individual intuition that she discovered in
the thought of Emerson and Theodore Parker was more appealing to her than the sterile reason heralded by Unitarians.
The transcendentalist belief in the immanence of God in
man and nature corresponded with Mott's belief in the God-
within and the identity of the laws of nature with the laws
of God.

More importantly, Mott found among transcendentalists
an affirmation of the Quaker notion of religious authority
within the individual. Divinity was within; it was a God-
given manifestation of truth inherent in each person. Authority emanated from that truth, and it was against that
personal truth that all beliefs and institutions had to be
measured and judged. Mott's slogan which she used extensively, "Truth for authority, not authority for truth,"
while rooted in the Quaker notion of the indwelling of the
Light, was also affirmed by transcendentalists. Drawing
from divergent sources, Mott molded together her various
insights into a coherent philosophy which we find best expressed in the sermons and speeches she delivered in the
course of her forty-year public career.

The principal theme of Mott's discourses is the moral nature of human life. It was her self-appointed task
to move her hearers, whether they be abolitionists, women's
rights supporters, peace advocates, Friends, Unitarians,
or anti-sectarians, to accept the belief that the goal of
human life was to live in righteousness and truth. Such a
life was possible only when the individual was freed from
custom, superstition and tolerance, from the physical
shackles of the chain, from impoverishment, and from legal
and social discrimination. Mott's quest for religious
self-perfection led her first to abolitionism. "I have
felt bound to plead their [the slaves'] cause in season and

out of season," she wrote,

> to endeavor to put my soul in their souls[']
> stead—and to give all my power and aid in
> every right effort for their immediate eman-
> cipation. This duty was impressed upon me
> at the time I consecrated myself to that
> Gospel which anoints 'to preach deliver-
> ance to the captive, to set at liberty them
> that are bruised'...[16]

Ultimately the liberation of all the oppressed became
Mott's self-chosen mission. She attempted not only to
awaken "the captives" to their own God-given powers, but
to attack institutions which continued their enslavement.

In Mott's eyes the contemporary state of religion
was deplorable. It was characterized by sectarianism and
dogmatism, emphasized priestcraft, theology, ritual and
ceremony, condoned injustice and inequality. It was for
Mott the antithesis of the practical religion of righteousness. Mott was particularly opposed to the churches' in-
sistence on the depravity of human nature. This, she maintained, not only contributed to human inaction and paraly-
sis, but necessitated another doctrine, the atonement of
Christ. Mott's rejection of both these dogmas made her
seem deviant to orthodox believers. She revelled in this
condemnation and proclaimed that she was a believer after
"the way called heresy." By this she meant that she saw
the function of religion not to proclaim dogma but to lead
the believer to follow the Spirit in a life of righteousness and truth. She continually railed against dogmatism
and called for free thinking and skepticism. She urged her
hearers to follow "true Christianity," "the word of God in
the soul," and to reject the priestcraft and superstition
which shackled them.

Mott condemned the church for its complicity with the
slave system and also vehemently castigated it for contin-

ued support of the subjugation of women. Her belief in the
necessity to crush its influence over women is evident in
the resolution she appended to the Declaration of Sentiments issued at the Seneca Falls Convention: "that the
speedy success of our cause depends on the zealous and un-
tiring efforts of both men and women for the overthrow of
the pulpit, and for the securing to women an equal participation with men in the various trades, professions and commerce."[17]

It is clear from her sermons and speeches that Mott
was aware of the systemic and institutional nature of evil.
She argued that all actions must be directed "to the overthrow of the outrageous system of American slavery."[18]
While she occasionally responded with personal support for
runaway slaves, she believed it essential to attack the
slave system itself; hence her unqualified support for the
boycott of slavemade goods. Likewise, she was concerned
that societal causes of poverty be examined. Although
throughout her life she scrimped and saved in order to
augment her gifts to the poor, she nonetheless claimed
that the Christian had to go beyond personal generosity
and seek the very sources of poverty.

Mott's hope for institutional re-evaluation and reform was at the center of her optimistic world-view. She
came to her analysis of societal problems with a positive
understanding of human nature which sprang from her religious belief in the indwelling of the Inner Light. She
recognized no fundamental dichotomy between reason and belief. Neither was there conflict between natural and divine laws: as God's creation, the world was governed by
laws people could understand. Although Mott proposed no
full-blown philosophy of history, like many of her contemporaries she was a firm believer in progress in history,
understood not as technological or intellectual progress,

but as moral advance, evidence of which she found in the
reformation of institutions. The establishment of equality,
the ending of injustice, and the elimination of superstition advanced the cause of humanity and were to her mind
holy works. The activities of the anti-slavery society,
she claimed, were "religious"; and of progress in ameliorating women's condition, she said, "I regard it all as divine."

    Although each of Mott's reformist activities was con-
gruent with her philosophy, it was her work in elevating
the condition of women which most clearly illustrates the
practical application of that philosophy. Unlike Stanton
and other later feminists, Mott's principal concern was not
with specific reforms like the franchise. Although she
consistently argued for equal rights and supported a myriad
of reform attempts, her central concern was always with
woman's self-definition and the expanding of the boundaries
of the female sphere. As Mott saw it, the condition of
woman was enervating and paralyzing: everywhere she was degraded. Any claim for her equality seemed ludicrous and
empirically indefensible.[19] Her degradation was attributable to the fact that she was defined not by herself but
by society. Mott argued that woman should disregard custom
and religious tradition, and attempt to define herself according to her God-given powers. Societal restrictions on
woman must also be challenged so that she might begin to
think of herself in a new way.

    To establish the fact that the degraded condition of
woman was neither natural nor divinely established, Mott
pointed to biblical and contemporary examples of strong,
heroic women. She believed that female inequality resulted
from the wages of sin. "The cause of the subjection of
woman to man," she said in her *Discourse on Woman,* "was
early ascribed to disobedience to the command of God. This
would seem to show that she was then regarded as not

occupying her true and rightful position in society."[20]
She also argued for the re-interpretation of the writings
of St. Paul which were often used to support the subordina-
tion of women. For example, as regards the Pauline admonition that women be silent in the churches, she said:

> All Bible commentators agree that the
> Church of Corinth, when the Apostle wrote,
> was in a state of great confusion. They
> fell into discussion and controversy; and
> in order to quiet this state of things,
> and bring the Church to greater propriety,
> the command was given out that women should
> keep silence, and it was not permitted them
> to speak, except by asking questions at
> home.[21]

At a time when evangelical religion was gaining increasing support from women, Mott pointed out that priestcraft was the greatest obstacle in changing the female condition. She set out as her goal the exposing of the untruth of its claims by contesting its authority on the basis of the authority of truth itself. Inspired by a deep
religious experience, yet free from the restraints of orthodox Christianity, Mott's position was unique and her attack powerful.

Scholarship on Mott has recognized her important role
as a transitional figure between the abolitionist and
woman's rights movements of the nineteenth century. More
than the Grimké sisters who preceded her or anyone who followed, Mott served as a bridge between these movements.
Throughout her long life she remained faithful to both
causes. It is not well known, however, that Mott frequently acted as a mediator between abolitionists and feminists
when they were at loggerheads over specific issues. For
example, when the bitter post-Civil War debates over the
fourteenth and fifteenth amendments strained the good will
between the two groups, Mott tried to reconcile them. This
role was particularly appropriate for her, given the

respect she had among these parties, her mediating personality, and her national stature as a reformer. Mott recognized that the substantive questions concerning these
amendments were made more difficult to resolve because of
personality differences among their proponents. Her inter-
vention proved frustrating and painful for her because it
often involved resolving animosities among her mutual
friends. She saw long-time ally Wendell Phillips, who defended the female delegation at the World Anti-Slavery Convention in 1840, claim that this was the "Negroes' hour"
and that votes for women should not jeopardize their long-
sought victory. While she lamented this position, she
criticized Stanton and Anthony for misunderstanding, for
being too hard on Phillips. On the other hand, she understood the sense of betrayal experienced by these women,
the "old pioneers" as she called them, and while she criticized their sometimes racist arguments, she remained their
staunch ally.[22]

Mott's efforts at reconciliation failed. The Equal
Rights Association formed in 1866 to secure political equality
for both Negroes and women was destroyed, as was the long-
time abolitionist-feminist alliance. The bitterness among
these groups contributed to the splintering of the woman's
rights movement as well. In 1869, Stanton and Anthony
formed the National Woman Suffrage Association. This was
quickly followed by the creation of the American Woman Suffrage Association led principally by Lucy Stone. The growing rift between conservative and radical factions within
the woman's rights movement was now public. While both
organizations supported suffrage, they differed on tactics.
Stone and the conservatives urged women to work only for
the franchise, while the more radical Stanton and Anthony
saw rights for women extending beyond the need for the vote.
In an effort to take up broader issues, the latter quickly became
associated with volatile causes such as divorce and free

love. Mott's sympathies were clearly with her old friends
Stanton and Anthony, although she continued to try to reconcile Stone and her followers with them.[23] She recognized that the central goals of the two suffrage organizations were not irreconcilable, even though the chasm between the leading personalities was too great to be
breached.

Not only did Mott serve the role of mediator among
reformers, as one of the oldest feminists she provided a
model for younger women. Elizabeth Cady Stanton, reminis-
cing of her 1840 meeting with Mott, wrote:

> Thus came Lucretia Mott to me, at a period
> in my young days when all life's problems
> seemed inextricably tangled; ....I often
> longed to meet some woman who had suffic-
> ient confidence in herself to frame and
> hold an opinion in the face of opposition,
> a woman who understood the deep signifi-
> cance of life to whom I could talk freely;
> My longings were answered at last.[24]

The even younger Susan B. Anthony, a fellow Quaker, recognized her debt to Mott when she claimed that when Lucretia
Mott was on her side she knew she was right.[25]

Besides her contributions as mediator and model for
abolitionists and feminists, Mott's eclectic philosophy
provided an important alternative argument to the natural
rights theory advanced by many mid-century feminists. The
Seneca Falls' Declaration of Sentiments, which represents
that latter type of thinking, was undergirded by secular,
rationalistic arguments. Like the Declaration of Independence on which it was modelled, it reflected Enlightenment
premises, different from those of older feminists such as Mott
who, while she accepted many of these rationalistic assumptions, appealed to religious experience and arguments as
well in her defense of woman's rights. Mott claimed that
woman's God-given powers were the basis for her equality
and that she had been naturally and divinely ordained as

the moral equal of man.   Her claim was rooted not in an
acceptance of   Deistic   principles but in the experience
of the indwelling of the Spirit in one's self.

Mott's pragmatic emphasis was different from that of
most mid-century feminists as well.   She saw that the
greatest need was not for suffrage or for any external
rights for women, but for the creation of a new female
self-image.   The notion that women could be moral, responsible beings was yet to be accepted; it was toward the realization of this idea that Mott directed her principal
energies.   She saw that the greatest obstacle to overcom-
ing both a degraded image of woman and the removal of limi-
tations on her rights was priestcraft.   More than any other
feminist she singled out the evils perpetrated against wom-
en by a dogmatic and sectarian religion.   The power of her
attack rested on the fact that, on the basis of religious
authority, she denounced as fraudulent the premise that
woman was divinely ordained as man's subordinate.   Mott
questioned the authority of such religion and rejected its
conclusions as spurious.

Lucretia Mott will be remembered as an important
force in shaping the woman's rights movement in the nineteenth century, as a tireless worker in the cause of numerous reforms, and as one who lent the credibility of her
person and the power of her presence to unpopular causes.
Although she continually complained that she was "much
overrated," even in her own time she was hailed as the
"Black man's goddess" and the "guiding light" of the woman's rights movement.   What is yet to be recognized is that
underlying her prodigious activity was a coherent philosophy which served as the basis not only for her critique of
institutions, but for her vision of the restructuring of
society.   At the heart of that philosophy was a religious
experience which both drove her to proclaim her message and
provided her with the personal authority to champion a new
consciousness of libertarian and egalitarian ideals.

NOTES

[1] Otelia Cromwell, *Lucretia Mott* (Cambridge, Mass.: Harvard Univ. Press, 1958). To appear in 1980 is Margaret H. Bacon's thorough and engaging *Liberating Woman, The Life of Lucretia Coffin Mott* (New York: Walker and Co.).

[2] Anna B. Hallowell, ed. *Life and Letters of James and Lucretia Mott* (Boston: Houghton, Mifflin Co., 1884).

[3] Mott's letters are principally in Mott Manuscript Collection, Friends Historical Library, Swarthmore College and in the Garrison Papers, Sophia Smith Collection, Smith College.

[4] Frederick B. Tolles, editor, *Slavery and the "Woman Question": Lucretia Mott's Diary of Her Visit to Great Britain to Attend the World's Anti-Slavery Convention of 1840* (Haverford, Pa.: Friends Historical Association, 1952).

[5] The following letters or articles of Lucretia Mott appeared in print: "Diversities," *Liberty Bell* (1844), 175-78; "What is Anti-Slavery Work," *Liberty Bell* (1846), 253-57; "Lucretia Mott to Edmund Quincy," *Liberator* (Oct. 6, 1848); "Lucretia Mott to The Woman's Convention to be Held in Salem, Ohio," *National Anti-Slavery Standard*, 4/13/1850.

[6] For treatment of this subject see Ellen Du Bois, *Feminism and Suffrage: The Emergence of an Independent Women's Movement in America, 1848-1869* (Ithaca, N.Y.: Cornell Univ. Press, 1978).

[7] Blanche Hersh in *Slavery of Sex* (Urbana, Ill.: Univ. of Illinois Press, 1978), begins this analysis.

[8] Mott MS. 1834-40. Notes by Lucretia Mott on her life given to Sarah J. Hale. Friends Historical Library, Swarthmore College.

[9] Hallowell, 123-24; 204-05; Cromwell, 112. Quoted from Lucretia Mott's 1842 letter to Richard Webb.

[10] For particulars on the Hicksite Separation, see Edwin Bronner, *'The Other Branch': London Yearly Meeting and the Hicksites, 1827-1912* (London: Friends Historical Society, 1975); Robert Doherty, *The Hicksite Separation* (New Brunswick, N.J.: Rutgers Univ. Press, 1967).

[11] Notes by Lucretia Mott on her life given to Sarah J. Hale.

[12]For a discussion of Quakerism and women see: Henry
J. Cadbury, "George Fox and Women's Liberation," *The Friends
Quarterly* (Oct. 1974), 370-76; Janis Calvo, "Quaker Women
Ministers in Nineteenth Century America," *Quaker History* 63
(1974), 75-93; Mary Maples Dunn, "Saints and Sisters: Con-
gregational and Quaker Women in the Early Colonial Period,"
American Quarterly XXX (1978), 582-601; Mary Maples Dunn,
"Women of Light" in *Women of America, A History,* ed. by
C. R. Berkin and M. B. Norton (Boston: Houghton Mifflin Co.,
1979), 114-32; J. William Frost, *The Quaker Family in
Colonial America* (N.Y.: St. Martin's Press, 1973); Keith
Thomas, "Women and the Civil War Sects," *Past and Present,*
13 (1958), 42-62.

[13]*William Lloyd Garrison, 1805-1879: The Story of His
Life Told by His Children* (N.Y.: Arno Press, 1969), I, 203-
04.

[14]For Mott's role in this Society see Ira Brown,
"Cradle of Feminism: The Philadelphia Female Anti-Slavery
Society, 1837-1840," *Pennsylvania Magazine of History and
Biography* (April 1978), 143-66.

[15]See *Slavery and the "Woman Question."*

[16]Notes by Lucretia Mott on her life given to Sarah J.
Hale.

[17]"Declaration of Sentiments: Seneca Falls Convention"
in the *Feminist Papers,* ed. by Alice Rossi (N.Y.: Columbia
University Press, 1973), 420.

[18]Mott, "Diversities," *Liberty Bell* (1844), 175-78.

[19]Lucretia Mott to Elizabeth, 3/16/1855. Garrison
Family Papers. Sophia Smith Collection.

[20]Lucretia Mott, *Discourse on Woman* (Phila.: T. B.
Peterson, 1850), 2.

[21]*Proceedings of the National Women's Rights Convention,* Cleveland, Oct. 5-7, 1853 (Cleveland, Ohio: Gray,
Beardsley, Spear Co., 1854), 61.

[22]Mott MS Lucretia Mott to M. Wright, 2/6/1867; Lucretia
Mott to ?, 5/8/1866; Lucretia Mott to Philadelphia, 6/11/1866.
Friends Historical Library.

[23]Mott MS. Lucretia Mott to Her Sister, 6/5/1869;
Lucretia Mott to Martha Wright, 7/16/1870. Friends Historical Library.

[24]Elizabeth Cady Stanton, ed. *History of Women Suffrage* (N.Y.: Arno Press, 1969), 1, 419.

THE TRUTH OF GOD...THE RIGHTEOUSNESS OF GOD

SERMON, DELIVERED AT MARLBORO CHAPEL,
BOSTON, SEPTEMBER 23, 1841

It is highly satisfactory to me, my friends, to meet
you. I rejoice to see so many fellow-beings without the usual distinctions which prevail in professing Christendom.
I believe that when they are so brought together, they may
hear, every man in his own tongue, the truths that may be
spoken; inasmuch as all truth is from "the sempiternal
source of light divine." There is no change in its principles. They are, and they have been, and will be, from everlasting: in their origin, divine—in their nature, eternal.

All who are believers in the truth of God, and in the
righteousness of God, must come to understand, that this
alone can set us free. But have we fully understood and
comprehended, how it is that only the truth can make free
indeed? In order to do so, educational prejudices and sectarian predilections should be laid aside; though to convince men of the necessity of doing so, might require as
notable a miracle as it did to convince men in a former age,
that in all nations, those who "fear God, and work righteousness, are accepted of him."

But what is it to fear God? and what is it to work
righteousness? It is as necessary now, as when the great
apostle uttered it, to say to men, "Let no man deceive you.
He that doeth righteousness, is righteous." But what is the
situation of most sects? What is their standard of righteousness? What evidence do they require of the fear of God?

25

Is it not the acknowledgment of some scheme of salvation,
or some plan of redemption, as insisted on in theological
systems, and taught in theological schools? Is it not a
confession of some creed, or a joining of some denomination?
And have not many thus blended the fear of God and the working of righteousness with outward and ceremonial rites, till
the result has been a lowering of the standard of peace and
righteousness, and of common honesty?

It becomes us to inquire, whether the plain precepts
and principles, which find a response in the soul of every
human being, and are confirmed by the inner sense which all
possess, and which have not their origin in any sect, or
body, or division, have not thereby been thought of less
importance than forms and ordinances. If this is so, and
if all see it in our various denominations, may we not all
profitably come together in the acknowledgment of principles and practices not dependent upon the reception of any
abstract doctrine, or form of worship? We may all feel here
in thus considering the principles and working of righteousness—the willing and the doing good—not as strangers, but
as much at home as in the town in which we were born: for
these principles are common to all, and are understood by
all. This is not presented by me as a Quaker tenet. I desire not to stand before you as a sectarian, but to hold up
principles of universal obligation.

I have seen that there is an objection, which seems
reasonable to many minds, against woman's stepping forth to
advocate what is right. Let me endeavor to remove these
prejudices and these objections: for I have often been made
sensibly to feel how hard it is to "do the work of the Lord,
where there is unbelief."

I know that many claim high apostolic authority against
this action of women. I am aware that the apostle Paul recommended to the women of Corinth, when they wanted information, to "ask their husbands at home." I am not disposed

to deny, that under the circumstances of the case, he did
it wisely. But do we find him saying, that they were not
to preach or prophecy? So far from it, that he has expressly given them directions how to preach and prophecy.
And what this preaching and prophecying were, is defined by
the same apostle as "speaking unto *men* to edification, and
exhortation, and comfort." Anyone will, I think, see that
to make a standing rule of the apostle's directions to the
ignorant Corinthian women, is to make him inconsistent with
himself, not only to those same Corinthian women, but in
his declaration to the Galatians, that, to as many of them
as had put on Christ, there was neither Jew nor Greek, male
nor female; and also in his expressions of gratitude to the
women helpers in the gospel.

Again, we find in the records of the evangelist, the
fact that four daughters of one man became public advocates
of the truth, and "honorable women not a few" are also
stated to have done the same thing. We read, also, of the
woman of Samaria going to the men of the city; and of Huldah, the prophetess. In the history of earlier times, we
read that the villages were in ruins through the land of
the Hebrews, and the highways unoccupied, till "Deborah
arose—till she arose, another in Israel."

This evening's opportunity would be far too short to
present the Bible argument, and I therefore refer you to
this volume itself, as its paramount authority is so generally acknowledged among you, to see whether there is not
far more plentiful testimony to the rightfulness of woman's
directly laboring for the gospel, than you had supposed from
perusing it without reference to this question.

Was it not one of the first acts of the apostles, to
announce, in the words of the prophet Joel, that the spirit
of the Lord was poured out upon all *flesh*; —and was not
this quoted to convince the people, that the prophesying and
preaching of both sexes was in fulfillment of ancient

prophecy? In the phrase in which "Phebe, the servant of the
church," is mentioned, those who are familiar with the original have found, that the same word, which is, in her case,
translated *servant,* is, in the case of men, translated *minister.* And has not conscious evidence been afforded by this
translation, of the priest-craft and monopoly of the pulpit,
which have so long held women bound? I ask the sticklers for
Bible authority, where they find the silence of women enjoined as a standing obligation. I find no such passage.
These objectors are bound to show that these injunctions
which they quote in favor of the silence of women, command an
obligation, binding on the church in all ages. But we find
them assuming the right to choose what they will consider
such. When the apostle recommends that widows shall not
marry, they do not agree with him, and therefore they explain
it as applicable only to those times of trouble and persecution; and do not consider it as a standing rule.

I long for the time when my sisters will rise, and occupy the sphere to which they are called by their high nature and destiny. What a change would then appear in the
character of woman! We should no longer find her the mere
plaything of man, and a frivolous appendage of society. We
should not find her so easily satisfied with a little domestic duty—with embroidering the light device on muslin
and lace, or with reading the sentimental novel. When I
look at the "Ladies Department" in our newspapers and magazines, I blush for my sex, and for the low sphere of action
they are content with. I believe that if woman would but
look seriously at herself, she would learn how great an
evil her nature suffers in being prevented from the exercise of her highest faculties. What a different race would
be brought forth—what a different and nobler generation
should we behold in the next, from that which preceded it,
if the high duties of women were all fulfilled! I believe
the tendency of truth, on this subject, is to equalize the

sexes; and that, when truth directs us, there will be no
longer assumed authority on one side or admitted inferiority on the other; but that as we advance in the cultivation
of all our powers, physical as well as intellectual and
moral, we shall see that our independence is equal, our
dependence mutual, and our obligations reciprocal.

It is this perception, my friends, that I long for. I
feel bound, when in company with my sisters who have thought
it improper or sinful to exercise their highest powers of
mind on the most important subjects, to beseech them to
think so no longer, and to come forth into that noble and
becoming freedom which they, in common with man, have received:——so useful will they then be in their own day, and
so happy will be their influence upon generations yet to
come.

I am aware that the imaginations of many have become
so depraved, and their minds so enervated, by appeals to
the passions and the imagination, from the inferior literature of the novelist, that it needs not only strong effort
to arouse them from the lethargy in which they live, to
true and noble activity; but a tender care is needed to
preserve them from the evils consequent upon their long inactivity. I am willing to incur ridicule——to become a
spectacle to angels and to men——if I thereby awaken any to
a sense of what the times demand of them. This is a day of
overturning and of change. Many are asking, "Who will show
us any good?" Theories and abstractions will not satisfy
them——outward observances will not be sufficient. The mul-
titude who are seeking, cannot attain what they desire, but
through the knowledge of themselves. I would speak to you
in the spirit of the gospel of the blessed God, of that un-
erring guide which shall direct you. I shall use in char-
acterizing it the language of a writer of your own: "All
mysteries of science and theology fade away before the simple impressions of duty on the mind of a little child."

We have each our different theories with regard to

creeds and forms; but let us not put them on a level with
what is of so much greater moment. While we tolerate (if
that can ever be a proper word to use in such a connection),
while we acknowledge the right of opinion, as regards the
various creeds and forms, let us not place these above the
pure and practical fruits of righteousness.

Is not this the reason why these fruits are so few in
the world? Look at the low state of public morals; look at
the prevalence and the general justification of war, and
slavery, and oppression; look at all the vices of society,
and see how the greatest abundance of creeds, and the utmost exactitude in forms, co-exist with them all; and judge
ye, whether these are not held up, rather than doing justice
and loving mercy.

What a field of labor does society now present! I rejoice to see the field white to the harvest. I rejoice in
a belief that the members of society are beginning to take
a practical view of its wants; and have, in some instances
at least, found that they cannot be satisfied with a mere
outward routine, but that something more efficacious is demanded by the present age. These are gathering themselves
together in the support of what is right; and let us bid
them Godspeed. Who can look at the crimes and sufferings
of men, and not labor for reformation? Let us put our own
souls in their souls' stead, who are in slavery, and let us
labor for their liberation as bound with them. Let us look
at the souls who are led away into hopeless captivity deprived of every right, and sundered from every happy association—the parents separated from their children, and all
the relations of life outraged; and then let us obey the
dictates of sympathy.

I cannot but rejoice in the efforts that they are making to
arrest the progress of war. The offering of a prize for
the best essay on the best mode of settling international
disputes, and the thousands of persons who thronged to hear

the addresses of George Harris at Birmingham on capital punishment, afford a cheering indication of an enquiring state
of the public mind in England. As enquiry proceeds, men
will discover the principle of forgiveness, and will feel
the power of the spirit of love. They will then become
more consistent with the Christianity they profess, and
will find that they must no longer indulge the spirit of
retaliation. In the course of our progress in the application of these principles, we shall have to put this sentiment in practice. We shall then understand the true spirit
of forgiveness, and conform our lives to its requisitions.
How is it that high professors of the Christian name can
forget the precepts of the blessed Jesus—"Love your enemies
—bless them that curse you—do good to them that hate you—
pray for them that despitefully sue you and persecute you."
Did not the apostle acknowledge the truth of this principle
of forgiveness, when he said, "Being defamed, we entreat—
being reviled, we bless?"

The time will not permit me to enlarge, or I would
turn your attention to further applications of gospel principles, and remind you, as we examined them together, that
"he that doeth righteous is righteous," of whatever sect or
clime.

I am aware that, in this city, the appeal has often
been made to you in behalf of the suffering slave. I am
sensible that most able appeals have been frequent here;
but the time has come for you, not merely to listen to them,
but to seek for the means of aiding in the working of this
righteousness. Whether you should act in organized societies, or as individuals, it is not for me to decide for any;
but we all have a part of the work to perform, for we are
all implicated in the transgression. Let us examine our
own clothing—the furniture of our houses—the conducting
of trade—the affairs of commerce—and then ask ourselves,
whether we have not each, as individuals, a duty which, in

some way or other, we are bound to perform.

When I look only over professing Christendom my soul
mourns over the doom to perpetual and unrequitted toil, the
entire deprivation of rights, the outrage of human affections, and the absence of all that makes life desirable,
which all unite to weigh down the lives of so many millions, while so few are ready to raise the cry of justice
and mercy on their behalf. Are there not men and women
here, whom these things shall yet constrain to exertion,
that they may be remedied? In how many ways may you not exercise your various powers for the alleviation of the miseries of those whose sufferings we have contemplated! You
have pens and voices to commend their cause to others, and
to portray their miseries so as to gain sympathy. To how
many towns you might go, and awaken their inhabitants to
the relief of these sufferings!

We are too apt to be discouraged, and to be impressed
with a sense of the difficulty of the work of reform: but
when we examine into the progress it makes, and behold the
effects of Temperance, and Peace, and Anti-Slavery, we may
be greatly encouraged, and bid each other Goodspeed, in
full confidence that, in due time, we shall reap, if we
faint not. We have sure evidence, from the success of
past efforts, that the same will be the effect in the future. Hard as was the labor at first, there [are] now far less
difficulties. Many hearts are now touched, and only need
the word of encouragement to come forth in aid of those who
so long struggled with so many disadvantages, under a load
of odium and opposition, to commence the work now so happily
advancing. Let me encourage the awakening soul to enter into the work. When the question arises as to the manner of
doing so, I can only say that what we sincerely desire to
do, we seldom lack means to accomplish. I know there is in
the community a growing dislike [of] organizations; but those
who adopt this view must remember, that it will not do for

them to do nothing.   "Herein is my Heavenly Father glorified, that ye bear much fruit."

It is too generally understood by men, that their labors must be connected with missionary and church efforts,
under submission to church-tests, and church forms: but it
is time we made a proper distinction between those who
merely cry,"Lord, Lord," and do not his righteous will, and
those who are bent on faithful obedience.   I am aware that
in this day of judging by verbal and ceremonial standards,
that such as have not submitted to the forms and rituals of
any church are obligated to suffer on that account in the
opinion of their fellow men. But those feel that they are
accountable to a higher power, and that "it is a small matter to be judged of any man's judgment."   They look for
guidance to their inner sense of right and wrong; and this
is coming more and more to be acknowledged as the voice of
God and his most intimate presence in the soul.   Let me
urge all, then, to be faithful to these manifestations of
his will.   It will [then] bring upon the reproach of high
professors.   But if they are faithful, they will be instant
at all times in raising high the standard of righteous action, and they will, by their practice, do more to recommend the faith of God, than those who are denouncing them.
Those who have regarded these good works more than plain
dress, or formal speech, or observance of times, or stated
reasons of vocal prayer, will be ready to proclaim that the
gospel is not in these outward things, while some, who make
high professions, are ignorant both of the scriptures and
of the power of the gospel.   Let us be faithful to the word
lying in the heart, and there is no need to doubt but we
shall be brought to love every good word and work, to promote
the progress of righteousness, temperance, and peace and to
keep ourselves unspotted from the world.

How often have I mourned, that so many in the cities
depart from the plain path of integrity! How much selfish-

ness and deception is there in trade!   "It is naught, it is
naught, saith the buyer; but when he hath gone his way, then
he boasteth." How many look not on the things of Jesus
Christ! But, do we not see that the principles of our holy
religion would reform commerce and trade, and lead every
man to do justly? Surely the cry of the oppressed is entering into the ears of the Lord of Sabaoth. Many who look at
other lands, and witness the sufferings of their people,
and see how the poor are crushed by oppression and taxation,
to maintain the existence and the prerogatives of an aristocracy, turn with delight to the hope of a reform co-
extensive with the earth. They realize that true republicanism is true Christian democracy. But it is because they
see not how reform is to be obtained, that they are slow of
heart to believe in its possibility. Let them not participate in the wrong they acknowledge. "If thy right hand offend thee, cut it off." If we applied the precepts of Jesus
to the direction of our own lives, how many that are now
rich would become poor. I believe that the principles of
righteousness can be carried out through the land, and that
we show our reverence for God by the respect we pay his
children. We do not sufficiently exercise our high moral
nature. We resist the benevolent principles and feelings
that would lead us forth into lanes and by-ways, that we
might comfort and save the outcast and afflicted. We forget that this is true religion and undefiled, and to keep
ourselves unspotted from the world. We may, after the manner that some call heresy, worship the God of our fathers;
but if we wish to serve him in the way prescribed by his
dear Son, we shall carry out the principles of righteousness in the service of our brethren and of society; nothing
doubting that if we do so, it will be well with us hereafter. Further we need not too curiously inquire, but be
content with the evidence of God's peace in our souls,
after having done his will.   [Liberator, October 15, 1841].

RIGHTEOUSNESS GIVES RESPECT TO ITS POSSESSOR

*SERMON, DELIVERED IN THE UNITARIAN CHURCH,
WASHINGTON, D.C., JANUARY 15, 1843*

"Righteousness exalteth a Nation, but sin is a reproach to any People."

I doubt not but that this scripture truth will be readily assented to by this congregation, for there is a universal admission of the truth, that righteousness gives respect to its possessor. It is equally true of individuals as of nations; and it is a fact worthy of our observation, that throughout all the scripture, through all the dispensation of which that scripture gives us an account, that religion, justice, mercy, and all the principles of righteousness are highly exalted above the various forms of worship—the speculative doctrines of the age. But we are prone to forget this in our zeal for sectarian theology; in our earnest endeavor to exalt our favorite forms and rituals, and in the idea that has prevailed to a considerable extent, that we are the favorites of Heaven, we come to regard our sect or our professions of religion more than the practice of righteousness, of goodness, of truth. We confound truth with our sectarian forms, our systems of faith and our theology. We should duly discriminate between that which has its origin in the schools of science, and theology, and those principles which are divine in their origin and eternal in their nature. Righteousness exalteth all who love it, and God in his gracious condescension to the children of men, has caused them to be exalted in pro-

35

portion as they have adhered to it through the variety of
the forms of worship and through gross misrepresentation
they have received the censure of devoted worshippers.
Those only are true worshippers who walk uprightly, and
love righteousness—who despise the gains of oppression—
those who do not close their eyes and shut themselves out
from their own flesh.

Such has ever been accepted with God. It is no new
doctrine. When Jesus and his apostles preached it, they
declared it was of God and was good. The people imagined
that he and his disciples had some new doctrine, but they
declared it was that which was from the beginning; it was
the same in all ages. The Jews, it is true, and Israel of
old, were so sunk in their forms and ceremonies that they
imagined they were the people of the Lord. They supposed
they must go forth with the rounds of ceremonies—go to the
temple of the Lord and even go forth unto the holy place
called by this name, so that their prophets declared against
them, "ye still burn incense and work after other gods whom
ye know not." And, "ye say the way of the Lord is not
equal." This has been the cry down to this day, that we
are so constituted that we must live in sin—that we are
more prone to evil than to good and we must depend on a vicarious atonement for our salvation; and this is called a
mysterious operation to cleanse us from our iniquity. It
proceeds from an unworthy examination of the scriptures,
"ye err, not knowing the scripture or the power of God"—
perverting the letter to your own destruction.

In no other way can I account for the great strength
of sin in professing christendom than for the long prevalence of this doctrine. Men have been taught that they
were more prone to evil than to good; hence they early fall
into temptation and yield to the sins that beset them, from
the very circumstances of being thus taught. "Oh House of
Israel, is not my way equal? Are not your ways unequal?

When a righteous man turneth away from his righteousness,
and committeth iniquity, and dieth in them, for his iniquity that he hath done, shall he die?"   Again, "when the
wicked man turneth away from his wickedness that he hath
committed, and doeth that which is lawful and right, he
shall save his soul alive, he shall surely live, he shall
not die, the soul that sinneth, it shall die."

     It is time the noble dignity of man was elevated to a
higher standard of goodness and truth—to that elevation
which God designed us to occupy.   I believe it to be high
time there was more christian boldness, more moral courage,
amongst mankind to speak to the sentiment of their hearts,
whether they be in accordance with the popular doctrines of
the day or not.   And there is already a bursting forth of
more independence of expression, of opinion among men—a
greater freedom in their declaration of thought and of belief; they are becoming dissatisfied with the dogmas and
theologies that they have been taught.   If we take a child
and teach him that he has a wicked heart, will he not be
more likely to fall into evil practices?   Teach him that he
is necessarily, and unavoidably corrupt, and will he not
feel discouraged?   But instead of this, instruct him in the
way he should go, then will conviction be daily implanted
in his breast, and he will feel the dignity of his nature
and the responsibility of his elevated station among created beings, and consequently be encouraged to works of
righteousness.   There is something in a child of heavenly
nature, which only needs to be cultivated; and well might
Jesus have held up the child in the midst of an assembly
and declare "of such was the kingdom of heaven."   How far
does this go to disprove the doctrine which has been taught?
Think ye that this child would have been held up as a fit
emblem of the kingdom of heaven if it had not been pure and
innocent?   The doctrine of natural depravity which has obtained so long in the world, does not appear to have any

connexion with the subject of righteousness, having no effect upon the conduct calculated to promote practical religion. But it would be a waste of time for me, at present,
to undertake to controvert this doctrine.

We all have a right to our own sentiments, we claim
this as a right, but when we find sentiments to effect the
conduct of men——when we find such opinions fastened upon
the community as the essential doctrine of christianity and
made a test of the christian character, and when this standard is regarded as more holy than the standard of practical
righteousness in order to elevate the faith, then would it
be well if there were more who would examine the subject and
declare what were their convictions upon it, even though
they should thereby subject themselves to the charge of
heresy or infidelity. Let us come to the disposition of the
apostle when he said, "it is after the manner that the world
calls heresy that I worship the father." Jesus taught the
heresy of that age, and it was his opposition to the cherished forms and creeds of that day that constituted his
greatest offense. We do not regard this heresy in its true
light——we are disposed to adhere to the systems we have
been taught, and to consider it heresy to call them in question, or even to endeavor to test their truth by the evidences of light and reason. As to the miracles which were
performed in that day, it is not a matter for us to dispute,
they were adapted to the age in which they were wrought, and
were performed to answer a great end; instead of questioning
them, ought we not rather endeavor to approach the Divinity
by purity of this life, which is emphatically said to have
been created for the glory of God. Thus will we come to be
the children of God. Let us love that Divinity of Christ
that is conformable to man's intelligence and reason, and
not be led by that construction of it which is tending to
divest him of some of the noblest feelings of his nature,
and to lower him in the scale of creative existence. The

objector may ask, does not this conflict with the doctrine
of the new birth? I think not. I think I understand the
scriptures. The new birth is not placed upon the principle
of the first birth being impure or wicked. We have a natural and a spiritual nature—that which partakes of the animal and that which partakes of the divine nature, and as we
receive more of the Divinity dwelling upon the spiritual
part we come to have our first nature brought out, and our
feelings exalted with the operation of the love of God upon
the soul. "That was not first which is spiritual." The
spiritual is one, the natural another. The carnal mind is
not subject to the law of God. But when he speaks of the
carnal mind, it is as men have given up to their propensities and yielded to the lust of the flesh.

But this Divine Goodness which is in every child, if
cherished and adhered to old age, will enable us to realize
all the christian enjoyments of communion with God and his
dear Son. Oh this kingdom, were it but understood—divested
of all the gloom and mysticism by which it is surrounded,
how beautiful would religion appear, and how readily would
it be embraced!

I come before you to preach no other righteousness, no
other gospel, but the righteousness of God, that which is a
spiritual righteousness—let that gloom which has been connected with it be removed; divest it of this, and of the
complicated system of theology, and I believe it will meet
conviction in every breast. Divest it of this, and men will
not reject the truth, let it come from what source it may.
But the minds of the people are instructed not to receive
truth except it come through the channel of certain rituals
and ordeals, and thus are their sectarian preferences prepared. These forms and rituals though they may have been
used in the days of the Apostles are but the shadow of
things to come—so with washing and other outward ordinances. Yet these are all to pass away—they are but a school-

master to bring us up to Christ. Do they contain any of the
real substances of religion? I ask you not with any desire
to shock the prejudices of any, but are these forms not
taking the place of the reality—of the principle? are they
not exalted to a higher estimate than the real practical
duties of life? has Jesus given any forms of worship? His
Prophets declare that these things were to pass away, and
that a new heaven and a new earth were to be created. I
know that speculative religionists have removed this to the
millenial day, and referred us to that day which should
bring about that glorious period when righteousness should
cover the earth as the waters cover the sea; but theology
is removing far the day instead of bringing it home close
to our doors. This is a state of things to be brought about
only when men prepare themselves to meet it, when men shall
have executed their nature and subdued their evil propensities. Then may we look for the fulfillment of that prophetic declaration that "the kingdoms of this world shall become
the kingdoms of our Lord and of his Christ." But those
forms of worship and those opinions and doctrines, may be
suited to those who practice them, and far be it from me to
judge anyone for praticing such things—but we may be teaching certain modes of speech, of observances, or peculiarities—no matter of what form—it may be music, it may be
vocal or silent exercise, any, or all of these may be the
gods we may be found worshipping; and while others may appear as idlers, performing none of these ceremonies, yet we
may be found to be as far off the true God as they, or even
they who are worshipping a heathen god; they worship heathen
gods, and we verbal ones. Now let us inquire as regards the
professors of the christian name in our strict adherence to
the rituals of our respective churches—are we not in as
much danger now of building up some images, as were those
who were denounced for such things in former days as guilty
of the grossest idolatry? And how shall we appear before

the Lord? No matter what were the customs in the Jewish
church—no matter what their offerings were—whether a lamb,
an ox or whether incense—they were not the rule for us.
"It is shown unto thee, Oh man,what is good, and what the
Lord thy God doth require of thee." "Who among us shall
dwell with everlasting burnings? He that walketh righteously and speaketh uprightly; he that despiseth the gain of oppressions, that shaketh his hands from holding of bribes,
that stoppeth his ears from hearing of blood, and shutteth
his eyes from seeing evil; He shall dwell on high, his place
of defense shall be the munition of rocks, bread shall be
given him, his water shall be sure." It was against those
who ground the face of the poor and practiced unrighteousness, that complaint was made. And we should contrast our
professions with our practices, and I think we will perceive
that the charge of neglecting our christian duties, is as
applicable to us as it was to those formerly, and that they
would be a reproach to any people. Does not Christianity
enjoin upon us to bring our principles to the practice of
everyday life? Did not Jesus Christ come immediately in
contact with the forms and customs of that day? It would
have been an easy thing for him to wash his hands before he
[ate],and it would be of small consequence, or appear so,for
him to conform in this respect; but it was his mission to
break down these forms and ceremonies, and institute a
practical religion. He was almost daily brought up before
the Jews of his day for offenses against their laws and
regulations. We have the account and it would be well for
us to compare it with the institutions of our day, and see
whether the effect would not likely be the same, were anyone
to rise up in the present age against prevailing practices,
and proclaim among the assemblies of the people the truths
which he did in those days. Would he not have to offer up
his life?

I am glad there are a few who have ventured to come

forward and declare the whole truth of God—who are placing
these things in their true light, and the consequence of
their labors I verily believe, will be to place the standard of true practical righteousness higher. For when we
live out the practical christian, and show by our love for
our brethren, and our consistent walkings, that we are the
followers of Christ, we shall elevate the standard of righteousness, though we shall manifest no tenacity for our forms
and creeds.

But as a community of christians, are we endeavoring
to preach to the poor—to plead for the widow, and striving
to promote that righteousness which exalteth a nation? are
we endeavoring to remove the great evils which beset us as
a nation? If this were the case would these great sins
which blight this country be suffered to remain? would war
still be slaying its thousands in our land? would slavery
be crushing its millions? would intemperance, and vice, and
wickedness in its various forms, continue to oppress the
weak, and harrass the poor, and corrupt the morals of our
citizens? Would the name or the depth of the purse, intelligence, or literary attainments be the criterion of respectability? would the principles of right be made subservient
to notions of honor or rank, and the standard of true piety
and virtue be thus lowered?

We see righteousness with many is nothing in comparison
to an adherence to the church ceremonies; the creeds of
faith and to the fashion and usage of society. They consider
this *faith* essential and that no one can enter into the
kingdom of Heaven without it. At the same time vice and
wrong are suffered to remain unrebuked, and teachers of
religion may glide along in the popular current with a faith
without works. It is considered a delicate subject to speak
of the slaveholder, and it is forbidden; and are there not
things done in secret of which it is a shame to speak and
must be passed over in silence? Is there not a fear as

regards the question of slavery, a fear to permit it to be
examined? I ask the question, not in the spirit of reproach; I do not wish to injure the feelings of a single
individual. If we could come together in a christian spirit, and with a right estimate of the true dignity of man,
we would calmly and profitably discuss our best interests;
the petition walls of prejudice,   sectarian and sectional
jealousies would be the standard which we would seek to
erect, and although we should retain many of our peculiar
views, we might enjoy them without enforcing them upon others. When we come to understand thoroughly our duties as
christians, we will not judge a brother, though we may warn
one another. We will be bound together in love without regard to denomination or sex. We shall then come to find our
petition walls [to] be broken down. The schoolmaster which
was to lead us unto Christ will no longer be needed, for
we shall then have attained to the substance of which the
old Jewish ceremonies were but the shadow.

I come before you this evening, my friends, with all
the disadvantages of a woman breaking through the proscribed
customs of the times, to endeavor to elevate the standard
of righteousness and to promote the common well being of
mankind; and I desire to be received in that spirit which
has induced me thus to appear before you. There has been a
great advancement among the people with regard to woman.
Her condition is destined to become improved and elevated—
she is already regarded in a very different light from that
assigned to her from the dark ages; and she should come also to appreciate herself and be seeking to something higher
than she has formerly done. She has already entered into
many of the scientific and literary subjects of the age,
and is enjoying the benefits of lyceums, and lectures and
literary associations. Joining in these enjoyments, go to
prove she is aspiring to something higher than the mere accomplishments and amusements of the day. Woman has long

been excluded from the privilege of speaking to the people,
and the bible has been applied to for a sanction of this exclusion of her right to speak, even to the men of the cities.
But the bible has been quoted to authorize nearly every
wrong in which the people have been found. The example of
darker times is considered a sufficient authority for the
present age; but is an unworthy application of the scriptures.

[A few sentences were here uttered which were not distinctly heard by the reporter, the import of which seemed to
be the incompatibility of the exclusion of females from ministerial services, with the spirit of christianity—that in
Christ Jesus male and female were one, and though it might
be considered as transcending the modesty of her sex, for a
woman to speak in public she did not understand Christ so.
She hoped to see a better use made of the scriptures in this
respect than had been done. She alluded to the announcement
of the disciples on the day of Pentecost, that the prophecy
of Joel was fulfilled—that daughters as well as sons should
prophecy—that Philip had four daughters who did prophecy
which was defined "speaking to men in edification, and exhortation and comfort"—that Tryphena and Tryphosa were
acknowledged co-laborers with Paul, as well as Phebe the
servant of Christ, which meant minister, &c.]

And I believe it is important that we should endeavor
to disabuse the christian mind with regard to this subject.
This idea has obtained to a great extent in the christian
world but will yet present itself in its true light through
the singleness of woman.

It is then under these disadvantages that I am constrained to appear before you, and to urge upon your consideration the plain principle of right that we should all in
our various sects and denominations, and those who are of
no denomination, contribute what we can to the advancement
of practical righteousness in the earth. I feel for those

of this age who are thus stigmatised and denounced because
they have not been willing to receive the orders and ceremonies that have been imposed upon them—for some of these
my feelings have often been enlisted; that they may be
faithful to that which they have seen, which will prove to them
to be their Saviour; that which was with them in their
youth, and was their comforter in their hour of affliction.

Oh ye who are not of any denomination, whose aspirations to God do nevertheless ascend with a confidence in
the impartiality of the arm of his protecting power, it
will not be by your outward profession but by your works
of righteousness that you will show forth your faith; if
you yield yourselves to him, and are willing to know his
ability—his glorious attributes—he will know you also—
he will set you above all the scoffs and frowns of the
world.

There are thousands who have stepped out of the common
round whose virtues will be admired by ages yet unborn. He
who is now gone, but whose benevolence even in other lands
has commanded respect and admiration; he who acknowledged
the universal brotherhood of man, and secured the love of
all, and that respect which gives evidence that righteousness exalteth—yes, the name of CHANNING will be long remembered and revered; he was willing so far to lose his popularity for the time being as to tread upon what is considered one of the most unpopular topics of the day; he
ventured to speak to the slaveholder—he was willing to
forego the small consideration of present popularity, for
the sake of lending the influence of his powerful mind to
the work of disenthralling this guilty nation.

The language in which he uttered his sentiments will
be felt, though his name will be no more heard among us.
His appeals to the intelligence of the people in this country in behalf of the African bondman—engraven upon the im-
perishable pages of history, will be transmitted to pos-

terity to be commended and admired. Though *he* is gone, the
labor of his pen is still doing its work, and his appeals
are not made in vain. There is in this nation an awakening
up—there is an increasing disposition to hear, not on one
subject only, but upon all.

I am aware of the place I stand; I know there are many
who will not allow anything to be said in behalf of the
slave. But I believe it to be my duty to plead the cause of
the poor and of the oppressed whether they will hear or
whether they will forbear. I have long believed that an
obedience to christian duty required that more mouths should
be opened upon this subject. Yet I do not regard this as an
evil resting upon any particular part of the country, but
"we are all verily guilty concerning our brother"; the manu-
facturers of the north, the consumers of the various commod-
ities of southern productions, are implicated in this matter,
and while the sweets of this system are found upon our tables we are partakers of other men's sins. I remember one
of your great statesmen of South Carolina, how he showed
that the north and east were deeply implicated in this subject, that we received as great profits as the immediate
agent in this unlawful, this unjust business. So regard me
not as coming here with vituperative language against any
particular part of the country; but let me implore you in
the name of justice and humanity, to examine and not fear
an investigation of this subject. Oh ye statesmen! if such
be present, fear not to speak aloud, fear not to discuss
this subject in your public councils, fear not to speak of
it by the way; let no apology, no plea of justification,
deter you from hastening the liberation of the bondman. The
only remedy is to break the bonds and let the oppressed go
free. Let no considerations of interest or expediency di-
vert you from the performance of this high and important
duty. Oh if we would but agree that this evil should be
removed from our land, would we not apply the rightful

remedy? What would this nation be—of what could not this
country boast, if she were free from this enormous system
of injustice! Nations that are subjecting their people to
wrong, might then admire our free institutions and the
prosperity and happiness of our land. We ought to feel for
the poor of our mother country, but we can never act effectively in their behalf, till we have removed this blot from
our country. I have seen thousands, if not tens of thousands, on the other side of the water, ground down with
poverty, their children with garments worn out and could
scarcely dress themselves—I felt that they were objects of
compassion and mercy. Again I have seen the poor peasantry
of Ireland calling upon the passenger by the way for aid;
yet I have beheld this, and the poor of England also who are
borne down by the proud hierarchy and the lordly aristocracy that have gained the ascendancy there. And when I beheld
these things how was my soul pained—how was my heart moved
within me for the oppressed of that land. But when I turned
my eyes to this country, what do I behold here? What kind
of an example do we set? The eyes of the nation are upon
us, and she compares our professions with our practices.
This country which professes to be one of universal liberty,
the assylum for the oppressed of every nation, and has not
only proclaimed it to the world, but inscribed upon her
parchments the principles of the inalienable rights of all
men to the enjoyment of liberty. And from these high professions of equality, we have led strangers to suppose that
this government would be the last to encourage monopolies—
that it would do anything but oppress its own subjects, but
when they look abroad in our land, and behold how we carry
out these principles they are ready to justify their own
system of aristocracy.

I was ready to inquire whether the oppression of the
peasantry was not equal in atrocity to that which existed in
our own land. But they have the right to plead for them-

selves, the most oppressed and indigent laborer in that
country, in his fustian jacket, can thrust himself into the
public meeting—he can retire to his home where he cannot
be invaded in his rights, and his domestic enjoyments; he
cannot be severed from his family forever, and have their
ties of affection riven asunder and sold to the merciless
taskmaster—he has the command of his own children, and as
they rise in education and usefulness, they are respected
and encouraged. And even in Ireland the poor children may
enter the public schools. But how is it here? We have
laws expressly enacted to perpetuate the ignorance of the
oppressed of our land! There is not only the first great
injustice of taking from them their liberty, but all the
concomitants of slavery are so many obstacles to their elevation. Oh look at it! I speak as to wise men. Look at
the subject. I would not unnecessarily endeavor to awaken
your sympathies; but I consider that the subject demands it.
There may be many here who would point to the comparative
humanity of slaveholders. But I would ask you whether
there are not necessarily connected with the system, those
evils of which I have spoken, and whether the humane masters
do not go to give sanction to the whole system. I would entreat them, to examine the history of emancipation in the
West Indies; the glorious result of that noble enterprise,
and hesitate not to strike off the fetters from our bondmen;
and so we may secure the republican principles of our country. Oh bear with me when I speak for those who may not
speak for themselves. Those who go forth with the single
purpose of doing good, under the influence of the power of
the living God, will ever find it their duty, "to cry aloud
and spare not, to lift up their voice like a trumpet, and
show the people their transgressions and the house of Jacob
their sins." Righteousness exalteth a nation but sin is a
lasting reproach. Let us then not hesitate to wipe from our
escutcheon, this disgrace—this foulest blot. And is this

the only crime in our land? Look at the Aborigines of our
country; what an amount has it cost this government to drive
them from their homes and from the graves of their fathers!
Millions have been expended in wars with this much injured
people. Alas, what little progress has christianity yet
made! The intelligent mind is however beginning to behold
the enormity of the crime of war. Is it not more difficult
than formerly to involve a nation in this great evil? There
is an obviously increasing love of right, and I believe
there are measures to which nations may resort for a pacific
adjudication of national difficulties. In England I know
there are means, not a few resorted to, to prevent the preparation for war——an evil which has disgraced the land from
age to age. In this country now, there are appeals made to
the public in behalf of peace principles, and they are beginning to claim considerable attention. I regard all these
things as favorable to the idea, that that desirable period
is approaching when "nation shall not lift up sword against
nation and shall learn war no more." Let us not think of
waiting till the millenium shall arrive, but even now, we
ought to know better and might do better. Oh have your
minds cultivated and your hearts enlightened, hesitate not
to speak of the evils which surround you——it may be unpopular for a time, but it is diffusing itself over the nation,
and I rejoice that the time may come when violence and war
will cease to crimson the land. I cannot but look forward
to that time when we shall understand the true character of
righteousness, and shall bring the great principles of
christianity to bear upon the conduct of our everyday life.
In how many ways are we in our social and commercial intercourse, striving to take the advantage of one another——how
we are oppressing, not only the slave, but the poor laborer?
Yes, bring our christianity to our everyday practices, let
our fruits test the purity of our profession, and when we
are making these contracts by which we are enriching our-

selves, let us look whether we are not indulging ourselves
in extravagance in life to such an extent as to bring misery and woe upon others. Let us not be looking to the political arrangement which can only bring about a temporary
relief until the *morals* of the people are changed; until
we bring our christianity to our everyday life; until this
comes to be the case, all our efforts, all our political
arrangements, can afford no permanent good. May we my
friends, see what part we have taken in the general oppression of the laboring classes, by our indulgences in fashionable life. I do not design to debar any from their enjoyments so far as true christianity will admit. We should
remember the poor, call in to see them in their abodes of
want and distress, call not in to see your rich acquaintances in preference to those who are objects of compassion
and charity—it is to the poor, the maimed and the blind,
that we are to administer. This is the principle which
must go to reform the world—to hasten the day when the
glory of the Lord will cover the earth as the waters cover
the sea.

I am aware I am lengthening out to an extent beyond
what might be agreeable to some, but I have but one opportunity, and this must be my apology.

[The speaker here alluded to the different customs of
opening and closing meetings and that in these respects she
might not accede to what was customary here. She knew that
she was not in these respects adhering to the taste of the
age—she spoke of the organs used in many churches, their
singing &c., and explained that the essence of true worship
consisted in the aspirations of the heart, and not in the
words of a prayer or the *forms* of worship. She approved of
vocal prayer, but not as a regular ordinance to be performed
at stated periods.]

And I ardently desire that that which has been offered
in much humility and sincerity this evening, may be received

in the spirit in which it is tendered, and that it may be
blessed and sanctified: and I believe God will bless all
who are sincerely approaching unto him, whether in the secret of their hearts or in the rounds of ceremony, so that
their hearts are filled with love to him and to their fellow creatures. He knoweth their hearts and he is full of
mercy. Oh that we understood the attributes of deity! We
should not be speculating upon abstract theory and contending about abstruse doctrines. Would that we understood the
attributes of his goodness. He is ever unfolding himself
to men, and as they obey this voice they will be led by his
spirit of which all men are endowed with a portion; and as
we are thus taught, and cease to look unto man for that instruction which God alone can impart, he will give us an
earnest of a better inheritance. Then shall we know that
we are all upon equal grounds as regards what we shall do.
Let us seek then to secure unto ourselves that which passeth the understanding of man, an inheritance that fadeth
not away, even an earnestness of the rock of the glorious
covenant where the Lord God enlighteneth the peaceful spirit in the highest [and] is the light thereof.

Let me now my friends express in tenderness of spirit
the obligation I feel, not only for the grant of this house,
but the respectful attention with which I have been heard,
and desiring the present and eternal welfare of you all, I
bid you adieu.

[B. B. Davis, Stenographer. Davis and Pound Printers,
Salem, Ohio, 1843.]

TO SPEAK OUT THE TRUTH

*SPEECH, DELIVERED AT THE SEMI-ANNUAL LENITORIAN
CONVENTION, PHILADELPHIA, OCTOBER 20, 1846*

I am gratified in having an invitation to speak out
the truth without clothing it in set theological language.
I liked the observation of the last speaker (Mr. Hedge)
especially in reference to this point. We make the cross
of Christ of no effect, by the ambiguous and deceiving
phraseology we throw around his precepts and doctrines. It
goes to perpetuate the erroneous views which prevail in
Christendom, of the divinity of Christ, and the vicarious
atonement. If we would disabuse Christianity of the errors
of theology we should do much towards advancing so great
and glorious a system if it can be called such. But when
preachers for fear of losing their reputation in the religious world, speak of their faith in the Divinity of Christ,
and the vicarious atonement, they are retarding Christian
progress by their want of simplicity and frankness.

Nothing is more fitted to impede this progress than
the popular theology, the generally received systems of
faith. A speaker has said (Mr. Clarke) that we ought not
unwillingly to allow ourselves to be cut off from the body
of the church. But, however vital that body may be and [he]
would not deny it much earnestness and worth, yet we must
be willing to be separated from it, in respect to the important doctrines. But who is there of you glorying so much
in that spirit of heresy in which St. Paul boasted—heresy
after the manner of men, who of you stands so fast in

liberty wherewith Christ has made us free, as to acknowledge the extent of their secret suspicions of views ordi-
narily professed? Who is ready to hold up the purity of human nature in place of its depravity? Who will speak of
Christ's divinity without mystery? Who will speak of the
importance of becoming Christ-like by following his example
of that which is meant when he is called "the Son of God
with power according the spirit of holiness," and not of
that greatness of his which is inexplicable or involves
mystery and miracle? We are too prone to take our views of
Christianity from some of the credulous followers of Christ,
lest any departure from the early disciples should fasten
upon us the suspicion of unbelief in the Bible. But should
we not feel free to speak of the narratives of those who
hand down the account of Christ's mission in their true
character? The importance of free thinking and honest
speech cannot be over-estimated. Be not afraid of the reputation of infidelity or the opprobrium of the religious
world. We must be willing to be severed from it if necessary. And our fruits and not our opinions will finally
judge us. There is but one criterion of judgment, and
everybody knows what love, truth, mercy are! If we seek to
bring forth righteousness exceeding the righteousness of
the Scribes and Pharisees, then we need fear little though
brother deliver up brother to death. It may become a small
thing to be judged of man's judgment. We ought to rejoice
that we are permitted to offer a pattern of Christianity
exceeding the common one. We need Saviors that shall be as
Saviors on our own Mount Zion. How great is the mischief
those false doctrines are doing which make men depraved and
then point to the vicarious suffering of Christ. We are
too prone to begin with the spirit and then seek to be made
perfect in the flesh. We clothe our thought in expressions
that deceive. There is too much image worship still practiced by Christians! We are apt to proselyte to sect

rather than to Christianity! It has been well said our
fathers made *graven* images, but we make *verbal* ones. God
has made man after his image and man has made God after his
image. If you have had Channing and Worcester to lead you
on, why are you not prepared to carry the work forward, even
beyond them? My heart was made humble and tender when I
came into the Convention and saw in the chair the son of an
old friend of my father; Samuel Parkman of Boston. Looking
at Calvinistic Boston as it then was, and considering how
Channing rose and bore his testimony and what results followed, we may be encouraged. But let the work advance, Lo!
the field is white to the harvest. There are some circumstances now tending to break the connection between religion
and death, and to substitute a connection between religion
and life. The graveyard and the church, religion and death
are not now as they were so closely and inseparably connected. Rural cemeteries have helped to bring religion into
view as belonging more to our present state than our future
condition! This divine gift of religion has been bestowed
rather to govern our lives than to gratify our curiosity!
We are fast settling down into satisfaction with the general
ignorance in relation to the future, and are no longer content to weave together a few texts about the nature of the
future state and play upon the superstitious feelings and
hopes of the people without moving them to good works. Religion is fast getting to be mingled with everyday life,
with common goodness.

The minister is ashamed to make such a use of the Bible,
as shall make it a store house of arguments against the most
sacred causes of humanity: to quote from the sensualist
Solomon texts in defense of intemperance, or to place obstacles in the way of those who are seeking to break the
fetters of the slave, by quoting texts of Scripture to prove
slavery a patriarchal institution! Look too at woman's
place in society here among ourselves. There is great zeal

for the relief of Hindoo woman, but let us look at home and
behold worse than their funeral pile, the immolation of woman at the shrine of Priestcraft. Has she leave to speak
out the gushings of her soul? Ah! Have you Brethren un-
fettered yourselves from a prejudice that is tending to im-
molate one half the whole human family? Some of us have not
so read the Scriptures so to find warrant for the exclusive
appropriation of the pulpit by one sex! I know where I
stand, I should speak with all delicacy. But shall not the
time come when you will consider if a great deal too much
of church machinery and ecclesiastical formality, does not
mingle with your Christianity? Are you not worse than your
teachers in keeping up ordinances which they would suffer
to decline, and will you not soon be able to see how much
more affectionate Christian Institutions might be if they
were not cumbered with a salaried class, how much less ex-
pensive and more efficient?

I hear you speak of Missionaries——I always like better
that name which the excellent Joseph Tuckerman chose for
himself, a minister at large. I desire to see Christianity
stripped of all names and things that make it technical, of
the gloomy appendage of a sect. Let it be a kingdom of God
in the soul, let the inward voice speak out, and it will
find a repose. I care not for the superstition of the
Quaker language. I feel myself to be one of you. Let me
urge you by all that is glorious in your principle to be
faithful to them. Do not reach to build up a demure piety,
but a true useful practical life. I wish there were more
extempore [speakers] among you. Then men who work with
their own hands and labor from day to day shall pour out
the gushings of their hearts upon you. If the ministry were
stripped of its peculiar and special support there would be
many preachers for one and a greater enlargement of heart in
all. Brethren, hearken to the spirit. He dwelleth with you
though you know it not. It is he that walketh with you by

the way.   Are not the aspirations for truth, proof that we have a present God with us?

   [*Christian Register,* October 31, 1846.]

PROGRESS OF THE RELIGIOUS WORLD

REMARKS, DELIVERED TO THE ANTI-SABBATH
CONVENTION, BOSTON, MARCH 23-24, 1848

I have little to add to what has been already said upon this subject [keeping the Sabbath]. Much that I could
not have spoken so well, has been said for me by others. I
am glad to be here, to have an opportunity of hearing the
discussions, and also to give countenance to this important
movement for the progress of the religious world. The distinction has been clearly and ably drawn, between mere forms
and rituals of the Church, and practical goodness; between
the consecration of man, and the consecration of days, the
dedication of the Church, and the dedication of our lives
to God.

But might we not go further, and shew that we are not
to rely so much upon books, even upon the Bible itself, as
upon the higher revelation within us? The time is come,
and especially in New England it is come, that man should
judge of his own self what is right, and that he should seek
authority less from the Scriptures. It is well, however,
inasmuch as the faith of a large part of the professors of
Christianity rests upon this book, to shew that certain also of their own teachers bear witness to the truth we advocate.

It seemed to me that the views of the last speaker went
further to sanctify the book, than his own principles would
justify. I thought the same of the remarks of Theodore
Parker, made yesterday, with regard to the day, and wished

to allude to it in his presence, but there was no opportunity. There seemed to be a little confusion, when he spoke of
not hallowing the day, and yet considered it essential that
there should be this religious observance. Does not such an
admission lead the advocates of it into a kind of compromise? and to "build again that which they are called to destroy?" It is observable, in nearly all the advance steps
in theological points, particularly when there is a reluctance to acknowledge the heresy, and a desire to appear
orthodox.

Those who differ from us would care little for an Anti-
Sabbath Convention which should come to the conclusion that,
after all, it would be best to have one day in seven set
apart for religious purposes. Few intelligent clergymen
will now admit, that they consecrate the day in any other
sense, or that there is any inherent holiness in it. If
you should agree that this day should be for more holy purposes than other days, you have granted much that they ask.
Is not this Convention prepared to go further than this? to
dissent from this idea, and declare openly, that it is lawful to do good on the Sabbath day? That it is the consecration of all our time to God and to goodness, that is required of us? Not by demure piety; not by avoiding innocent
recreation on any day of the week; but by such a distribu-
tion of time as shall give sufficient opportunity for such
intellectual culture and spiritual improvement, as our mental and religious nature requires. There would not then be
the necessity of a devotion of the seventh part of our time,
even for the rational improvement that our friend yesterday
considered so essential.

In the Scripture authority, however, as it has been
cited, it might have been shown, that, even in the times of
the most rigid Jewish observance, it was regarded as a shadow only of good things to come. "I gave them also my Sabbaths to be a sign unto them." The distinction was then

made, by the more faithful and discerning of their people,
between mere formal worship and practical goodness. "Lord,
who shall abide in the tabernacle? Who shall dwell in thy
holy hill? He that walketh uprightly, and worketh righteousness, and speaketh the truth in his heart." When these
things were not done, even the temple-worship became an
abomination; the Sabbaths, the holy meetings, he was weary
of them. Their clear-sighted prophets spoke in the name of
the Highest, to those who had violated the law of right: "I
hate, I despise your feast-days. The new moons and Sabbaths,
the calling of assemblies, I cannot away with; it is iniquity, even the solemn meeting." They were called to amend
their ways and their doings——to do justly, love mercy, and
walk humbly. There is now, as there ever has been, but one
test——one standard of true worship.

If we were better acquainted with the doctrines and
principles of the ancients, of those who are not regarded as
coming within any divine enclosure, but who are looked upon
as heathen, we should find abundant recognition of practical
Christianity. Who is it that tells us that the testimony of
a Socrates is not equally corroborative of truth, with the
testimony of a Paul? That certain authorities, bound in a
certain way, are of higher credence, than that which has
come through other channels? Man is man, and his rational
and spiritual natures are worthy of respect. His testimony
is corroborative in every age of the world, let it come from
what source it may, while in accordance with truth.

It has been said here, that we are not bound by the Old
Testament; but are we to bind ourselves to the New Testament
authority? Enough has already been quoted from that book,
to prove all that we would ask, with regard to the day.
There is no testimony, no evidence there found, that will
authorize the consecration of one day above another. Jesus
recognized no such distinction; and the Apostle Paul said,
"Let every man be fully persuaded in his own mind. He that

regardeth the day, unto the Lord he doth regard it; and he
that regardeth not the day, unto the Lord he doth not regard it." These equally give God thanks.   There is all this
liberal view, and it is well to bring it before the people.
But, after all, are we to take this as our sufficient authority?   Suppose some of them had been so under their Jewish prejudices, as to teach the importance of the observance of the day; would that have made it obligatory on us?
No, we are not called to follow implicitly any outward authority.   Suppose that Jesus himself had said, with regard
to the day, as he did in allusion to John's baptism, "Suffer
it to be so now," would that have made it binding on us?   Is
the example of the ancients, whether Prophets or Apostles,
or the "beloved Son of God" himself, sufficient for the entire regulation of our action at the present day?   No: Jesus
testified to his disciples, that when the spirit of truth
was come, they should be taught all things, and should do
the things which he did, and greater.   The people were not
then prepared for more.   The time would come when that which
was spoken in the ear, in closets, should be proclaimed on
the house-top.   He urged upon his disciples to keep their
eye single, that their whole body might be full of light.

His practice, then, in any of these observances, is not
sufficient authority for us.   We are not required to walk in
the exact path of our predecessors, in any of our steps
through life.   We are to conform to the spirit of the present age, to the demand of the present life.   Our progress is
dependent upon our acting out our convictions.   New bottles
for new wine now, as in days past.   Let us not be ashamed
of the gospel that we profess, so far as to endeavor to
qualify it with any orthodox ceremonies or expressions.   We
must be willing to stand out in our heresy; especially, as
already mentioned, when the duty of Sabbath observance is
carried to such an extent, that it is regarded, too generally, a greater crime to do an innocent thing on the first day

of the week—to use the needle, for instance—a greater
crime to engage in harmless employment on the first day,
than to go into the field of battle, and slay our fellow-
beings, either on that or other days of the week! While
there is this palpable inconsistency, it is demanded of us,
not only to speak plainly, but to act out our convictions,
and not seem to harmonize with the religious world generally, when our theory is not in accordance with theirs.

Many religionists apparently believe that they are consecrating man to the truth and the right, when they convert
him to their creeds—to their scheme of salvation, and plan
of redemption. They, therefore, are very zealous for the
tradition of their fathers, and for the observance of days;
while at the same time, as already mentioned, they give
countenance to war, slavery, and other evils; not because
they are wholly reckless of the condition of man, but because such is their sectarian idea. Their great error is in
imagining that the highest good is found in their church.
Hence their zeal and proselyting spirit.

The religious world ought to be disabused of this idea,
and made to understand the real consecration of time. In
order to do this, not only should this Convention be held,
and resolutions, urging the carrying out of our principles,
be passed; but we should be prepared to issue tracts, and
scatter them over the land. This has been done, to some extent. There are several copies here, of a tract published
a year or two ago in Philadelphia, on this question, by one,
who, not feeling qualified to write, spoke to his friend who
could write, but had not the means to publish, and agreed to
furnish the means. This is the right kind of zeal, leading
to individual labor, not mere conventional interest. The
more it is called for, on account of the extraordinary efforts in holding Sabbath Conventions, &c. Men of talents and
reputed religious worth are going about the country, making
exertions to establish a Sabbath, to increase its obligations,

and the necessity of its observance, on the part of the
people.

The editors of some of the daily papers in Philadelphia, especially since the issue of the Anti-Sabbath Call,
are catering to the religious sentiment, praising the labors of Edwards and others, in travelling about for this
purpose. In proportion as these publications go forth,
should there be zeal on the part of the Anti-Sabbatarians,
as they are called by way of distinction, to spread clear,
intelligent, and liberal views on the subject. There
should, therefore, be a generous appropriation of means and
funds to circulate information, and to enlighten the people,
and a reasonable portion of our time and talents devoted to
the cause. The reformer should advocate a portion of every
day of the week, for mental and spiritual improvement, as
well as innocent recreation, rather than give sanction to
the idea, that the present arrangement is a wise distribu-
tion of our time.

In the existing state of society, while the laborer is
over-tasked, and has so little respite from his toil, we
may indeed rejoice, that, by common consent, he has even
this one day in seven of rest; when if he chose, he ought
to be encouraged to go out with his family, in steamboats
and railroad cars; and in the fields and woods he might offer acceptable homage and worship to the Highest. This exercise of his right need not interfere at all with the conscientious action of those, who believe they may more acceptably worship God in temples made with hands. But if we
take the ground, that all should rather assemble on that
day, to worship, and hear what is called religious instruction, there is danger of our yielding the very point for
which we are called together.

Many of us verily believe that there is, on the whole,
material harm done to the people, in these false observances,
and in the dogmas which are taught as religious truth. So

believing, we should endeavor to discourage this kind of
devotion of the time, and correct these errors, by plain
speaking and honest walking—rather than, by our example
and our admissions, do that which shall go to strengthen
superstition, and increase idolatry in the land.

[Other speakers intervene. Mott continues.]

I did not ask for the reading of these resolutions
again, with the intention of speaking upon them, but that,
in justice to him who presented them, they should have an
intelligent hearing and understanding, and passage, if it
be so judged, in this Convention.

Some of them do not appear in accordance with the resolutions already passed here; and the tendency of them, I
fear, would be rather to strengthen the superstition that
prevails on this subject, than to lessen it. The object of
this Convention is to remove this superstition, as well as
to take measures for the repeal of all penal enactments to
enforce the observance of the day. So far, its course has
been in accordance with its object, as published to the
world. It is important that we should carry out consistently our principles and proposed measures.

Is it needful that reformers should ever express themselves in the manner in which some of these resolutions are
expressed, with regard to any institutions that they believe might rightly pass away? Those who are prone to adhere to their cherished customs and forms, will not lightly
yield them. The sectarian will not give up his Sabbath too
soon.

The right has been sufficiently admitted, in the
speeches made here, and the resolutions passed, that all
who choose should voluntarily associate themselves in the
observance of the day, for as long a time as it may yield
them any profit. But it would be too much to ask of us,
that we should propose to do anything to continue the sacredness of the day.

If we assert that, in the attempt to strengthen its observance by appeals to superstition and ignorance, more harm
will accrue to the cause of pure religion than good. Do we
fear that our devotion and piety will be called in question?
I trust the reformers of this character will give practical
evidence, in their everyday life, of their allegiance to
God. If their fruits shall testify to their faith, they
need not fear the stigma or the opprobrium of the bigoted
worshipper, because of their not holding up one day above
another.

There are various reasons for keeping this Convention
on very simple ground—not blending it with any of the popular views of the subject, which prevail to such an extent.
We shall do more, in this way, to promote the cause of practical Christianity, than by yielding to the prevailing idea,
that worship is more acceptable on one day in seven, than
doing right every day of the week. The character of many of
these reformers—their interest in the various concerns of
humanity, the sacrifices they have made for the good of
their fellow-beings—all testify to their devotion to God
and humanity. They feel it incumbent upon them to be exceedingly careful in their conduct on all the days of the
week, so that those who speak evil of them as evil-doers may
be ashamed when they falsely accuse their good conversation
in Christ. Numbers of these have seen to the end of gathering together for religious worship. They understand the
vision of John in the Revelations, describing the New Jerusalem, the holy city; and he "saw no *temple* therein, for the
Lord God Almighty and the Lamb are the temple of it." These
cultivate the religious sentiment every day. They feel in
their hearts the raising of praise and hallelujah unto their
God, when they go forth into the fields and groves. God's
temple is there; and they no longer need to enter the outward temple to perform their vows, and make their offerings.
"Let every man be fully persuaded in his own mind."

There are signs of progress in the movements of the
age. The superstitions and idols in our midst are held up
to the view of the people. Enquiring minds are asking, "who
shall shew us any good?" These are dissatisfied with the
existing forms and institutions of religious sects, and are
demanding a higher righteousness-uprightness in everyday
life. The standard of creeds and forms must be lowered,
while that of justice, peace, and love one to another, must
be raised higher and higher. "The earth shall be filled
with the knowledge of the glory of the Lord." We wait for
no imagined millennium—no speculation or arithmetical calculation—no Bible research—to ascertain when this shall
be. It only needs that the people examine for themselves—
not pin their faith on ministers' sleeves, but do their own
thinking, obey the truth, and be made free. The kingdom of
God is nigh, even at the door. He dwelleth in your midst,
though ye know it not. One of your own poets hath said:

> "All mankind are one in spirit, and an instinct
> bears along,
> Round the earth's electric circle, the swift
> clash of right or wrong."

This is no longer the peculiar creed of the Quaker. It
is coming to be universally acknowledged in the hearts of
the people, and, if faithful, the bright day of liberty, and
knowledge, and truth, shall be hastened.

Many clear views have been held out before us during
this Convention, to which there has been a ready response,
shewing that we are ripe for advancement—that it is of more
importance to live up to our convictions of right than to
subscribe to the creed of any church. May we let our light
so shine, that men may see our good works, and glorify our
Father in heaven, even though our worship of him may be
after the way called heresy. We may be instructed by the
prayer of the Apostle Paul for his brethren: "I pray to God
that ye do no evil; not that we should appear approved, but
that ye should do that which is honest, though we be as

reprobates; for we can do nothing against the truth, but for the truth."

Is it not indicative of great progress that here, in Boston, in Puritan New England, where the Sabbath has been so long regarded with much zeal and religious devotion— even here, there can be a large gathering of the people from day to day, and the interest continued to the end of such a Convention as this? that they can listen and bear so much? that they can receive the resolutions read here, and passed almost unanimously? I rejoice herein; yea, and will rejoice.

Some remarks have been made, tending to discourage any appeal to the State Legislatures on this subject: we have nothing to do with "the powers that be," but must trust the subject entirely to the moral sentiment of the people. But is not the very act of petitioning an appeal, and often an effective one, to the moral sense of the people? It is sometimes only by demonstrances and petitions to the rulers and statesmen of the land, that the ear of a great portion of the people is reached; and by going from house to house to obtain signers, an opportunity presents itself to scatter truth, and to enlighten the mind.

It has been so, to a great extent, in the Anti-Slavery movement. Converts have been made in this way, who are now devoting themselves to the cause of human freedom; and by reiterated appeals to the Legislatures, much has been effected for the bondman. In Pennsylvania, every facility for recovering the fugitive, and the law by which man could be held as property for six months, were removed from the statute books, last year, by the unanimous vote of both houses of the Legislature.

The success attendant on these measures should encourage us to adopt similar modes of action on this subject. Let us go away impressed with the importance of making every effort, that will induce inquiry among the people.

What is done here, will be limited in its extent; but if we
carry the subject home with us, and act there, we may effect
something.

The Abolitionists endeavored early to enlist the pulpit
and the press in behalf of the suffering and dumb. They organized societies, scattered tracts, and sent forth the
living agent; and, behold, the whole country is aroused to
the subject. May it prove a healthful agitation, resulting
in proclaiming liberty throughout the land, unto all the inhabitants thereof!

In this case, may not similar measures be resorted to,
with equally good effect? Every fetter which superstition
and sectarian bigotry have imposed, must be broken, before
the mind of man will be free. The pulpit and the press may
yet be enlisted even in this cause. There are many thinking
minds. The people do not love to have their prophets prophesying so
falsely as they have done; and they will demand an examination into this subject. If the reformer be faithful to his
convictions, and make no compromise with the religion of the
day; if he do[es] not seem to believe that for which he has no
respect; if he come[s] not to the table of the Lord unworthily; the time will not be long, before the clergymen of the
various sects will investigate this subject with other spectacles than those they have hitherto worn.

The zeal now manifested to increase the sanctity of the
Sabbath, is not in accordance with the spirit of the age. In
travelling through New York and Ohio, last year, I mourned
the evidence of this sectarian zeal. Tracts were scattered
through the length of the cars, on this subject, appealing
to ignorance and credulity, and gross superstition. The
judgments of Heaven in numerous anecdotes, were stated as
falling on the Sabbath-breaker. It is unworthy the age,
when we have such works as Combe on the Constitution of Man,
so freely circulated, as well as others, shewing the true
workings of the natural laws, and their unavoidable results.

We must, then, do our part to counteract these injurious influences of wide-spread error.

This is no new subject. I am one of the older members
of this Convention. I have been familiar with these views
from my early days, being accustomed to hear the remarks of
the venerable Elias Hicks, who bore his testimony against
all penal enactments for enforcing the observance of the Sabbath. He travelled extensively through New York and Pennsylvania, and after much observation, came to the conclusion,
that crime and licentious indulgence were greatly increased
by the existing arrangement of society on this subject. He
remarked for himself, that he was careful on the first day
of the week, as on the fourth, not to do so much work in the
morning, as would unfit him for the enjoyment of his meeting;
but, after meeting, on either day, if he had a field of wheat
which needed cradling, he would not hesitate to do it; and
the law forbidding it on the first day was oppressive on his
conscience. His view was, that there should be such regulation of time as should over-tax none with labor on any day
of the week——that darkness was spread over the land half the
time, when man might rest; and after such devotional exercises as he might choose for himself, he should have the advantage of innocent relaxation. A person present, opposing
him, stated how he observed the day——that he wished all to
be quiet——no secular business &c. Elias replied, "I consider thee as much under the effect of superstition, as thou
would be in the observance of any other of the Jewish rites."

During the discussion, impressions were made which I have
ever remembered. They were strengthened, in after years, and
now I feel the more prepared, by my feeble expression, to encourage those who have been pioneers in other labors of reform.

[*Proceedings of the Anti-Sabbath Convention.* Port
Washington, N.Y.: Kennikat Press, 1971.]

LAW OF PROGRESS

*SPEECH, DELIVERED AT THE FOURTEENTH ANNUAL
MEETING OF THE AMERICAN ANTI-SLAVERY
SOCIETY, NEW YORK, MAY 9, 1848*

There is not a more interesting object for the contemplation of the philosopher and the Christian—the lover of man, and the lover of God, than the law of progress—the advancement from knowledge to knowledge, from obedience to obedience. The contemplation of it is beautiful, the investigation of it is exceedingly interesting, as manifested in the history of the world. We find in the earliest records, the command to advance—"to get thee from thy kindred, from thy father's house, and to come into the land which I shall show thee." And, again: "ye have encompassed this mountain long enough; speak to my people, that they go forward." In the declaration of the Prophets of old, it was men of clean hands who were to grow stronger and stronger; it was the righteous who held on his way: and in later times we find the recommendation of the Apostles to their brethren was, "to go on unto perfection not laying again the foundation for repentance from dead works." And, indeed, was not the teaching of Jesus particularly directed to lead the people onward,—"Ye have heard that it was said by them of old time, thou shalt do thus or so?" then assailed those orders and institutions which they regarded as sacred; speaking directly in opposition to their alleged Heaven ordained law. In contradiction to this law of retaliation, he taught them to love their enemies and to do good to all, embracing all mankind in the love which he so beautifully inculcated,

71

and so happily exemplified.

In coming down to later times, this law of progress is
most emphatically marked in our day, in the great reformatory movements which have agitated the truth-loving and sincere hearted, engaged in the work of blessing man. This may
not be a fitting occasion to dwell much upon this topic; but
there are those present who can look back to the early days
of the great peace reformation. The first efforts were to
arrest the progress of *offensive* war; while they claimed to
themselves, in extreme cases, the right of resort to self-
defence. But a reformer now, the Jesus of the present age,
on the Mount Zion of Peace, says: "Ye have heard that it was
said by them of old, thou shall war only in self-defence,
but I say unto you, take not up the sword at all." The language is not now in only prophetic vision, as of old; it
does not, as the current theology has attempted, explain the
prophecies of peace on earth, to refer to some future, far
distant millenium, but its language now is "sheath the sword";
"render good for evil"; little children are taught to return
a "kiss for a blow." Do we not see the progress that these
principles have made? Was there ever a period in history
when nations were so prolific of events as at the present
moment, giving promise of being consummated by the ultimate
realization of the higher principles of "peace on earth, and
good will to man," calling into action the high moral sentiments of the people and tending to arrest the sword of the
destroyer?

Truly, this law of progress is worthy of our admiration.
Look at it in the temperance reformation: those interested
in that cause, can remember how it was said by them of old
time: "thou shalt drink wine moderately, and abstain from
the unnecessary use of intoxicating liquors." What is the
language now of the Saviour on the Mount Zion of Temperance?
"I say unto you, drink not wine at all—practice 'total abstinence' from all intoxicating liquors."

And how has it been (let me touch upon it ever so lightly) with the subject of priestcraft? It was said by them of
old time, "down with your hierarchies." The Protestant reformers said, "away with your popery, away with priests of
that particular church," and let us have in lieu thereof,
the Protestant and dissenting priesthood. What now is the
language of the reformer from among those who begin to have
God for their high priest—himself the teacher of his people?
"Thou shalt judge for thine own self what is right, and God
alone is, and shall be thy teacher." Look at your pulpits;
they are widening; they are not the little, high, narrow,
isolated boxes they were wont to be in olden time; there is
room for several, and occasionally a *woman* is found to occupy a place there. Is not this then an evidence of progress
even in the greatest and highest of Christian principles?

How is it in the Anti-Slavery cause? It is now more
than ten years since it was my privilege—and a great one I
esteemed it—to attend an anniversary of this kind in this
city. I remember the tone of the speeches, how that only
the first principles of Anti-Slavery were brought into view.
And, indeed, looking back to a period shortly before this,
when a little handful gathered together in the city of Philadelphia [illegible] [to] declare, not merely self-evident
truths—to reiterate the simplest truisms that were ever uttered. Read the declaration of the Anti-Slavery Convention
of 1838, and see what it was found necessary then to declare
in Convention. The people were asleep on the subject with
some few exceptions. There had been solitary individuals,
such as Lundy, and Elias Hicks, and the Benezetts, the Clark-
sons, and the Wilberforces. But the labours in England for
twenty years were simply to arrest the progress of the Slave-
Trade; and it was the work of a *woman* to declare, that "Immediate, not Gradual Abolition" was no less the duty of the
master, than the right of the slave. In this Convention in
Philadelphia, the great principles of human freedom were

uttered that every man had a right to his own body, and that
no man had a right to enslave or imbrute his brother, or to
hold him for a moment as his property—to put a fellow-being
on the auction-block, and sell him to the highest bidder,
making the most cruel separations in families. At that time
these things were scarcely known; the people had scarcely
considered them. It was now made known to very many in the
Northern States, that there were then more than two million
held in this abject bondage, who were claimed as property,—
that men had this irresponsible control, this legal right to
their persons. This Convention resolved what it should do:
first—efficiently to organize itself, and then to seek to
form other Anti-Slavery Societies throughout the country.
They were to go forth and endeavour to enlist the pulpit and
press in behalf of the suffering and the dumb. The work it
had to do was a Herculean task; it was, to meet the priests
of the Church, and to endeavour, by bringing Bible texts,
to oppose them to others, in order to prove that man had no
right to hold his fellow-being as a slave. What has resulted from their labours? Look at the law of progress in this
particular: read this appeal of the women of Scotland to the
women of America: see what they there say with regard to
going to the Bible to claim authority for holding human beings in bondage. It is not sufficient now to quote the example of the ancients, on which modern slaveholders claim
the rights to oppress their fellow-beings, and that to an
extent greatly transcending slaveholding in ancient times.

     But time is no longer occupied by Abolitionists in
meeting the ministers in this way. The labours of these
few pioneers have been sufficient to awake the nation to
the consideration of this subject, and there is a response
in the hearts of those who have not been blinded by their
sectarian prejudices, by the tradition they have received,
or by the god of this world which blinds the eyes of them
that believe not. These have heard the truth, and having

received it, gladly have come forward; and in their inmost
heart there is a response to the truth as it was once uttered by a speaker of the House of Assembly in Barbadoes: that
"every man knows in his heart that slaveholding is wrong."
It was needed that some should first come forth thus armed
and give their views to the people; and may not the pioneer
in this cause of immediate abolition, who trod the wine
press alone in the beginning of this work, say in the language of the Prophet, "with my staff I passed over this Jordan, and now I have become two bands." Look around you over
the country, and see whether he spoke in vain, when he declared that he *would be heard*. Observe the progress in the
labours of this reform, that both the pulpit and the press
are enlisted to some extent in behalf of the suffering and
the dumb. Also, as has been already remarked in the legislative halls of the land, the National Assembly is engaged
with it. Scarcely a Legislature in the several States but
discovers at every move on the great question of American
Slavery, something cheering to the Abolitionist. Even
though the slaves are increasing in numbers, even though
their territory is being enlarged at every circle, yet, when
we look abroad and see what is now being done in other lands,
when we see human freedom engaging the attention of the nations of the earth, we may take courage; and while we perceive how it is assailed in our own land, still we know how
impossible it will be to separate it from the question of
the freedom of the slave, in that it is inseparably connected with it in France, and is beginning to be so in other
countries.

Have we not evidence of progress even in our own country on this subject? A large public meeting was called the
other day to hail the events of France. Mark the difference
in this from former meetings. Why it was scarcely ten years
since Pennsylvania Hall was burned by a mob, because the
liberty of the coloured man was advocated by white and

coloured people intermingled. What are now the facts with
regard to this large meeting in the great public square in
the same city? Not only were the movements in regard to
Freedom in the French colonies hailed by the white people
present, but the coloured people also came forward and were
helped onward; they had their stand also: and was it confined to themselves alone? No, it was an *amalgamation meeting!* Was it by privilege, as women sometimes have the
privilege to hold a kind of play meeting? No, the white
people of that large gathering left their own speakers, to
go among the coloured crowd, and hear their speaker.

Look also at the condition of the coloured people in
respect to the ridicule which was once heaped upon them.
Who are *they* now who ridicule us, because coloured people
are mingled in this meeting? It is those whose ridicule is
the scorn of the intelligent and wise of the nation. Now
we find the coloured people coming forth in intelligence, in
moral worth, with increasing self-respect, and are respected
by their white brothers; we see them stand side by side with
those who have thus cruelly treated, oppressed, and trodden
them down.

These, then, are the evidences of progress. Let the
Abolitionist, who should be as the Jesus of the present age
on the Mount Zion of Freedom, continue to say: "Ye have
heard that it was said by them of old, thou shalt treat thy
slaves kindly, thou shalt prepare them for freedom at a
future day; but I say unto you hold no slaves at all, proclaim liberty now throughout the land to all the inhabitants
thereof." Let this be the loud sounding jubilee that shall
be uttered. Let us no longer be blinded by the dim theology
that only in the far seeing vision discovers a millenium,
when violence shall no more be heard in the land—wasting
nor destruction in her borders; but let us behold it now,
nigh at the door—lending faith and confidence to our hopes,
assuring us that even we ourselves shall be instrumental in

proclaiming liberty to the captive. But let there be increasing activity on the part [of] Abolitionists; they must
not cease their labours and fold their hands, thinking their
work done, because they have effected so much: they must not
be satisfied with coming to these anniversary meetings, they
must continue to work at home. It is the righteous that
holds on his way, it is those who are faithful to the light
that obtain more light; "he that is faithful in a little,
shall be made ruler over more." "But if the light that is
in you be darkness, how great is that darkness." Have we
not some apostates in the cause, who give evidence of the
truth of this? Are there not some of whom it may be said,
"it were better they had never known the way of righteousness, than that they should have turned from the commandments delivered unto them?"

Let us go on, then, and make advancement by our faithfulness. When the pulpit cannot be enlisted, nor the Church
aroused, it is the duty of Abolitionists to have no longer
any fellowship with those unfruitful works of darkness, but
rather reprove them, by separating from them, and touching
not the unclean thing. Here is the advanced step the Abolitionists have made; in the beginning of their work many of
them were enlisted, as some of them still are, with the political movements of the land —the party politics of the
nation. They hoped by thus uniting with these powers, to
effect their work; but they have discovered that the situation of the country, the legal enactments, the statutes that
the slaveholders have made, have been altogether tending to
rivet the chains of the oppressed. They have, therefore,
found it their duty to declare in the progress they have
been called upon to make, that they must obey the command;
"get thee from thy father's house, and come into a land that
I shall show thee." They have found it their duty to come
out against the Constitution and Government of the country,
as it is at present construed. I know little, however, how

to treat this part of the subject.   I am glad, however, of
the progress evident in this.

Glad also, of the Evidence of advancement among Abolitionists as to the commercial and manufacturing relations of
the country; it being made known that these are carried on
by the gain of oppression, [with] the North, equally with the
South, in "building its house by unrighteousness, and its
churches by wrong, using its neighbour's service without
wages, and giving him not for his work." It is beginning to
be seen that they must despise the gain of oppression, and
deny themselves the blood-bought sweets and the blood-
stained cotton that has come through this corrupt channel.
They feel that they are called upon not to be partakers of
other men's sins, and not to participate in this matter, except so far as in the general admixture of things, they are
necessarily involved, while they live in the country.   The
fact that they are also implicated in other oppressive systems—by the use of the products of human labour, ought not
to discourage them.   The Abolitionists have also developed
the oppression existing in other lands.   They have disclosed
the sufferings of those engaged in the various laborious
employments in England, Scotland, Ireland, and other portions of Europe.   The axe was first laid at the root of the
corrupt tree of human slavery, and through this their eyes
have been anointed more clearly to behold what are the universal rights of man.   None are more ready to assist the oppressed labourer to obtain his rights than they.   Let them
be faithful to their trust, so shall their work be blest,
not only to the poor slave, but to all those who are in any
way wronged and injured.   If they are not true to their
trust, if they are not united to go on in our work, but suffer themselves to slumber at their posts, what will be the
result?   Will there not then be reason to fear the language
of the martyr, Charles Marriott, will be fulfilled: "that
America, Republican America, will be the last stronghold of

slavery in the civilized world."

    [*National Anti-Slavery Standard*, May 18, 1848.]

SERMON TO THE MEDICAL STUDENTS

DELIVERED AT CHERRY STREET MEETING,
PHILADELPHIA, FEBRUARY 11, 1849

"Thee we reject, unable to abide
Thy purity, till pure as thou art pure;
Made such by thee, we love thee for that cause,
For which we shunned and hated thee before.
Then we are free. Then liberty, like day,
Breaks on the soul, and by a flash from Heaven
Fires all the faculties with glorious joy.
A voice is heard, which mortal ears hear not,
Till thou hast touched them; 'tis the voice of song,
A loud Hosanna sent from all thy works;
Which he that hears it, with a shout repeats,
And adds his rapture to the general praise."

This inspired language of the simple and artless poet,
arose in my mind, as the secret prayer was offered:

"Oh Thou my voice inspire,
Who touched Isaiah's hallowed lips with fire!"

Aware that, to many present, the opening of a meeting
of this kind, without the harmonious note—the sacred hymn,
would be, to say the least, novel; if, indeed, it would not
divest it of the character of a religious meeting; and the
service, of the nature of divine service;—aware also, that
many are accustomed to the offering of prayer on their behalf; it is due to these to say, that some of us believe we may
understand the sacred harmony and melodious note, arising in
the soul—singing and making melody in the heart, without a
dependence upon measured lines or the music of the voice;
that we may no less in the secret of the heart, offer aspirations to him who heareth the sincerely-devoted always, and

81

maketh them "joyful in his house of prayer," without the in-
tervention of words, or the aid of the priest or minister.

Is not the time arrived, that intelligent, spiritually-
enlightened minds, should have such free access to this
throne of grace, as to render less necessary, in the assemblies of the people, the delivery of the oral prayer? The
recommendation of Jesus—the beloved, the blessed of God—
appears to be to this end. "Enter into thy closet, and
there pray in secret." Even while he bowed before the Father in outward prayer, he said: "I knew that thou hearest me
always, but because of the people which stand by, I said it,
that they may believe that thou hast sent me."

My prayer is that this occasion may be blessed both to
the hearers and to the speaker. That the hearers may be impressed with the importance of coming together for the consideration of their highest and best interests; and that the
speaker also may be benefitted, by the deep impression that
without divine aid, no good result can be expected or received.

I have desired for months, aye, for more than a year
past, this opportunity with you, my friends; those of you
for whom this meeting was especially called. In walking the
streets of this city, at this season of the year, and approaching the places where ye are wont to gather for your
instruction, maternal desires have often flowed from a heart,
touched with solicitude for young men, separated from the
tender care, the cautionary admonition of parents, of a beloved mother or sister; that you may be preserved in inno-
cence and purity, while surrounded with the allurements of
this city—the many temptations to vice of almost every description. While I may not speak of the things that are
done in secret—delicacy may revolt from an exposure of the
"rioting and drunkenness, the chambering and wantonness,"
that abound in our midst; due regard to the conviction of
duty to invite you hither, will not allow me to be silent,

and avoid an allusion to vices, of which some may think it,
"a shame to speak."

I called you not here for any theological discussion.
The religion we profess—the principles of Christianity we
believe it our duty to inculcate, are not wrapped in mystery,
or in the theories that are dividing and sub-dividing Christendom. In the view of many, the gospel is not preached,
unless it embrace a certain scheme of salvation and plan of
redemption. Faith in Christ has become so involved with a
belief in human depravity and a vicarious atonement, imputed
sin and imputed righteousness, that a discourse is divested
of the character of gospel preaching, and regarded as little
other than a mere lecture, if this scheme and plan—this
system or theory, be not embraced.

I confess to you, my friends, that I am a worshipper
after the way called heresy—a believer after the manner
which many deem infidel. While, at the same time, my faith
is firm in the blessed, the eternal doctrines preached by
Jesus, and by every child of God from the creation of the
world; especially the great truth that God is the teacher
of his people himself; the doctrine which Jesus most emphatically taught, that the kingdom of God is within man—
that *there* is his sacred and divine temple. This religious
doctrine is simple, because it appeals to self-evident conviction. It is divested of mystery and mysticism, for it
is not necessarily connected, with anything miraculous or
extraordinary.

This noble gift of God, is as legitimate a part of
man's being, as the moral sense with which he is quickened,
the intellectual power with which he is so abundantly endowed, or as the animal propensities which are bestowed for
his pleasure, his comfort, his good. All these are equally
of divine origin. The religion offered to our acceptance
tends in no wise to degrade man, to lessen his proper self-
respect, or lead him to undervalue any of the gifts of the

great Creator. I believe man is created innately good; that
his instincts are for good. It is by a perversion of these,
through disobedience, that the purity of his soul becomes
sullied. Rejecting, then, the doctrine of human depravity,
denying that by nature we have wicked hearts, I have every
confidence, every hope, in addressing an audience of unso-
phisticated minds, that they may be reached, because I know
that the love of God has previously touched their hearts;
that he has implanted there, a sense of justice and mercy,
of charity and all goodness. This is the beauty and divinity of true religion, that it is universal. Wherever man is
found, these great attributes of Deity are there found—a
nice sense of justice, a quick perception of love, a keen
apprehension of mercy, and of all the glorious attributes of
God; without puzzling the mind with attempts to reconcile
his imagined infinite justice, with his prescience or his
infinite power.

Christianity has been lamentably marred in its glory
and beauty, by the gloomy dogmas of the schools. Many, however, are now enquiring for themselves, and acknowledging
the heavenly light within them. They begin to understand
the divine mission of Jesus; how it is that his coming was
and ever is to bless mankind, by turning every one from his
iniquities; that in him, in the great truths which he
preached, all nations shall be blessed.

In the exercise of the intellectual powers, in the advancement and discoveries in science, the vague theories of
past ages are yielding to fact and demonstration, so as to
require no dry argument to prove their truth to the hearer.
So also in religion, the highest concern of man. Theories
long held in darkness, are now brought to a strict examination; the people are exercising their rational powers, and
bringing that which is offered them, to the light of truth
in themselves. In this there is much to hope. The intelligent mind receiving truth in the obedience of a little child,

comes to be quick in its perception and understanding, of
all that belongs to the soul's salvation. This is no mere
Quaker doctrine. Certain also of your own writers bear this
testimony: "All mysteries of science and theology fade away,
before the grandeur of the simple perception of duty, which
dawns on the mind of the little child. He becomes subject
from that moment to a law which no power in the universe can
abrogate. He hears a voice which, if faithfully followed,
will lead him to happiness, and, in neglecting which, he
brings upon himself inevitable misery." This is the faith
that we preach. It commends itself to the understanding and
heart of the hearer, bringing him to a close examination of
his daily life and practice. Another writer has observed:
"The divine principle in man is given, not for the gratifi-
cation of our curiosity, but for the government of our
lives." Were this kept in view, the tone of the preaching
on this day of the week would be changed. Abstract theories,
as well as the attempted descriptions of a future world,
would give place to the enforcing of the great practical
duties of life. For while any verbal or ceremonial standard
shall obtain, as the essential of Christianity, the standard
of pure morality and practical righteousness is proportional-
ly lowered. Especially so, if the theory shall teach, that
good works are of no avail, making a wide separation between
faith and practice. We have not so learned Christ.

I would then urge upon your consideration how far you
are faithful to that in your hearts, which you have felt to
be near you, in your solitary moments, when your prayer has
ascended, as I doubt not it has at seasons, from the altar
of every doubt now present. When the quick response of the
Father's love has shewn you in what your duty consists, how
far, I would appeal to your best feelings, does your conscience acquit you, that you have been obedient to the heavenly vision, that you have confessed this divinity before
men? Are ye willing to acknowledge to your companions, oh

ye young men, that you cannot conscientiously do this, or are
conscientiously bound to do that? Believe me, this confession of the Saviour is of afar more consequence to you, than
a belief in a mysterious divinity. The divinity of Christ
was not in mystery or miracle. It was in doing the will of
his Father. He was "the Son of God with power according to
the spirit of holiness."

Cultivate this ennobling view; be obedient to the
truth; so will you make advancement in your several neigh-
bourhoods and become wiser than your teachers. You will exalt the standard of justice and mercy above that around
which your Fathers have rallied. One object in inviting
you here this evening was, to speak plainly, as regards the
prevailing errors and sins of the time. This is a most important day —a notable age in which we live. Great principles of truth, noble views of humanity are being advocated.
Faith in human nature is increasing, and many are coming,
from every department of society, and investigating great
questions of human concernment. The former dependence on
the monopoly of the pulpit is broken, the people are thinking and acting for themselves and their fellow beings, in
their various relations in society. And what is the result?
Look at the great temperance movement. Is not this reformation one of the greatest moral miracles of our age? Many
are the families in this city, as well as elsewhere, in
this and other lands, many the mothers, daughters, and sons,
who are hailing the temperance reform; who behold the rescue of their husbands and fathers, and are offering praises
unto him, who has put it into the hearts of the people to
plead on their behalf, and to restore such as have fallen.
Are you willing, my young friends, who are just coming upon
the stage of action, in your various relations in society,
to aid in carrying forward this great movement? Will you
be faithful in this great work, by example and precept,
and "walk worthy the vocation unto which ye are called?["]

By practising total abstinence from that which intoxicates,
by ceasing to hand the wind as as act of hospitality to a
friend, and by going forward to rescue those who have sunk
to the lowest degradation, you may be instrumental in setting the feet of many upon the rock of Temperance, and putting the song of total abstinence into their mouths.

Your growing knowledge of the system of man impresses
the importance of observing every law of his physical being,
in order to be preserved a perfect whole. The light of
truth has revealed to you your noble powers, and the responsibility of exercising them in the purity with which they
have been bestowed. If then by your studies you are made
intelligently acquainted with these things, and if super-
added, you have a quick sense of the divinity in the soul,
responding to and according with this knowledge, how increasingly incumbent is it upon you to carry out your principles among your associates, so that you be not found in
the background in the great reformation that is taking place
in human society.

This is a part of my religion—a part of true Christianity, and you must bear with me, my friends, if I press
upon you duties, having reference to your different relations in society, to your intercourse with men, wherever you
are placed. It has been my privilege and pleasure to meet
with some of you in our Anti-Slavery Rooms. When these have
been disposed to come there, though perhaps from mere curiosity, to see what the despised abolitionist was doing, I
have been glad to meet them, and to offer such considerations as would induce a reflection upon the relation which
they bear to our fellow beings in their own country and
neighborhood. This, in the view of many, is a subject of
delicacy—lightly to be touched. Still it is an essential
part of Christianity; and one object in asking your audience
this evening, was to offer for your consideration some views
connected with it, in the hope that you would at least patiently hear, and "suffer the word of exhortation."

There are many now looking at the subject of slavery
in all it[s] bearings, who are sympathizing with the condition of the poor and oppressed in our land. Although many
of you may be more immediately connected with this system,
yet it is coming to be regarded as not a mere sectional
question, but a national and an individual one. It is interwoven throughout our country, into so much with which we
have to do, that we may well acknowledge we are all, all
"verily guilty concerning our brother." There is, therefore, the greater responsibility that we first examine ourselves and ascertain what there is for us to do in order
that we may speedily rid ourselves of the great evil that is
clinging to us. *Evil?*——this mightly *sin* which so easily be-
sets us. There are those here who have had their hearts
touched, who have been led to feel and have entered into
sympathy with the bondman, and have known where the evil
lies. I believe there is a work for you to do, when you return home, if you will be faithful to yourselves. You will
be brought more deeply to enter into feeling with the poor
and oppressed slave; you will find that the mission of the
gospel is "to bind up the broken hearted, to preach deliverance to the captive." It would be a reflection upon the intelligence and conscience of those who are here, to suppose
that they would always resist the wisdom and power with
which truth is speaking to their hearts upon his subject.
There are many disposed to examine, to cultivate their minds
and hearts in relation to their duties in this respect. May
you be faithful, and enter into a consideration as to how
far you are partakers in this evil, even in other men's
sins. How far, by permission, by apology, or otherwise, you
are found lending your sanction to a system which degrades
and brutalizes three millions of our fellow beings; which
denies to them the rights of intelligent education, rights
essential to them, and which we acknowledge to be dear to
us.

Is this an evil that cannot be remedied? A remedy is
nigh at hand, even at the door. The voice has been heard
saying, "Proclaim liberty to the captive, the opening of
the prison to them that are bound." "Proclaim ye liberty
throughout all the land unto all the inhabitants thereof."
To this land peculiarly is the language applicable. In
this land especially are we called to be faithful in this
subject. Be true to your convictions of duty then, oh my
brethren, and you will have the blessing of beholding your
own country purged of this iniquity, and be brought to acknowledge that the divine hand of mercy and love has been
stretched over our land.

It is not strange that the allusion to this subject
should create some little agitation among you; and while I
can but regret it, I stand here on behalf of the suffering
and the dumb, and must express the desire, that there may
be a disposition to hear and reflect, and then judge. I
speak unto those who have ears to hear, who have hearts to
feel. May their understandings not be closed! May they be
willing to receive that which conflicts with their education,
their prejudices and preconceived opinions. The subject of
slavery you must know, is now agitating the country from one
end to the other. The Church and the Legislative Hall are
occupied with its discussion. It will be presented to you
in all its various bearings, and let me urge such faithfulness to the light which you have, as shall prepare you to
become able advocates for the oppressed. So shall the blessing descend upon you as well as upon those for whom the appeal is made. I should not be true to myself did I not thus
urge this subject upon your consideration. When you have
opportunities for mediation and reflection, when your feelings are soothed by the circumstances around you, may you be
led to reflect upon your duties, and the responsibility of
your position in society.

I long for you my friends, that you may be so true to

your best feelings as to be preserved from the temptations
with which you are surrounded, that your hearts may be preserved in unsullied purity. And in so far as any of you
have swerved from the right, and have gone down to the chambers of dissipation, or been found in any indulgence from
which your better nature would revolt, oh, be persuaded to
make a stand in your course, to return, repent and live.
The God with whom we have to do, our tender Father "who is
plenteous in redemption, and abundant in mercy," requireth
only that those who have departed from the right shall return, shall give up their practices and walk uprightly. "As
I live, saith the Lord, if the wicked shall depart from his
wickedness and do that which is right in my sight, his wickedness shall no more be remembered. In the righteousness
which he doeth he shall live." Are any of you, then approaching the state of the poor prodigal, in your indulgences, in giving unbridled license to your propensities? Remember, that the Father's love is ever near, that he will
meet you as you may be disposed to turn from your course and
return to his love. He will meet you, as the parable beautifully illustrates, and conduct you to his heavenly mansion,
where his banner over you will ever be love.

When we read the numerous revelations unto the faithful of the present day, the advancement in truth and knowledge, in moral duty and obligation, we may well hail the age
in which we live, the generation coming on the platform of
humanity. Even now behold the nations, beginning to discuss
the great question of peace. It has recently been brought
before the British Parliament, as well as our own National
Legislature, by the statesmen of the age, whether there is
not a more rational mode of settling national disputes, than
a resort to arms. The labors of an Elihu Burritt, and others not a few, to enlighten the people on both sides of the
Atlantic, on the blessings of peace, the glorious principles
of the Messiah's reign——the readiness on the part of many,

who have been heretofore wedded to their forms and religious services, now to regard war in its just light, as belonging to a barbarous age, unfit for the intelligence and
spiritual growth of this time—the increasing faith that
true principles are capable of being applied *now,* and that
it is no visionary idea that the "sword may be beaten into
the ploughshare and the spear into the pruning hook," that
"nation shall not lift up sword against nation, neither
shall they learn war anymore" —these all give evidence
that "the kingdom of God is at hand," when "violence shall
no more be heard in the land, wasting and destruction within her borders."

Not only is this hope filling the minds of many of
the faithful, but they behold the spirit of mercy spreading
over the country:—The prisons are visited; insane hospitals
are erected for meliorating the condition of suffering humanity; efforts are made to remove the gallows and other
barbarous inflictions from our midst; and an increasing regard for the poor and the lowly, leading many to give
countenance to systems which shall raise these, and tend to
equalize the condition of the human family. If that equality which is our nation's boast were recognized, we should
not see large classes, crushed by existing monopolies, laboring for their scanty pittance. True Christian democracy
and republicanism would lead us not to "look upon our own
things merely, but also upon the things of others." The
practical precept of the Son of God requires, "whatsoever
we would that men should do unto us, even so should we do
unto them."

This then is the religion that is offered to your acceptance. I would not weary you with words, fully believing
that each has a Teacher within himself; and obeying this, we
need not that any man should teach us. It will be found
superior to any other revelation, to everything external.
Come then, to this principle, this Word of God in the soul,

and you will be led into all righteousness and truth, though
you may now shrink from their presentation here.

We have the revelation of God as much in this age as
in any that has gone before us, and if we have faith, we
shall do the things done in former times and greater—that
which has been spoken in the ear in closets, shall be heard
upon the house-top.

May all the difficulties that have hindered the progress of true religion be removed. May it be stripped of
the gloomy appendages of the sects, and presented to view
in its pristine purity and beauty, bearing the impress of
the Divinity. Nothing of gloominess, nothing of dullness
connected with it; nothing that debars from innocent cheerfulness, or conflicts with any of the rational powers with
which we are gifted. The noble intelligence of man has not
been allowed its proper place. There is ever a blessed harmony between every revelation of truth and reason, when not
corrupted by the false dictates of appetite, or clouded by
tradition and superstition.

Let us then be true to our calling, preserving the
holy union of faith and righteousness, religion and humanity; so shall all the mists and clouds of ignorance and
prejudice be dispelled. "The light of the moon shall be as
the light of the sun, and the light of the sun as the light
of seven days."

These great and glorious principles filling our hearts,
liberty, like day, would break upon the soul, and fill all
the faculties with glorious joy. A voice would be heard
that mortal ears hear not till Thou, Oh God, hast touched
them.

> "But oh, Thou bounteous giver of all good
> Thou art of all thy gifts thyself the crown;
> Give what thou canst, without thee we are poor,
> And with thee rich, take what thou wilt away."

And in acknowledging, O God, that every good and perfect gift is from above and cometh from thee, the Father of

lights, we are bound to prostrate ourselves before thee and
to bless thy holy name, and in remembrance of thy many mercies, to ask of thee a renewed clothing of that spirit which
breathes glory to thee in the highest, on earth peace and
good will to men; even thine own spirit which resisteth not
evil, nor revengeth wrong, but which through thy power, is
enabled to bless them that curse and to pray for them that
persecute. We are sensible that this cannot be attained by
our finite comprehension, that thou has veiled it from human understanding; for thou continuest to hide these things
from the wise and simple and reveal them unto babes.

Grant, then, O Father, that we may be brought unto
such a child-like state as to receive all the mysteries
that belong to thy kingdom. We would ask to be kept so humble by thy mighty power that we vaunt not ourselves, saying
that by our own hand we have gained any victory. But we
would acknowledge that thou only hast the power, and that
to thee alone belongs all the glory.

[Philadelphia: Merrihew and Thompson, 1849.]

UNITY OF SPIRIT IN THE BOND OF PEACE

SERMON, DELIVERED AT CHERRY STREET MEETING

PHILADELPHIA, SEPTEMBER 2, 1849

How are we my friends to attain the state, so desirable, as just described, when there will be true unity of
spirit in the bond of peace; when strife and contention
shall no more enter, but when we shall experience the truth,
that they shall not hurt or destroy in all God's Holy mountain? We may so far forget our sectarian predilections,
and bury our prejudices as to feel great charity for those
who have not found this spirit. We may even say as did the
Apostle," It was that through ignorance ye did it as did also your Rulers," but if we attain to the State when we can
say "Father forgive them, for they know not what they do";
we must come to understand that spirit, and by obedience be
established in this high mountain of the Lord above the influence of sectarian feelings. We desire this attainment
but in what manner shall we seek and how shall we find it?
In no other way, than by aiming and arriving at the great
truth that the highest righteousness is the true condition
of man; exalting the standard of justice and mercy, truth and
honesty above all sectarian attachments in theological
speculations. If we read understandingly and intelligently
the religious history of ages long past, [we] find this
standard of truth set above all forms and ceremonies by the
prophets and righteous servants of God, from generation to
generation.

When the people were just coming out of great barbar-

ism; when, in order to satisfy their religious zeal, they
even sacrificed their own children; and when in the progress of time, their veneration led them to build magnificent temples and palaces to the Highest, and bring their
burnt offerings to the altar; the more spiritual and enlightened among them discovered that the Lord accepted not
these things at their hands, as a substitute for true worship.

Practical goodness was at that day required, and not
burnt offerings or sacrifices. Their worship in outward
temples was not sufficient. They only ascended His holy
mountain, and entered His temple, who were found walking
uprightly and working righteousness. So long as they continued to take up a reproach against their neighbor, "to
sit and speak against their brother, or slander their own
Mother's son," the rebuke went forth: "What hast thou to do
to declare my statutes, or that thou shouldn't take my covenant in thy mouth, seeing thou hatest instruction and
castest my words behind thee?"

The Jewish history as we have it handed down to us,
inhibiting as it does that there is one universal practical
religion and that the God, our God has lived righteousness
and hated iniquity in every age of the world, we find that
no man has acceptably bowed before him who has not done
justly, loved mercy, and walked humbly. But let us come
down to a later period; for it is with the present we have
to do. We may profitably look back and examine the history
of past ages but true religion does not consist in a veneration of the past, not in receiving the errors of any age as
the word of God. The word of God we have to do with is
that which is manifested to our souls in our day, which
teaches our every duty, enlightens our understanding and
leads us to discriminate between that which is erroneous,
and that which is really and substantially true. In reference to the religious observances of our day, we may well

say as did the ancient servants of God "these things are
not required at your hands" as a substitute for true religion. When we behold the imposing ceremonies of the present age, the magnificent temples and places of worship in
Christendom, to say nothing of the so-called heathen world,
who amid rude forms still exhibit that divine spirit
breathed in all God's children the world over, we must come
to the conclusion that the universal church, of which we
have just heard, is not composed of mere ceremonial worshippers. The fast which God has chosen, is to
"loose the bonds of wickedness, undo the heavy burdens, and
let the oppressed go free, and that ye break every yoke."

Is there not as in ancient times a tendency to depend
upon religious teachers rather than our own selves judging
what is right, and obeying the testimonies committed to us?
Instead of daring to reject the Jewish errors, lamentably
prevalent in early time, we have them engrafted upon the
Christian stock—not by Jesus—blessings-heavenly, divine
blessings be ever upon His exalted memory—but by some of
the early converts and apostles, introducing their theology
into the primitive church. These errors have been handed
down to us, declared the word of God, and believed in or assented to in all Christendom, as the true religion—the
saving faith of the Christian.

This creed based upon the assumption of human depravity and completed by a vicarious atonement—connected with
a belief in mysteries and miracles as essential to salvation—forms a substitute for that faith which works by love
and which purified the heart, leading us into communion
with God and teaching us to live in the cultivation of benevolence, to visit the widow and the fatherless in their
affliction and to entertain charitable feelings one unto another. While we see much error in the worship now practiced and feel bound to express our dissent and to become
nonconformists, still in the present condition of the people

it may be necessary that they should have their temples,
their imposing forms, their psalmody, and their prayers,
but it is not the highest idea, the most enlightened view
of the exercise of spiritual worship of our God. These
things may be aids to the piety of those who perform them
in sincerity. Among the ignorant coloured people of our
city they seem to require this animal excitement, these appeals to the imagination, in order to arouse them to a consideration of that religion which will regulate their everyday life and conduct. So also with others who have their
chosen ordinances—baptism of the communion and Sabbath day
observances—these may be as school masters to lead them to
Christ, but having come to the substance, what need they
any longer of the shadow? While we recommend to all therefore not to continue in them after their end shall be answered,we must cultivate that charity which will leave all
in the enjoyment of such forms and outward devotions as
shall seem to them most fitting. Our religious Society may
derive spiritual strength from our silent communion, by
mingling together and setting on "the quiet"; and by this
spiritual exercise we may more nearly approach unto Him who
is a spirit and who requireth of the children to worship in
spirit and in truth. But let us beware how we imagine silence to be of itself acceptable worship.

It may be a means of quickening our devotions and
we can respond to the sentiments expressed in this meeting,
that there is a sympathy of hearts leaving us to come together and mingle feelings of devotion and tears of sympathy with those who have mourned because they have been be-
reaved. But when our better nature has been ministered unto, our higher and holier affections called forth, and
our spirits drawn together in love, and in divine feeling
one with another, let us not regard this as the sum and
substance of our religious duty.

We should feel the importance of daily watching over

ourselves, and striving to obtain the mastery over our animal propensities, wisely bestowed by Him, who "giveth us
richly all things to enjoy." We should strive to establish
the eternal, the divine principle of righteousness and
truth. And when we come together, we should try our faith,
and our professions by this unvarying standard. Then, instead of going away self-satisfied with our forms and devotions, our belief or our faith, we should feel that we have
something more to do, to make our actions consistent with
our profession of Christianity. We should set a higher
value upon good works than too many now do and we should endeavor to promote that righteousness which "exalteth a nation."

Were this the acknowledged and practised religion of
Christendom think you that the spirit of war would still be
so rife in the world? Would justice be prostrate in our
streets and mercy be crying at our doors as now emphatically
in the persons of the millions who are trampled to the dust
by the iron hoof of depotism and oppression? In vain [is]
all your temple worship, in vain your faith in trinity, or
unity, in human depravity and original sin, the atonement
by an imagined sacrifice—in vain all your forms and observances, while ye thus grind the face of the poor, give countenance to this most crying inequity of the land, this
great sin of the nation.

Look abroad also into other lands. With all the high
profession of religious worship[,] all the [illegible]
church establishments, are not a proud aristocracy, a de-
vouring hierarchy and a manufacturing monopoly in these
countries crushing the oppressed people to the very dust
and bringing upon them all the evils which are the concomitants, of such a state of poverty and wretchedness? Who is
so unenlightened as to regard the sufferings as the direct
visitation of Providence? As though God did not design
that all his children should be happy. Let us in view of

all these things be concerned to discover how far we are
implicated, individually and nationally, in war, slavery
and other oppressions, in the famine and pestilence which
we find abroad through the earth. I believe there is a
heavy and mighty responsibility attached to us. The more
intelligent and educated in physiological science teach us
that by a violation of the established laws of our Creator
we bring upon ourselves these evils and destroy the blessed
harmony which belongs to God's creation and which can only
be brought about by human beings coming into an observance
of these laws, recognizing within us that holy glorious
light which lighteth every man that cometh into the world.
Implanted in every human soul are there not many now present who know this truth, who have made the discovery that it
is more blessed to give than to receive, who heed the
claims of the poor and of the fatherless and visit them and
minister to their wants? These hear the welcome message,
"Come ye blessed of my Father; inherit the kingdom prepared
for you from the foundation of the world for I was hungry
and ye gave me meat, I was thirsty and ye gave me drink. I
was a stranger and ye took me in, naked and ye clothed me,
I was in prison and ye came unto me."

    May these principles spread, so shall we be brought
into unity, one with another, and introduce that harmony which in
faith we see in its approach when knowledge of the glory of
the Lord shall cover the earth as the waters cover the sea.

        [Sermons. MSS. Friends Historical
        Library, Swarthmore College.]

IMPROVING OUR HEARTS AND ENLARGING OUR SOULS

SERMON, DELIVERED AT CHERRY STREET MEETING,
PHILADELPHIA, SEPTEMBER 16, 1849

It is for the purpose of improving our hearts, and
enlarging our souls that we come here, [that] we may spend
this hour profitably. We may feel desirous of having a devout heart, and the effect of endeavouring to acquire this,
is the enlarging of the understanding in the fear of the
Lord. We behold the commandments of the Lord to be exceedingly broad. The mind that is accustomed to approach unto
the Highest, in prayer and praise, cultivates the feeling
of veneration, and adoration. Difference of religious opinion need not prevent us from seeing the magnitude of the
works of the Lord and feeling that our duty is not limited
to our own particular sphere. The liberal mind is often
led to take a view of the world as it is. I have remembered in this meeting the language of one who may well be
venerated by those who are accustomed to acknowledge, as
saints, the apostles and such as have fulfilled their duty
in their day—one who might well be ranked with these—the
Sainted Channing. In the view he took of the world, of the
state of society as he says: "Mighty powers are at work in
the world, and who shall stay them. God's word has gone
forth and it will not return unto him void." A new comprehension of the Christian spirit, a new reverence for humanity, a new feeling of brotherhood, and of all men's relations to the common Father, this is among the signs of our
times. Amid all the commotions, the jarrings, the marrings,

and the bloodshed in the earth, and these are mournfully
prevalent in various portions of the world, still there is
to some extent, truth in the sentiment he offered. Would
that it were more general, that it were more immediately
felt! There is need of prayers to the Lord to increase our
faith in the sufficiency and efficiency of this divine
world, that it may be exalted high above everything of human contrivance; that in obedience to it, we may go forth
and labour in the great harvest field. Oh that there might
be an increasing number of labourers going forth to arrest
the evils and miseries that are in the world, and to aid
the progress of knowledge and virtue. It needs that the
people should be awakened, that they should be aroused to a
sense of their condition, and be brought to the disposition
to come into the pure walk of righteousness, peace, and
love. There is need of this in order to effect a change so
desirable, so greatly to be coveted, to be prayed for and
laboured for. We have cause to rejoice, that there are already so many labourers in this field, that there are enlightened minds, and purified hearts going forth at the
command of the Highest, to turn the feet of those, who have
gone far in the broad way that leadeth to destruction, into
the way of peace and love. We may be glad that the voice
of peace is being proclaimed not only in our midst, but
afar off among the nations of the earth; that the spirit of
war is being held up in just abhorrence, and the benign and
pure principles of the blessed Messiah, of all who have
known the truth are spreading, leading the people to turn
away from these destructive practices, from an indulgence in
every spirit which engenders [them,] and to bring forth in their
place the beautiful, the divine principles of the blessed
son of God. Truly this is cause of rejoicing and well may
we say in reference to these and other great movements, having
the good of man for their object, and the removal of oppression and injustice for their end that "mighty powers are at

work in the world and who shall stay them? God's word has
gone forth and it shall not return unto him void." We behold Divinity, not in differences of religious opinion but
in the increasing regard for the right, which arises from
this "new comprehension of the Christian spirit," this "new
feeling of brotherhood, this new reverence for humanity."
There are many who are viewing it in such light as to lead
them to make sacrifices for the purpose of bettering the
condition of the world; of effecting a more united brotherhood, where the relations which man sustains to man shall
be acknowledged, and where there shall not be continued monopolies and the facilities for oppression and grinding the
face of the poor, which are now existing, not only in our
own country, but in various parts of the world. "A new
feeling of brotherhood and of all men's relation to the common Father," is beginning to be manifested, tending to modify mere sectarian preferences, and bring us to acknowledge
one universal test of righteousness and love. This is apparent not only in one society or two, but it is being professed and acted out in a way that is cheering to every observer of signs of the times. Let us hope that this spirit
will spread and show man his true relation to his fellow
beings. Then will be overthrown systems of oppression which
have been conformed to so long, and which still are upheld
by the corrupt and selfish, as well as by many in the ignorance under which unfavourable circumstances may have placed
them. But these evils are not the less afflicting to humanity, they cause not less misery in the world, because acted
out through ignorance or thoughtlessness; or as some may
claim by the peculiar circumstances of their situation.
They are nevertheless, evils most deeply to be deplored;
sins to which countenance should be given; no, not for an
hour; sins which require the united action of the good, the
benevolent, the truly virtuous, to overthrow. Let all these
go forth in their might—in the might which heaven will

bestow upon them, for God blesses these with his gracious
name. He is ever ready to aid the efforts of those who are
rightly exercised for the good of humanity. Their confidence will be thus strengthened, and they cannot fail of
success. Then there will be that growth in the earth of
good principles, which will make her wilderness as Eden, her
desert the garden of the Lord, joy and gladness shall be
found therein, thanksgiving and the voice of melody. Can
we not believe my friends that it is the design of our
Heavenly Father, that these things should be so that our
millenium should be now at hand, that we should enter the
kingdom of heaven now? The language of Jesus was "the kingdom of heaven is at hand. It cometh not by observation or
observances but behold it is within you."

    Much as we say of this fundamental doctrine of our
profession, we need greater faith in it. There is need of
spreading this truth, that the kingdom of heaven is within
man, that it is a kingdom not of mysteries or miracles but
of righteousness, peace and joy in a holy spirit. Were we
not overlooking the simplicity of the truth as it is in
Jesus, and seeking some greater display of the divine power
than is manifested, we should acknowledge the divinity of
this religion in the simplicity of its coming. We should
prove it to be a power, mighty in deed yet having connection
with our everyday conduct one with another. Were we to carry out our principles in practice, our religious society
might be instrumental in impressing the divinity of this
truth, in offering more enlarged views for the people's
consideration, as well as spreading and promoting more virtuous practices. Blessings even rest upon those who practise mercy, love, benevolence and goodness, and who are
continually hungering after righteousness. If there is anything that our souls should aspire to above all earthly considerations, it should be for greater purity of heart and
the growth of more practical righteousness among men.

The author introduced to your notice and whose life
has been present with me in this meeting has done much to
direct the religious world from erroneous creeds and to the
pursuit of truth and the right. Why may we not as profitably contemplate the life of such a man as Channing, and
offer his views for consideration, so far as they are in
accordance with the truth, as those of any minister of the
Gospel in Christendom? Why not indeed, as profitably, as
the life and practice of Abraham and Isaac and David of old,
or even of the Apostles of a later age?

It is interesting and instructive to review the life
of this great and good man, in so far as he was faithful to
the work assigned him. He proclaimed unpopular truths, at
variance with the theology of his sect, and adopted a more
liberal creed, submitting it to the people's consideration;
and urged a life and practice more in accordance with the
doctrine of Christ and the spirit of Christianity, than had
obtained in the religious sects. He was not appreciated by
the believers in a dark and gloomy theology and the wor-
shipers in the timeworn ceremonies of their church. But
standing fast in his liberty, he was an instrument of good
to many.

This generation is indebted to such as Worcester and
Channing and Elias Hicks, as well as other honorable men
and women, not a few. Let me name Hannah Bernard who came
forth amid the darkness and error that prevailed, and in
this country as well as in England, bore a noble testimony
to truth, as opposed to superstition and tradition. She
exposed the benighted reliance on Jewish authority, which
led the people to find sanction for war and other evils
and abuses; rebuking them for their sin and great wrongs,
sustained by an unwarrantable use of the Scriptures. Her
name was cast out as evil and trampled upon by those high
in authority, both in England and in this country. But
she lived to see the spread of true principles, in the

ministry of Elias Hicks and others, and could say "now lettest thou thy servant depart in peace." In view of these
and other laborers in the vineyard of truth, we may well
say that, "Mighty powers are at work in the world, and who
shall stay them?"

[Sermons. MSS. Friends Historical
Library, Swarthmore College.]

LIKENESS TO CHRIST

SERMON, DELIVERED AT CHERRY STREET MEETING,
PHILADELPHIA, SEPTEMBER 30, 1849

It is time that Christians were judged more by their
likeness to Christ than their notions of Christ. Were this
sentiment generally admitted we should not see such tenacious adherence to what men deem the opinions and doctrines
of Christ while at the same time in every day practise is
exhibited anything but a likeness to Christ. My reflections
in this meeting have been upon the origin, parentage, and
character of Jesus. I have thought we might profitably
dwell upon the facts connected with his life, his precepts,
and his practice in his walks among men. Humble as was his
birth, obscure as was his parentage, little known as he
seemed to be in his neighborhood and country, he has astonished the world and brought a response from all mankind by
the purity of his precepts, the excellence of his example.
Wherever that inimitable sermon on the mount is read, let it
be translated into any language and spread before the people, there as an acknowledgement of its truth. When we come
to judge the sectarian professors of his name by the true
test, how widely do their lives differ from his?

Instead of going about doing good as was his wont,
instead of being constantly in the exercise of benevolence
and love as was his practice, we find the disposition too
generally to measure the Christian by his assent to a creed
which had not its sign with him nor indeed in his day. Instead of engaging in the exercise of peace, justice and

mercy, how many of the professors are arrayed against him
in opposition to those great principles even as were his
opposers in his day. Instead of being the bold nonconform-
ist (if I may so speak) that he was, they are adhering to
old church usages, and worn-out forms and exhibiting little
of a Christ like disposition and character. Instead of ut-
tering the earnest protests against wickedness in high
places, against the spirit of proselytism and sectarianism
as did the blessed Jesus—the divine, the holy, the born of
God, there is the servile accommodation to this sectarian
spirit and an observance of those forms even long after
there is any claim of virtue in them; a disposition to use
language which shall convey belief that in the inmost heart
of many they reject.

Is this honest, is this Christ like? Should Jesus
again appear and preach as he did round about Judea and
Jerusalem and Galilee, these high professors would be
among the first to set him at naught, if not to resort to
the extremes which were resorted to in his day. There is
no danger of this now, however, because the customs of the
age will not bear the bigot out in it, but the spirit is
manifest, which led martyrs to the stake, Jesus to the
cross, Mary Dyer to the gallows. This spirit is now showing itself in casting out the name one of another, as evil,
in brother delivering up brother unto sectarian death. We
say if Jesus should again appear — He *is* here; he *has* appeared, from generation to generation and his spirit is now
as manifest, in the humble, the meek, the bold reformers,
even among some of obscure parentage.

His spirit is now going up and down among men seeking
their good, and endeavoring to promote the benign and holy
principles of peace, justice, and love. And blessing to
the merciful, to the peace maker, to the pure in heart, and
the poor in spirit, to the just, the upright, to those who
desire righteousness is earnestly proclaimed, by these

messengers of the Highest who are now in our midst. These
the preachers of righteousness are no more acknowledged by
the same class of people than was the messiah to the Jews.
They are the anointed of God, the inspired preachers and
writers and believers of the present time. In the pure example which they exhibit to the nations, they are emphatically the beloved sons of God. It is, my friends, my mission to declare these things among you at the hazard of
shocking many prejudices. The testimony of the chosen servants of the Highest in our day is equally divine inspiration with the inspired teaching of those in former times.
It is evidence of the superstition of our age, that we can
adhere to, Yea that, we can bow with profound veneration to
the records of an Abraham, the sensualist Solomon, and the
war-like David, inspired though they may have been, and I
am not disposed to doubt it, more than to the equal inspiration of the writers of the present age. Why not acknowledge
the inspiration of many of the poets of succeeding ages, as
well as of Deborah and Miriam in their songs of victory of
Job and David in their beautiful poetry and psalms, or of
Isaiah and Jeremiah in their scorching rebukes and mournful
lamentations? These are beautifully instructive but ought
they to command our veneration more than the divine poetic
language of many, very many, since their day, who have uttered
truth equally precious? Truth speaks the same language in
every age of the world and is equally valuable to us. Are
we so blindly superstitious as to reject the one and adhere
to the other? How much does this society lose by this undue veneration to ancient authorities, a want of equal respect to the living inspired testimonies of latter time?
Christianity requires that we bring into view the apostles
of succeeding generations, that we acknowledge their apos-
tleship and give the right hand of fellowship to those who
have been and who are sent forth of God with great truths
to declare before the people; and also to practise lives of

righteousness, exceeding the righteousness of the scribes
and pharisees, and even of many of the chosen ones of former times. The people in their childish and dark state,
just emerging out of barbarism, were not prepared to exhibit
all those great principles in the near approach to fulness,
to the perfection that is called for at our hands. There is
this continued advance toward perfection from age to age.
The records of our predecessors give evidence of such progress. When I quote the language of William Penn, "it is
time for Christians to be judged more by their likeness to
Christ than their notions of Christ," I offer the sentiment
of one who is justly held in great regard if not veneration
by this people, and whose writings may be referred to with
as much profit as those of the servants of God in former
ages; and we may well respect the memory of him and his contemporaries as well as of many not limited to our religious
society, who have borne testimony to the truth.

It is of importance to us also, to speak of those
whom we know, those whose characters we have [fuller] acquaintance with, than we can have with such as lived in ages
past, that we should bring into view the lives of the faithful in our generation.

Jesus bore his testimony-doing always the things which
pleased his Father. He lived his meek, his humble and useful life—drawing his disciples around him, and declaring
great truths to the people who gathered to hear him.

His apostles and their successors were faithful in
their day—going out into the world, and shaking the nations
around them. Reformers since their time have done their work
in exposing error and wrong, and calling for priests of
righteousness in place of vain forms. The bold utterance of
Elias Hicks and his contemporaries aroused the sectarian and
theological world in our day. Their demand for a higher
righteousness was not in vain. Their examples of self-de-
nials and faithfulness to duty should be held up for imita-

tion. We overestimate those who have lived and labored in
days long past, while we value not sufficiently the labors
of those around us, who may have as high a commission as
had their predecessors.

Let us not hesitate to regard the utterance of truth
in our age, as of equal value with that which is recorded
in the scriptures. None can revere more than I do, the
truths of the Bible. I have read it perhaps as much as any
one present, and, I trust, with profit. It has at times been
more to me than my daily food. When an attempt was made
some twenty years ago to engraft some church dogmas upon
this society, claiming this book for authority, it led me
to examine, and compare text with the content. In so doing
I became so much interested that I scarcely noted the passage of time. Even to this day, when I open this volume, so
familiar is almost every chapter that I can sometimes scarcely lay it aside from the interest I feel in its beautiful
pages. But I should be recreant to principle, did I not
say, the great error in Christendom is, in regarding these
scriptures taken as a whole as the plenary inspiration of
God, and their authority as supreme. I consider this as
Elias Hicks did one of the greatest drawbacks, one of the
greatest barriers to human progress that there is in the
religious world, for while this volume is held as it is,
and, by a resort to it, war, and slavery, wine drinking,
and other cruel, oppressive and degrading evils are sustained, pleading the example of the ancients as authority
it serves as a check to human progress, as an obstacle in
the way of these great and glorious reformers that are now
upon the field. Well did that servant of God, Elias Hicks,
warn the people against an undue veneration of the Bible,
or of any human authority, any written record or outward
testimony. The tendency of his ministry was to lead the
mind to the divine teacher, the sublime ruler, that all
would find within themselves, which was above men's teaching,

human records, or outward authorities. Highly as he valued
these ancient testimonies, they were not to take the place
of the higher law inwardly revealed, which was and should
be, the governing principle of our lives. One of our early
friends, Richard Davies, attended a meeting of the indepen-
dents, and heard the preacher express the sentiment that
the time would come when Christians would have no more need
of the Bible than of any other book. He remarked on this
saying of the preacher, "Hast thou not experienced that
time already come." Does not this imply, or may we not in-
fer from this, that our worthy friend has experienced that
time already come; was it a greater heresy, than that uttered by the apostle Paul, when he declared that those who
had known a birth into the gospel, had no more need of the
law? that they were under a higher dispensation than were
they who were bound by their statutes and ceremonies? Let
us also not hesitate to declare it, and to speak the truth
plainly as it is in Jesus, that we believe the time is come
when this undue adherence to outward authorities, or to any
forms of baptism or of communion of church or sabbath worship, should give place to more practical goodness among
men, more love manifested one unto another in our every day
life, doing good and ministering to the wants and interests
of our fellow beings the world over. If we fully believe
this, should we be most honest, did we so far seek to please
men, more than to please God, as to fail to utter in our
meetings, and whenever we feel called upon to do so in our
conversation, in our writings, and to exhibit by example,
by a life of non-conformity, in accordance with these views,
that we have faith and confidence in our convictions? It
needs, my friends, in this day that one should go forth
saying neither baptism profiteth anything nor non-baptism,
but faith which worketh by love, neither the ordinance of
the communion table profiteth anything, nor the absence
from the same, but faith which worketh by love. These

things should never be regarded as the test of the worshipper. Neither your sabbath observance profiteth any thing,
nor the non-observance of the day, but faith which worketh
by love. Let all these subjects be held up in their true
light. Let them be plainly spoken of—and let our lives be
in accordance with our convictions of right, each striving
to carry out our principles. Then obscure though we may
be, lost sight of almost, in the great and pompous religious associations of the day, we yet shall have our influence and it will be felt. Why do we wish it to be felt?
Because we believe it is the testimony of truth, and our
duty to spread it far and wide. Because the healthful
growth of the people requires that they should come away
from their vain oblations, and settle upon the ground of
obedience to the requirings of truth.

I desire to speak so as to be understood, and trust
there are among you, ears blessed that they hear, and that
these principles will be received as the Gospel of the
blessed son of God. Happy shall they be, who by observing
these, shall come to be divested of the traditions and superstitions which have been clinging to them, leading them
to erect an altar "to the unknown God."

In the place of this shall an altar be raised where
on may be oblations of God's own preparing. Thus may these
approach our Father in Heaven and hold communion with him—
entering his courts with thanksgiving, and his gates with
praise, even though there may be no oral expression. He
may unite in prayer and in praise, which will ascend as
sweet incense, and the blessing will come which we can
scarcely contain.

[Sermons. MSS. Friends Historical
Library, Swarthmore College.]

THE DUTY OF PRAYER AND ITS EFFECTS

SERMON, DELIVERED AT CHERRY STREET MEETING

PHILADELPHIA, OCTOBER 14, 1849

In the short time we have been sitting together this morning in silent meditation my thoughts have been occupied with the duty of prayer and its effects upon our souls.

We know that at this hour, on this day of the week, throughout Christendom, the all monopolizing clergy are saying: "We will begin the worship of Almighty God by singing such a hymn;" then follows the delivery of the oral prayer. This is a regular habitual thing, until the act and duty of worship has come to be almost inseparably connected with some performance of this kind. We too partake of it my friends, when we virtually say we will begin the worship of God by sitting still and saying nothing. All these things tend to confuse our ideas of worship and to confound that which is in spirit and in truth, in active deeds, in practical righteousness, in love to God and love to man, with mere forms and ceremonies. Whether these religious exercises be with the tongue or in silence, they may be equally formal, without life or spirit and in many cases, doubtless, they are so. We need therefore to draw the distinction clearly between that which is merely ceremonial and that which is really spiritual, proceeding from a sincere and devout heart. Does this imply that we should be without prayer, that we should not acknowledge our dependence upon a power higher than we for strength to do that which is right, that we feel no need of asking that

115

we may receive, or seeking that we may find or of knocking
that it may be opened unto us? By no means. The true spirit of prayer may be fully lived in, without a word of oral
delivery in the assemblies of the people. If we understood
the caution of Jesus to his disciples not to be found
praying as did the hypocrites in synagogues and in the corners of the streets to be seen of men, but to retire in
secret and offer up prayer in the closet and their Heavenly
Father would hear them and reward them openly, if this enlightened recommendation of the beloved son of God, of one
of the beloved sons of God permit me to say, were appreciated there would be less public prayer; for the inspiring
confidence of the obedient soul is such that with Jesus it
says, "I know that thou hearest me always, I am assured
that there are means adequate to every end to be attained,
that it is our duty to use the rightful means, to depend
more upon our own efforts, upon watching and labor, and
that ultimate success will be our abundant reward. We lack
this confidence, we lack effort and so we come to substitute prayer for action. We need the fable repeated, to put
shoulder to the wheel before we call upon Hercules to help
us. Abundant prayers are put up that this, that or the
other good may be brought about, that an end may be put to
oppression, to slavery and the multiplied wrongs that are
afflicting, crushing mankind.

     The true philosophy, the enlightened knowledge that
is spread before this generation, must teach us that if we
would have any evils removed, physical, mental, moral, or
spiritual, we must sue the legitimate means and the desired
end will as certainly follow as any result in natural science. To pray that health may be restored to a city, to
have a national fast on account of the cholera and to humble ourselves for our sins and pray for a mitigation of
these evils, without observing the laws by which health
shall be restored, is the darkness of superstition, a blind

trust and we shall fail to receive the blessing. Prayers
are now offered in the churches of the land for this, that
and the other blessing, for the kings of the earth, the gov-
ernors and potentates of the land, prayers for physical comfort and for spiritual growth, while the rightful means for
the acquisition of all these blessings are wholly neglected.
True, then, it is, that you ask and receive not, because
you ask amiss. We are crying unto the Lord and he is not
answering our prayer, and calling unto him and he is not
saying, "Here am I". If we ask for that which is good—if
we desire to cease to do evil and learn to do well, to do
justice, to relieve the oppressed, to plead for the widow
and the fatherless, and the stranger; if we are disposed
to bring our deeds to the light and not wait in culpable
idolence for the light to bring our deeds to us; then may
we all with confidence, apply unto the Highest in a sense
of our dependence, and our humility will be increased and
we shall feel that it is of his strength, and be ready to
say, "Not unto us, but unto thy name O Lord, thy great and
marvellous power, belongeth all the honor and glory. This
is a state that the soul is brought into, that rightly understands practical prayer, and in conjunction with this
prayer, is disposed to do that which is right, to resort to
and be obedient to that "light which lighteneth every man
that cometh into the world." When the father of John the
Baptist had been dumb for a season, his mouth was opened
and he praised God because the "dayspring from on high had
visited us to give light to them that sit in darkness and
in the shadow of death and to guide our feet in the way of
peace. Have confidence in the light. Do we really believe
in it, or is it only a tradition professed among us? It is
a light that is ever manifesting all unrighteousness, all
iniquity, injustice and oppression. If we obey it, bringing our deeds to it, suffering ourselves to be guided by it,
shall we go on, continuing in these sins, waiting for the

Lord's own good time to remove these mighty evils from
amongst us? I tell you, my friends, it is impious for us
to declare before the people, that we have not seen the
right time to cease to do wrong. The word has gone forth,
"Cease to do evil and I learn to do well." The fact ever
has been that all unrighteousness is sin, and we need to impress this upon our own hearts because there is such
a proneness in us, to put that off upon others, to say
that it is because of the providential arrangements of society, the influences of circumstances over which we have
no control, that these great and mighty evils are overwhelm-
ing the land; we let the destroying sword go unsheathed
without the exertions we might use to enlighten the people,
to lead them to put up their swords in their sheaths, for
"He that uses the sword shall perish by the sword."

     We want more zeal; we need to be zealously affected
always in a good cause; and especially our society which
claims to have these testimonies descend to us from our
fathers. We should show emphatically by our own fruits that
they are testimonies of conviction and not of tradition.
Other men have labored, we should be prepared to enter into
their labors, and into far higher labors than it was their
lot to perform. The times are ready, the advancing spirit
of the age is prepared for higher and more advanced labor
than in the days of Jesus and his disciples and apostles;
than in the days of Luther, Fox and Penn. This is a day
when the fields are white unto harvest and blessed are those
eyes that are lifted above the things calculated to shut
them, the cares and deceitful things of this world, the
money-getting spirit and honor-getting spirit. Blessed are
they whose eyes are so anointed in "heartfelt devotion" to
their God, whose continual aspirations are for his blessing,
his crowning power over their exertions. They lift up their
eyes and behold fields white unto harvest. They pray that
laborers may be sent into this harvest.

Many are now prepared to receive the principles of
peace and love in lieu of hatred and the sword. Many are
prepared to heed the claims of justice and mercy, and to
continue no longer in oppression and cruelty and the multiplied wrongs heaped upon our fellow-beings. There is a
disposition to hear the truth on these subjects. Happy are
they who were willing to go with their staff in their hands
over this Jordan in a time when there was little to encourage. Happy they who having done this look abroad and behold! They have become two bands and can say, "How could
one thus chase a thousand, and two put ten thousand to
flight had not the Lord been on our side?" On the side of
truth, justice and mercy. Is this spiritual pride, is this
arrogance? By no means. It may be the language of the
deepest humility. Was it spiritual pride in Jesus, when he
declared that by obedience he was enabled to do always the
things that pleased the Father? And that when he judged,
his judgment was just because he sought the will of his
Father who sent him? No, I want evidence of his humility
and yet of strong confidence, the true religious trust. If
I honor myself my honor is nothing; it is my Father that
honoreth me. A similar spirit is now operating in us if we
will but receive and believe in it, that we may always do
the things which please our Father and we may have similar
confidence that he will hear us also. Then that which began in prayer will be concluded in praise, eternal praise
to his great and glorious name who is everlastingly worthy.
Let us then understand prayer and our duties. Be not so
superstitious as to go about praying for temporal blessings
or even for moral results before we have used the means
that are placed within our reach and for which, as accountable beings, we are responsible. We are placed here as
agents of the Highest and the language unto us is "Arise,
shine, for thy light is come and the glory of the Lord has
risen upon thee." Do we believe this? If so, we shall go

forth, though it be in great weakness.

The true philosophy is, that he who is faithful in a
little shall be made ruler over more, while he that is unjust or faithless in the little becomes so also in that
which is greater. He who runs well for a time and then suffers himself to be hindered from obeying the truth, the
light that is in him becomes darkness, and how great is
that darkness. These are great philosophical truths in the
spiritual creation as much so as any in the natural or physical world. Christianity and true philosophy are never at
variance. There is this harmony, and we are so constituted
that prayer and effort are so necessary for our spiritual
sustenance as is labor for the things which belong to our
material existence. Let us then, be faithful to the light;
be obedient even though it may lead us into greater non-
conformity and be the means of our names being cast out as
evil. We are very unworthy of the name of disciples of
Jesus if we are not willing to drink of the cup which he
drank of, and be baptized with the baptism with which he
was baptized, to be faithful without regard to sectarian
consideration, or the denunciations or anathemas of the
church. What are they? They are less than nothing when
rightly viewed. It is a small thing to be judged of men's
judgment. Formerly when Popish denunciations were more
popular and society's denunciations were decisions more
venerated, it required a great deal of moral courage to
stand fast in the liberty wherewith Christ had made free,
but in this day it is no great matter to stem the torrent
of popular odium. It is rather creditable because the
church has gone into merited rebuke. It has substituted
lifeless forms for practical goodness attaching undue importance to sacraments and ordinances, to Sabbath day observances and silent meetings, to hoary creeds and venerated disciplines. It is neglecting the claims of justice,
mercy, and truth. What then are the denunciations of such

a church? Nothing at all. When Jesus was to walk alone,
when of the people there were none with him, when even his
disciples forsook him and fled, and one declared in the
hour of extremity, "I know not the man," when this was the
case with Jesus, did he flinch, did he give up? No, he declared that though he was left alone he was not alone for
the Father was with him. This strong confidence is what we
need, so that when the fathers and mothers of the church
forsake us, we may rest reassured that the Lord on high
will take us up; that he will give us ability to do and suffer whatever may be necessary for the truth's sake and his
angels will be our abundant consolation and comfort. I can
bear testimony here in favor of enlightened spiritual
prayer and though I seldom find it my place or duty to
bring my own actions into view, yet I can say that when I
have risen in the assemblies of the people and with solemn
sense of dependence upon a higher power I have asked in humility for his aid to stand by and strengthen and support
me, I have been blessed, abundantly blessed. I have felt
this divinity rising in my soul—I speak it with all reverence and without arrogance—and I can recommend to others
this trust, this dependence upon a divine power, believing
him to be not far off, but a God near at hand. Let our
prayers be for strength to do our duty, for the overthrow
of all evil and the bringing in of a higher and better
righteousness; for the bringing in of that great and glorious day when the knowledge of the Lord shall cover the
earth as the waters cover the sea, when "peace on earth and
good will to man" shall be proclaimed with as much zeal as
any of the senseless "Glory to God in the highest," in the
absurd forms by which this language is poured forth on this
day of the week. Let there be that which shall proclaim
justice to all, breathe deliverance to the captive and the
opening of the prison to them that are bound; preach the
acceptable year of the Lord and this shall be the highest

evidence that we shall give, that our mission is from above,
that the spirit of the Lord is upon us. Because he hath
anointed us to do these things, the true fact he has chosen
is to break the bands of wickedness, undo the heavy burdens
and let the oppressed go free and   break every yoke. We
forget my friends, that true freedom, true Christianity
brings unto true liberty. He that abideth in the word of
God, he only understandeth true liberty, true freedom. May
we endeavor to do this; may we be faithful in our day, then
we may rest assured that our prayers will be abundantly answered and we may have confidence that the Lord has kept
the city, and the labourers have not labored in vain.

[Sermons. MSS. Friends Historical
Library, Swarthmore College.]

ABUSES AND USES OF THE BIBLE

SERMON, DELIVERED AT CHERRY STREET MEETING,
PHILADELPHIA, NOVEMBER 4, 1849

What are the abuses and what are the proper uses of
the Bible and of this day of the week? This question is of
some importance for us to seek to answer aright lest we
should fall into the popular error that prevails upon this
subject. Mingling as we do in religious society generally,
adopting some of its forms and some of its theories, we have
need to be upon our guard lest we fall into the superstition
and error and before we are aware become bigoted in our
opinions and denunciatory in our conduct. We know well that
in Christendom generally it is assumed that the Bible is the
word of God, while we from the earliest date of our religious society have declared and believe we have been sustained by Scripture testimony in the view that the word of
God is a quickening spirit or as beautifully expressed in
what are called the apocryphal writings: "Thine incorruptible spirit Oh Lord filleth all things. Therefore chastiseth
thou them by a little and little that offend, and warnest
them by putting them in remembrance wherein they have offended, that leaving their wickedness they may return unto thee O Lord." A portion of this blessed, this divine and
all pervading spirit of which there is an acknowledgment to
a greater or less extent everywhere, is found wherever man is
found, darkened to be sure and clouded by very many circumstances. This divine and holy spirit which is a quickening
spirit and has even been believed to be by this Society

123

the word of God and the only word of God; that it has been
through the operation and inspiring power of this word that
the testimony to the truth has been borne in various ages
of the world; that this testimony wherever it be found
either in Scriptures or out of them is but a corroboration
of the word and not the word itself and that word of God,
which is quick and powerful[,] which showeth the thoughts
and intent of the heart, that engrafted word which is able
to serve the soul, we find so spoken in the Scriptures, but
we no where find the Scriptures called the word of God by
themselves. We read of one of the ancient Hebrew writers
who after being converted to a purer faith, commended the
Scriptures as being able to give knowledge of that which is to
come, being able to make wise into salvation; giving knowledge of a purer way, but only through the faith of Jesus
Christ. What is this faith of Jesus Christ; not as theologians define it, faith in the Trinity and a vicarious
atonement, not faith in a system, a mere scheme of salvation, a plan of redemption? Faith of Jesus Christ is faith
in the truth, faith in God and in man. The life that I now
live in the flesh, said the Apostle, I live by the faith of
the son of God, who loved me and gave himself for me. Well
what is this other than a faith similar to that which Jesus
held, the faith of the Son of God How many chosen sons of
God are there who have not loved their lives unto death, who have
given themselves for their brethren even as the Apostle
recommended; that as he, Jesus, laid down his life for the
brethren so do we also lay down our lives one for another.
This then perhaps is the more intelligent reading of these
Scriptures and of what is spoken of as the word of God and
as the saving faith of the Christian. The great error in
Christendom is that the Bible is called the word, that it
is taken as a whole, as a volume of plenary inspiration and
in this way it has proved one of the strongest pillars to
uphold ecclesiastical power and hireling priesthood. What

has been the power of this book? Is it not uniformly taken
among all the professors to establish their peculiar creeds,
their dogmas of faith and their forms of worship, be they
ever so superstitious? Is not the Bible sought from beginning to end for its isolated passages wherewith to prove
the most absurd dogmas that ever were palmed off upon a
credulous people; dogmas doing violence to the divine gift
of reason with which man is so beautifully endowed; doing
violence to all his feelings, his sense of justice and
mercy with which the Most High has seen fit to clothe him?
The Bible has been taken to make man from his very birth a
poor corrupt sinful creature, and to make his salvation depend upon the sacrifice of Jesus in order that he should be
saved. When his understanding has been imposed on by a
Trinity and Atonement in the manner that it has, well may
we say that the abuse of the Bible has been a means of
strengthening priestcraft, and [giving] sanction to sectarian ordinances and establishments. We find the religionist,
especially those whose greater interest it is to build up
sect than to establish truth and righteousness in the
earth, and probably many of these in the main idea that by
this means they shall do the other more effectually, ready
to flee to the Bible for authority for all their mysteries, their nonsensical dogmas, that have been imposed as
articles of belief, as essential doctrines of Christianity.
But also my friends has there not been an unworthy resort to this volume to prove the rightfulness of war and
slavery, and of crushing woman's powers, the assumption of
authority over her, and indeed of all the evils under which
the earth, humanity has groaned from age to age? You know
as well as I do how prone the sectarian has been to flee
to the Bible to find authority for war, and indeed in the
very existence of war, and there is a disposition because
of the undue veneration of these records, to regard our
God, even now as a God of battles. We do not duly discrimi-

nate between that comparatively dark age, when they set up
their shouts of victory for their successes in their wars,
whether aggressive or defensive, and the present. There is
not sufficient allowance for the state that they were in at
that time. Because of the veneration paid to the Bible, we
find, even down to the present time, the overruling providence of God is claimed as giving countenance to the most
barbarous and horrid wars, that are even in this day, curs-
ing and disgracing the nations of the earth. Slavery, you
know how ready the apologists for slavery and these apologists, to the shame of the church be it spoken[,] have been
abundantly found in the pulpit, have screened themselves behind their imaged patriarchal institution and what sanction
has been given to this greatest of all oppressions, this
most wicked system which the English language furnishes no
words wherewith rightly to depict the enormity of its cruelty. And this is done even at the present time by these
priests of sect,these monopolizers of the pulpit. These
ecclesiastics of our day have sought authority from the
Bible and made it the plea for the sabbath, by quotations
there from, that it was of God's sanction, that it was a
patriarchal institution. You know as regards sensual indulgence the great obstacles that were thrown in the way of the
temperance reformation by the use that was made of the Bible,
by authority sought, for indulging in the intoxicating cup.
We may rejoice that truth has been found stronger than all
these, that thus the great efforts that have been made in
our day for peace[,] for human freedom, for temperance, for
moral purity, for the removal of all oppressions and monopolies that are afflicting mankind, have been to a considerable extent successful notwithstanding such obstacles as a
popular priesthood, a popular clergy and a popular belief
and the use of the Bible, have placed in the way of these
great reformations. See now the resort to the Bible to
prove the superstitious observances of a day. The manner

in which this day is observed is one of the strongholds of
priestcraft. It forms one of the pillars which must be
broken down and which will be broken down, before an enlightened Christian faith. But then it needs that there
should be boldness to declare this faith. It needs there
should be faith to act in accordance with this and to declare the abuse that is now made of the Bible, in seeking
to establish forms of worship which long since should have
passed away. Superstitions, baptism, communion tables and
devotions of various kinds and orders, have there found
their sanction by improper reference to this volume. Thus
by taking the examples of the ancients, even though they
may have been comparatively modern, though they may have
been disciples of Jesus in his day, yet I believe there is
no rightful authority, no Scripture authority, for taking
their example as sufficient authority for the continuance
of the practice in the present day. We are not thus to use
the example or practice of the ancients. It may have been
well for them, coming from under the cloud of superstition
formerly. They may still have needed their outward
school master to bring them to a higher position, a higher
sphere, a higher understanding, a higher dispensation, but
are we because we find that they continued their type under
the law, or their baptism which was of John[,] because they
continued in their Sabbath observances, are we to do these
things? I tell you nay. This divine word which we believe
to be our sufficient teacher, draws us away from a dependance upon books, or everything that is outward, and leads
us onward and upward in the work of progress toward perfection. Were we to come to the light we should have less
need of the ordinance, for it would lead us away from customs of the religious world. If we have come as a babe,
like stated in the language of the Apostle, what need he
says have we any more of these ordained; touch not, taste
not, handle not for all are designed to punish with the

using but the substance is of Christ. And if ye come to
this then let no man judge you as regards meats and drinks
or new moons, or Sabbath days.

Remember the Sabbaths are but a shadow of things to
come but the substance is of Christ. Those whose dependance is upon apostolic authority cannot find it, but there
is notwithstanding a superstitious veneration put in the
clerical explanation of that authority which has led many
most mournfully to pin their faith upon ministers sleeves.
Therefore we see the religious world gone on satisfying itself with its mysteries, with its nice theories of religion.
These they regard as useful but which are really anything
but true religion. We see them going out satisfied with
their forms and devotions, taking comparatively little
interest in the great subject of truth and humanity.

But are those all or the only uses that are made of
the Bible and of the first day of the week, for the day has
been consecrated to the expounding of these dogmas and the
enforcing of useless forms? Are there not also other uses
of these, has there not been another reading of the Scriptures? The proper use of them I can verily believe has
been understood and is increasingly understood by very many
and that the day is a day also for strengthening good feelings, for exciting religious veneration in a profitable way.
We can freely admit that the Bible, in the intelligent reading and growing intelligence with which it is pursued with
proper discrimination, without taking it as a volume of
inspiration but only acknowledging that which is inspired,
the truth which is eternal and divine being of value to the
soul, had used not a few with a proper appreciation
of the day, it also had its uses. How many have found
consolation in Scripture testimonials suited to their
almost every state? When they were in the low dungeon,
then the Lord delivered his angels and those who are now
in a similar state can understand these testimonies and they

too sing their song on the banks of deliverance: These find
true consolation in these corroborating testimonies for
they have passed through similar scenes with those who are
now suffering and who are now rejoicing. These are feelings leading to praises and acclamations unto the highest.
How many are the testimonies of these Scriptures which suit
the state of those who are desirous for truth and righteousness to prevail on the earth, how beautiful is the testimony
from the beginning to the end of the Scriptures, to the discriminating servant of the highest that is born to righteousness, truth, uprightness, justice and mercy, peace and universal love? The law of the Lord is declared to be perfect,
to be pure, upright and clear, and to abide forever and those
who obey this word, are made clear sighted. This truth when
heard and suffered to be as a law is as a candle, as a light
leading and enlightening the path that leads into the right
way. How satisfactory then are the corroborating testimonies of Scripture but not more so than the testimonies of
many other servants of God. Why not regard all the testimonies of the good, as Scripture, recorded in every age and
in every condition of life? These Scriptures are valuable
because they bring together the testimonies of so many
ages of the world, but are there not equal testimonies
born to the truth that are not bound in this volume? Certainly there are and we do err not knowing the Scriptures,
nor the power of God when we limit the Scriptures, when we
limit the truth or indeed when we set so high a value on
these Scriptures as to suffer our veneration to lead us to
receive truth more from this source than from any other.
There is one source which is higher than this, and when we
come to it we are drawn away, to some extent from all external dependances, from all outward authorities. And further as regards these Scriptures, intelligently we shall
not fasten upon ourselves any form of worship or conversion
because those in ancient time were in the practice of them.

We shall look at these and make all allowance for the state
that they were in and suffer them to pass by. As regards
days, we shall not be venerators of days because the ancients were, and indeed I have too often thought that the
veneration which professing Christians paid to this day far
exceeds that which was enjoined upon the Jews, among whom
the observances were instituted. Well has a modern writer
said, that the consecration of the Sabbath or one day in
seven, indicates the desecration of the other six, that the
consecration of our churches indicates the desecration of
our homes, the consecration of a class leads to the desecration of the great mass of the people, the consecration
of this leads to the desecration of others, rather than the
dedication of them to holiness and sacredness. I knew a
woman some years ago who would spend every day in the week
reading all the novels that were issued from the press and
on the first day she would take her Bible and read a chapter and one of Blair's sermons, then close up the books,
and state what she had done, and look with a kind of religious horror upon those who would be engaged pursuing some
innocent occupation, and whose every time was consecrated
to truth and duty, God and humanity. This latter class
find a portion of every day for religious devotion and instructive reading. Oh my Friends, the abuse that there is
in this day; leading people to regard with a kind of pious
horror anything which is innocent in itself. This is a
superstition which we at least ought to be rid of. Our
Fathers suffered enough in bearing their testimonies to
the equality of days for us not to be found going back to
the beggarly elements. Let us hail, in the present state
of society, the existence of this day as set apart as a
day of rest and it may be too of innocent recreation to the
toil worn labourer, while there is a disposition to exact
so much of him through the week, leaving little time for
rest and innocent recreation, and for religious improvement,

on other days. Let us hail this as a season that shall
give such time though it may not be so used. Let us also
hail it as a day furnishing opportunity for exciting the
religious veneration of those who still require this for
their better nature, be that either in psalmody, in melody
and in prayer or in some other way suited to their views of
what belongs to the day.

    I also enjoy while I am coming down to my chosen
place of gathering, the liberty, the freedom that is manifested in our fellow citizens, going each to his chosen
place of worship. I also enjoy the cleanliness of our
courts and alleys, and the little children who one day in a
week have on what they call their Sunday clothes and go
forth in a feeling of cleanliness and innocent enjoyment.
While we feel that there may be these advantages let us
earnestly protest against the superstition which had led
to penal enactments to enforce the observance of this day.
Let us protest against this spirit for it is a spirit of
priestcraft. It is the clerical and ecclesiastical power
that's gaining the ascendency in this country so far as
it is allowed by the public opinion of the country. It's
gaining upon the people and it will make inroads upon us
until our liberties are sapped, until we are brought under
a yoke which neither we nor our fathers were able to bear.
Let us then my friends cherish a religion which shall be
rational and which shall be reasonable in its observances
and in its requirements. Let us keep hold of the faith
that is in accordance with reason and with the intelligent
dictates of the pure spirit of God. Let us ever hold up
the supremacy of this spirit[,] of this divine guidance,
as far above all the leadings of men and the teaching of
books or the veneration that is imposed by the observance
of these, or by worship in meeting houses. We need to understand the worship that is more in our everyday life that
is manifested more by efforts of love and of devotion to truth and
righteousness. We need to consecrate ourselves more to God and to

humanity and less to forms and ceremonies and to ritual
faith. With the proper uses of the day and of the Bible
and with the proper use of the church and of our religious
institutions we may then be greatly benefited to improved.
But there will be division and subdivisions until we come
to fully to understand that truth which leadeth unto the
liberty; That he that upholdeth truth designs that there
should be no inspiration, no power delegated upon one portion of the people over another. Until we come to this,
until there is an intelligent testimony born against ecclesiastical usurpations, against hierarchical institutions,
against the favored few in the congregation, there must be
divisions and subdivision among us. These things must
needs be; therefore when we hear of wars and rumors of wars
in our midst let us not be troubled but know full well that
the end is not yet, but that we must trust in the growing
light and intelligence which is spreading over the human
family and which is marking those who are desirous to obtain the right, who are hungering and thirsting after greater righteousness. That in this growing intelligence, these
evils which still cling to sect, will be removed, and one
great means of removing these, is the diffusion of knowledge among both male and female. The usurpations of the
church and clergy, by which woman has been so debased, so
crushed, her powers of mind, her very being brought low,
and a low estimate set upon these, are coming to be seen in
their true light. But woman must avail herself of the increasing means of intelligence, education and knowledge.
She must rise also in a higher sphere of spiritual existence and suffer her moral nature to be developed, her mind
to be made right in the sight of God. Then will the time
speedily come when the influence of the clergy shall be
taken off of woman, when the monopoly of the pulpit shall
no more oppress her, when marriage shall not be a means of
rendering her noble nature subsidiary to man, when there

shall be no assumed authority on the one part nor admitted
inferiority or subjection on the other. One of the abuses
of the Bible (for Apostolic opinion has been taken and no
doubt false opinion, for there have been abundant quotations and some mistranslations in order to make the Apostle
say what the priests declare he did say) has been to bind
silence upon woman in the churches, fasten upon her that
kind of degrading obedience in the marriage relation which
has led to countless evils in society and indeed has enervated, and produced for us a feeble race. Oh my friends,
these subjects are subjects of religious interest and of
vast importance. I would that there were successors coming
forth in this great field of reform. The Almighty is calling upon both man and woman to open their mouths and judge
righteously, to plead the cause of the poor and needy and
many sure are thus emphatically called to lift-up the voice
and declare the truth of God and this will give evidence of
the divinity of their mission just as Jesus did. The Spirit
of the highest is upon me; The Spirit of the Lord is upon me,
because he hath anointed me to preach the gospel, because
he hath anointed me to bind up the broken-hearted to preach
deliverance to the captive, the opening of the prison to
them that are bound, and so preach the acceptable ear of
the Lord. May they then not be afraid, may they not be
ashamed to lift up their voices for the right so let the
sound be heard far and wide and let it go forth to the ends
of the earth; The Spirit of the Lord is come upon them and
they are called to go forth on this mission. A blessing
will be to them for they will acknowledge that the highest
has been their mouth and wisdom, their tongue and utterance
have been of the Lord that whereas they were a few and
feeble but that they have been made strong and mighty in
him who is ever with his children. Whoever giveth them
mouth and wisdom, tongue, and utterance to speak that which
he commandeth, strength and perseverance in accordance with

right; preaching and doing that which is right by a blessed
example, by a pure life, for this is almost effectual
preaching of righteousness.

        [Sermons.   MSS.   Friends Historical
        Library, Swarthmore College.]

QUARTERLY MEETINGS, NO ORDINARY OCCASIONS

SERMON, DELIVERED AT CHERRY STREET MEETING,
PHILADELPHIA, NOVEMBER 6, 1849

Rachel [Rodgers] in her sermon stated that if we kept our eyes singly directed to the light we should not be concerned about the existing evils in Society. I view these Quarterly meetings as no ordinary occasions. They are opportunities for us to compare ourselves and our progress with our predecessors, with our fathers, and with the great principles upon which they were established, and which we also profess to act upon. They are occasions when we may confer together, and seek to provoke one another to love and good works, when we may endeavor to stir up the pure mind one in another by way of remembrance. I have believed that if this Society continues with any degree of prosperity, if it be marked as any living thing, as having any life in it, it must be by the evidence furnished in these examinations of ourselves, in our Quarterly meetings and other opportunities. If we have any evidence furnished of its progress it is by our progress and advancement in the truth. There is in all religious associations a constant tendency to retrogression. Having begun in the spirit there is a disposition too manifest to seek to be made perfect by the flesh, to go back again to the weak and beggarly elements and to desire, and be willing, to be brought into bondage again. The only way in which we can be preserved from this downward step, from this backsliding, is that we go forward, that we follow the light, not that we

sit down in listless indolence. The great heresy that is
proclaimed in our Society, sometimes is of waiting in a
kind of indifference for the light to come to us. This has
been one of the most fatal heresies, the most fatal to the
progress of this religious body, of any that has ever been
proclaimed. That we may be serving him, whoever seeketh
fruits at the hands of his children, by doing nothing, by
as has been expressed, waiting and failing to enter into
the great harvest field, the great vineyard of the Lord
with the paltry plea that no man hath hired us, that we
have not been called to this or that work. In every principle[,] in every testimony that the fathers of this people
held[,] there is progress, there is advancement, in none
more than in the great fundamental one of the guidance of
the divine light to the souls of the children of men; that
in obedience to this as our fathers were led out of the
traditions that specially marked their age, they had to
bear their emphatic and loud testimony against the great
theological errors that were existing among the people presenting their progress, as well as against the great practical sins of their day. They were going actively against
these having their hearts in the work, being troubled because of these great evils that were afflicting society.
Many went forth endeavoring to enlighten the people being
concerned to strengthen their brethren, and we if we continue to make progress and advance and become established[,]
strengthened and settled on this immutable foundation of God,
this in speaking word in the soul,will manifest it by our
works. There is no more certain law of God[,] of his providence[,] no more certain evidence of the invariable nature
of his law, than the stamp that has set up a people, upon
religious society as well as upon nations, and individuals,
showing just what they are by their fruits. If this society through the means of its Quarterly and other meetings
wherein to take cognizance of the state of its progress,

shall not give evidence of progress of advancement, as the
light is increasingly opened unto us, surely then in the
eternal providence of God, Ichabod will be written upon thy
walls[,] the glory will be departed from thee. And vain
will it be for us to cling to the outward habitiments of
sect to say, master behold what a beautiful building is
ours, verily it may be said not one stone shall be left upon
another of all these systems[,] of all these outward build-
ings[,] glorious though they may have been in their day,
which shall not be thrown down. Then in the advance of society as has been declared here, that people[,] that society,
that individuals cannot advance while they have the clogs
of superstitions and tradition around them holding them
back[.] [I]t is incumbent upon us my friends[,] if we be
made sensible of this superstition that we be faithful to
the light which we have entering our dissent and it may be
our earnest protest against them. There are many in this
society who have as much occasion to protest against the
traditional views of the scripture[,] of the sabbath or of
the first day of the week[,] of the church ordinances therein performed as ever any had in any age of the world. I
would that these were not in any disposition to please men
rather than to please God. I would that these were a disposition in us to be willing to be made of no religious
reputation among the Orthodox people of our day but to declare openly [uncompromisingly] and without reserve and without clothing our sentiments in mystical forms of expression[,] our faith in simplicity[,] the truth as it is in
Jesus, as we comprehend it in Jesus; That we may not be
bound to bible traditions, to sabbath traditions, by
imagined divinity of Christ's tradition, by the absurd doctrine of atonement, but that we may stand by the truth as
simply and clearly manifested and be willing to take the
consequences of all charges that may be made of infidelity
or unsoundness of doctrine even though it lead us to be

cast out of the synagogue and our names cast out as evil
for truth sake. Shall we not be able to drink of the cup
which Jesus drank, shall we not be able to bear the Baptisms with which he was baptized? I believe we shall and
also be kept in the very spirit, that would say, father
forgive them for they know not what they do, forever blessed[,] eternally blessed be the name of our father and we
should feel the invaluable nature of this treasure. There
is a spirit as one said formerly, that I feel, that resisteth not evil nor revengeth wrong but which enables us to
bear all things. Paul spoke of a spirit on the outward,
which is of a contrary nature. The former spirit may be
attained, is attainable. Then let us not fear of any consequences for ourselves. Let us not hesitate to declare
openly the whole counsel of God, as we may be called upon
to do it. We behold society holding back. We see that it
is not keeping pace with the great advances in the church
of Christ.

     Remember that the church of Christ is not our little
petty society, nor any other sectarian organization. That
church is composed of living members and these living members are sent forth even as Jesus was sent forth, with the
glorious gospel of peace to proclaim in the earth. The
highest evidence that these give of the divinity of their
mission, is that the spirit of the highest is upon them,
because they are thus anointed because they thus go
forth to bind up the broken hearted, to preach deliverance
to the captive, the opening of the prison doors to them
that are bound. Well then we know that in this church of
Christ there are living members now going abroad in the
earth spreading the benign doctrines of the blessed principles of peace, seeking to put an end to the wars that are
savaging the earth and despoiling nations, that are bringing lamentations and woe unto the families of men. The
harvest truly is great[,] pray ye therefore to the Lord of

the harvest that he will send forth labourers into this
field. We should all be filled with this spirit which shall
desire, the universal spread of peace on earth and goodwill
among men. Let it be regarded as a zeal without knowledge,
though you may be accused of being over zealously effected.
I tell you nay it is good to be zealously effected in a good
cause, and I rejoice in the great efforts that are being
made for the spread of the true principles and the carrying
of them out in our intercourse with our fellow beings. We
should all advance beyond what our fathers saw, and hence it
was that Elias Hicks hesitated to put his own sentiments upon paper, because he believed that the generations following
him would see truth more clearly than he and his contemporaries saw it. It is the beauty of the glory of truth that
there is this progress in it. It is beautiful to behold
this. We see many giving up their undue attachment to political parties and to governments, giving up their consti-
tutional veneration and refusing to have any lot or part in
a government and constitution which are based upon the
sword, the ultimate resort of which is the destroying weapon. We see this progress in the divine principle of nonre-
sistance, and we hail the day when there shall be greater
advances upon this subject. If any sect, be it our own self
styled favoured society or any other society or organization[,] shall set its face against this progress[,] if any
minister in society shall be found endeavoring to give check
to any such progress, mark it my friends, derision will come
upon these. Ichabod will be written upon its walls, the
glory has departed, will be stamped upon any such society.
It is well for us then in these Quarterly meetings, in our
examinations, to query now whether those who are chosen messengers, officers and high seat occupants of this society
are those who are keeping up to the advance guard of progress in the peace reformations; whether they are full of
the political periodicals of the day[,] whether

they are going to the polls and voting for warriors and
slaveholders, whether they are showing they have the true
allegiance to peace principles which their profession would
lead us to look for. So also as regards the great testimony against slavery. We are called, as I believe every
living member of the church of Christ is called, to bear a
testimony against all oppression, all wrong and all unrighteousness. There are many such living members of the
church of Christ up and down in society who are indeed
earnestly protesting, who are indeed going against this vast
iniquity and seeking to enlighten the public mind upon this
subject. If this society or any of its accredited ministers, its members[,] its officers or high seat occupants,
shall be found giving their influence against this great
progress, and this great and mighty reformation that there
is in the earth; more than this, if they shall be found enriching themselves with the gain of oppression and reveling
in the sweets of unrequited labor that comes through such a
polluted channel; if they shall be found engaging in building their houses by unrighteousness and chambers of wrongs
living upon their neighbors service without hire, giving
him naught for his work, it is certain that declension will
follow, and we will be scattered and divided. On the other
hand if there be any consistent testimony upon this subject
it will lead to practises far in advance of any practises
of our fathers, for they were involved in it to a greater
or less extent than we now are. However a profession may
be made that a testimony against slavery belongs to this
society, there will be a declension among us, we will be
marked as a declining people that can never make progress
unless we do something. Our fathers never made progress
but by holding up righteousness and uprightness, high above
all speculations, even the speculation that we may be faithful to the light and do nothing. Beware of this heresy.

Beware of the heresy that will lead us into the belief,
that we should do nothing to remove the great evils that
are in the earth. I rejoice that the church of Christ is
manifested, is marked, is stamped by the inviolable seal of
the highest, in that its members are found arrayed against
all unrighteousness and wrong, against all iniquity in high
and in secret places, against all monopolies that exist in
society. I rejoice that Christian Democracy is spreading
in society at large. Both in other countries and in this,
there is beginning to be, at least, a better appreciation
of the rights of man. We hail this true Christian understanding of the equal brotherhood of man. If we as a society continue to uphold aristocracy and give countenance
to monopolies which furnish facilities to the rich to become richer, and cause the poor to become poorer, our society can never prosper. It must go down, it will go down,
let us cling ever so tightly to its forms, to its outward
dress or address, to its arrangements and disciplinary ex-
pedients, however these may have been and are useful.
There is nothing that will preserve the life and growth of
this people but by living in its principles, and being
faithful in working them out. Therein will my heavenly
father, the heavenly father of Jesus, be glorified that his
children bring forth much fruits. Mark if there are among
the parables one more than another impressing active duties
upon the people and the necessity of being fruit bearing
branches it is this, which Jesus held up to view, showing
the importance of actively pursuing and fulfilling the
great duties of life, by bearing fruits. How is it in the
temperance reformation? Have we by our own practice and
occasionally by our accredited preaching, in our meetings
giving a check to this noble reformation. As we show by
the stamp upon our countenances that we are still indulging in the intoxicating wine, beer and cider while this
great reformation has reached almost to the uttermost

ends of the earth. Depend upon it if this be the case,
our testimony against intemperance will be but a show as a
form and we shall not have evidence that we are advancing
in this also. I hope better things my friends. I trust
that this great testimony has found its place among the
younger members at least of our society, influencing the
fathers and mothers as far to banish the decanters, and
bringing us down to the pure water, by which our minds are
kept clearer to discriminate, our morals purer and our
hearts cleaner for the reception of the blessed light of
Christ. May then these Quarterly meetings be seasons of
self-examination, and for holding up great principles
wherein there is progress one unto another. I could not
let this opportunity pass without holding up these things
before us, so that we may be profited. If we are really
profited by these, it must be by coming home and bringing
these principles to bear upon our every day conduct in
life. Blessed shall he be who is ready to say here am I, O
Lord, send me into the great harvest field of reform where
there shall be labor and this labor shall be done.

        [Sermons. MSS. Friends Historical
        Library, Swarthmore College.]

DISCOURSE ON WOMAN

DELIVERED IN PHILADELPHIA,
DECEMBER 17, 1849

There is nothing of greater importance to the well-being of society at large—of man as well as woman—than the true and proper position of woman. Much has been said, from time to time, upon this subject. It has been a theme for ridicule, for satire and sarcasm. We might look for this from the ignorant and vulgar; but from the intelligent and refined we have a right to expect that such weapons shall not be resorted to,—that gross comparisons and vulgar epithets shall not be applied, so as to place woman, in a point of view, ridiculous to say the least.

This subject has claimed my earnest interest for many years. I have long wished to see woman occupying a more elevated position than that which custom for ages has alloted to her. It was with great regret, therefore, that I listened a few days ago to a lecture upon this subject, which, though replete with intellectual beauty, and containing much that was true and excellent, was yet fraught with sentiments calculated to retard the progress of woman to the high elevation destined by her Creator. I regretted the more that these sentiments should be presented with such intellectual vigor and beauty, because they would be likely to ensnare the young.

The minds of young people generally are open to the reception of more exalted views upon this subject. The kind of homage that has been paid to woman, the flattering appeals

which have too long satisfied her—appeals to her mere fancy and imagination, are giving place to a more extended
recognition of her rights, her important duties and responsibilities in life. Woman is claiming for herself stronger
and more profitable food. Various are the indications to
this conclusion. The increasing attention to female education, the improvement in the literature of the age, especially in what is called the "Ladies' Department," in the periodicals of the day, are among the proofs of a higher estimate of women in society at large. Therefore we may hope
that the intellectual and intelligent are being prepared
for the discussion of this question in a manner which shall
tend to enoble woman and dignify man.

Free discussion upon this, as upon all other subjects,
is never to be feared; nor will be, except by such as prefer
darkness to light. "Those only who are in the wrong dread
discussion. The light alarms those only who feel the need
of darkness." It was sound philosophy, uttered by Jesus,
"He that doeth truth cometh to the light, that his deeds
may be made manifest, that they are wrought in God."

I have not come here with a view of answering any particular parts of the lecture alluded to, in order to point
out the fallacy of its reasoning. The speaker, however, did
not profess to offer anything like argument on that occasion,
but rather a sentiment. I have no prepared address to deliver to you, being unaccustomed to speak in that way; but I
felt a wish to offer some views for your consideration,
though in a desultory manner, which may lead to such reflection and discussion as will present the subject in a true
light.

In the beginning, man and woman were created equal.
"Male and female created he them, and blessed them, and
called their name Adam." He gave dominion to both over the
animals, but not to one over the other.

> "Man o'er woman
> He made not lord, such title to himself
> Reserving, human left from human free."

The cause of the subjection of woman to man, was early ascribed to disobedience to the command of God. This would seem to show that she was then regarded as not occupying her true and rightful position in society.

The laws given on Mount Sinai for the government of man and woman were equal, the precepts of Jesus make no distinction. Those who read the Scriptures, and judge for themselves, not resting satisfied with the perverted application of the text, do not find the distinction, that theology and ecclesiastical authorities have made, in the condition of the sexes. In the early ages, Miriam and Deborah, conjointly with Aaron and Barak, enlisted themselves on the side which they regarded the right, unitedly going up to their battles, and singing their songs of victory. We regard these with veneration. Deborah judged Israel many years—she went up with Barak against their enemies, with an army of 10,000, assuring him that the honor of the battle should not be to him, but to a woman. Revolting as were the circumstances of their success, the acts of a semi-barbarous people, yet we read with reverence the song of Deborah: "Blessed above woman shall Jael, the wife of Heeber, the Kenite be; blessed shall she be above women in the tent. *** She put her hand to the nail, and her right hand to the workman's hammer; she smote Sisera down dead." This circumstance, revolting to Christianity, is recognized as an act befitting woman in that day. Deborah, Huldah, and other honorable women, were looked up to and consulted in times of exigency, and their counsel was received. In that eastern country, with all the customs tending to degrade woman, some were called to fill great and important stations in society. There were also false prophetesses as well as true. The denunciations of Ezekiel were upon these women who would prophesy out of their own heart, and sew pillows to all armholes," &c.

Coming down to later times, we find Anna, a prophetess of four-score years, in the temple day and night, speaking of Christ to all them who looked for redemption in Jerusalem. Numbers of women were the companions of Jesus —one
going to the men of the city, saying, "Come, see a man who
told me all things that ever I did; is not this the Christ?"
Another, "Whatsoever he saith unto you, do it." Philip had
four daughters who did prophesy. Tryphena and Tryphosa
were co-workers with the apostles in their mission, to whom
they sent special messages of regard and acknowledgement of
their labors in the gospel. A learned Jew, mighty in the
Scriptures, was by Priscilla instructed in the way of the
Lord more perfectly. Phebe is mentioned as a *servant* of
Christ, and commended as such to the brethren. It is worthy of note, that the word *servant,* when applied to Tychi-
cus, is rendered *minister.* Women *professing* godliness,
should be translated *preaching*.

The first announcement, on the day of Pentecost, was
the fulfillment of ancient prophecy, that God's spirit
should be poured out upon *daughters* as well as sons, and
they should prophesy. It is important that we be familiar
with these facts, because woman has been so long circum-
scribed in her influence by the perverted application of
the text, rendering it improper for her to speak in the
assemblies of the people, "to edification, to exhortation,
and to comfort."

If these scriptures were read intelligently, we should
not so learn Christ, as to exclude any from a position,
where they might exert an influence for good to their fellow-beings. The epistle to the Corinthian church, where
the supposed apostolic prohibition of woman's preaching is
found, contains express directions how woman shall appear,
when she prayeth or prophesyeth. Judge then whether this
admonition, relative to *speaking* and asking questions, in

the excited state of that church, should be regarded as a
standing injunction on woman's *preaching,* when that word
was not used by the apostle. Where is the Scripture authority for the advice given to the early church, under peculiar
circumstances, being binding on the church of the present
day? Ecclesiastical history informs us, that for two or
three hundred years, female ministers suffered martyrdom,
in company with their brethren.

These things are too much lost sight of. They should
be known, in order that we may be prepared to meet the assertion, so often made, that woman is stepping out of her
appropriate sphere, when she shall attempt to instruct public assemblies. The present time particularly demands such
investigation. It requires also, that "of yourselves ye
should judge what is right," that you should know the ground
whereon you stand. This age is notable for its works of
mercy and benevolence—for the efforts that are made to reform the inebriate and the degraded, to relieve the oppressed and the suffering. Women as well as men are interested in these works of justice and mercy. They are efficient co-workers, their talents are called into profile exercise, their labors are effective in each department of reform. The blessing to the merciful, to the peacemaker is
equal to man and to woman. It is greatly to be deplored,
now that she is increasingly qualified for usefulness, that
any view should be presented, calculated to retard her labors of love.

Why should not woman seek to be a reformer? If she is
to shrink from being such an iconoclast as shall "break the
image of man's lower worship," as so long held up to view;
if she is to fear to exercise her reason, and her noblest
powers, lest these should be thought to "attempt to act the
man," and not "acknowledge his supremacy"; if she is to be
satisfied with the narrow sphere assigned her by man, nor
aspire to a higher, lest she should transcend the bounds

of female delicacy; truly it is a mournful prospect for woman. We would admit all the difference, that our great and
beneficent Creator has made, in the relation of man and woman, nor would we seek to disturb this relation; but we deny that the present position of woman is her true sphere
of usefulness; nor will she attain to this sphere, until
the disabilities and disadvantages, religious, civil, and
social, which impede her progress, are removed out of her
way. These have enervated her mind and paralysed her powers.
While man assumes that the present is the original state
designed for woman, that the *existing* "differences are not
arbitrary nor the result of accident," but grounded in nature; she will not make the necessary effort to obtain her
just rights, lest it should subject her to the kind of scorn
and contemptuous manner in which she has been spoken of.

So far from her "ambition leading her to attempt to
act the man," she needs all the encouragement she can receive, by the removal of obstacles from her path, in order
that she may become a "true woman." As it is desirable
that man should act a manly and generous part, not "mannish,"
so let woman be urged to exercise a dignified and womanly
bearing, not womanish. Let her cultivate all the graces
and proper accomplishments of her sex, but let not these
degenerate into a kind of effeminacy, in which she is satisfied to be the mere plaything or toy of society, content
with her outward adorning, and with the tone of flattery
and fulsome adulation too often addressed to her. True,
nature has made a difference in her configuration, her physical strength, her voice, &c.—and we ask no change, we are
satisfied with nature. But how has neglect and mismanage-
ment increased this difference! It is our duty to develop
these natural powers by suitable exercise, so that they may
be strengthened "by reason of use." In the ruder state of
society, woman is made to bear heavy burdens, while her
"lord and master" walks idly by her side. In the civiliza-

tion to which we have attained, if cultivated and refined
woman would bring all her powers into use, she might engage
in pursuits which she now shrinks from as beneath her proper
vocation. The energies of men need not then be wholly devoted to the counting house and common business of life, in
order that woman in fashionable society may be supported
in their daily promenades and nightly visits to the theatre
and ball room.

   The appeal of Catharine Beecher to woman some years
ago, leading her to aim at higher pursuits, was greatly encouraging. It gave earnest of an improved condition of woman. She says, "The time is coming, when woman will be
taught to understand the construction of the human frame,
the philosophical results from restricted exercise, unhealthy modes of dress, improper diet, and other causes, which
are continually operating to destroy the health and life of
the young. *** Woman has been but little aware of the high
incitements which should stimulate to the cultivation of her
noblest powers. The world is no longer to be governed by
physical force, but by the influence which mind exerts over
mind. *** Woman has never wakened to her highest destinies
and holiest hopes. The time is coming when educated females
will not be satisfied with the present objects of their low
ambition. When a woman now leaves the immediate business of
her own education, how often, how generally do we find her,
sinking down into almost useless inactivity. To enjoy the
social circle, to accomplish a little sewing, a *little* reading, a little domestic duty, to while away her hours in
self-indulgence, or to enjoy the pleasures of domestic life,
—these are the highest objects at which many a woman of
elevated mind, and accomplished education aim. And what
does she find of sufficient interest to call forth her cultivated energies, and warm affections? But when the cultivation and development of the immortal mind shall be presented to woman, as her especial and delightful duty, and

that, too, whatever be her relations in life; when by example
and experience she shall have learned her power over the
intellect and the affections, *** then we shall not find
woman, returning from the precincts of learning and wisdom,
to pass lightly away the bright hours of her maturing youth.
We shall not so often see her, seeking the light device to
embroider on muslin and lace (and I would add, the fashionable crochet work of the present day); "but we shall see her,
with the delighted glow of benevolence, seeking for immortal
minds, whereon she may fasten durable and holy impressions,
that shall never be effaced or wear away."

A new generation of women is now upon the stage, improving the increased opportunities furnished for the ac-
quirement of knowledge. Public education is coming to be
regarded the right of the children of a republic. The hill
of science is not so difficult of ascent as formerly represented by poets and painters; but by fact and demonstration,
smoothed down, so as to be accessible to the assumed weak
capacity of woman. She is rising in the scale of being
through this, as well as other means, and finding heightened
pleasure and profit on the right hand and on the left. The
study of Physiology, now introduced into our common schools,
is engaging her attention, impressing the necessity of the
observance of the laws of health. The intellectual Lyceum
and instructive lectures room are becoming, to many, more
attractive than the theatre and the ball room. The sickly
and sentimental novel and pernicious romance are giving
place to works, calculated to call forth the benevolent affections and higher nature. It is only by comparison that
I would speak commendatory of these works of imagination.
The frequent issue of them from the press is to be regretted.
Their exciting contents, like stimulating drinks, when long
indulged in, enervate the mind, unfitting it for the sober
duties of life.

These duties are not to be limited by man. Nor will

woman fulfill less her domestic relations, as the faithful
companion of her chosen husband, and the fitting mother of
her children, because she has a right estimate of her position and her responsibilities. Her self-respect will be
increased; preserving the dignity of her being, she will
not suffer herself to be degraded into a mere dependant.
Nor will her feminine character be impaired. Instances are
not few of woman throwing off the incumbrances which bind
her, and going forth in a manner worthy of herself, her creation, and her dignified calling. Did Elizabeth Fry lose
any of her feminine qualities by the public walk into which
she was called? Having performed the duties of a mother to
a large family, feeling that she owed a labor of love to
the poor prisoner, she was empowered by Him who sent her
forth, to go to kings and crowned heads of the earth, and
ask audience of these; and it was granted her. Did she
lose the delicacy of woman by her acts? No. Her retiring
modesty was characteristic of her to the latest period of
her life. It was my privilege to enjoy her society some
years ago, and I found all that belonged to the feminine in
woman—to true nobility, in a refined and purified moral
nature. Is Dorothea Dix throwing off her womanly nature
and appearance in the course she is pursuing? In finding
duties abroad, has any "refined man felt that something of
beauty has gone forth from her?" To use the contemptuous
word applied in the lecture alluded to, is she becoming
"mannish"? Is she compromising her womanly dignity in going forth to seek to better the condition of the insane and
afflicted? Is not a beautiful mind and a retiring modesty
still conspicuous in her?

Indeed, I would ask if this modesty is not attractive
also, when manifested in the other sex? It was strikingly
marked in Horace Mann when presiding over the late National
Educational Convention in this city. The retiring modesty
of William Ellery Channing was beautiful, as well as of

many others, who have filled dignified stations in society.
These virtues, differing as they may in degree in man and
woman, are of the same nature and call forth our admiration
wherever manifested.

The noble courage of Grace Darling is justly honored,
leading her to present herself on the coast of England,
during the raging storm, in order to rescue the poor, suffering, shipwrecked mariner. Woman was not wanting in courage in the early ages. In war and bloodshed this trait was
often displayed. Grecian and Roman history have lauded and
honored her in this character. English history records her
courageous women too, for unhappily we have little but the
records of war handed down to us. The courage of Joan of
Arc was made the subject of a popular lecture not long ago,
by one of our intelligent citizens. But more noble, moral
daring is marking the female character at the present time,
and better worthy of imitation. As these characteristics
come to be appreciated in man too, his warlike acts, with
all the miseries and horrors of the battle-ground, will sink
into their merited oblivion, or be remembered only to be
condemned. The heroism displayed in the tented field must
yield to the moral and Christian heroism which is shadowed
in the signs of our times.

The lecturer regarded the announcement of woman's
achievements, and the offering of appropriate praise through
the press, as a gross innovation upon the obscurity of female life——he complained that the exhibition of the attainments of girls, in schools, was now equal to that of boys,
and the newspapers announce that "Miss Brown received the
first prize for English grammar," &c. If he objected to so
much excitement of emulation in schools, it would be well;
for the most enlightened teachers discountenance these appeals of love of approbation and self-esteem. But, while
prizes continue to be awarded, can any good reason be given
why the name of the girl should not be published as well as

that of the boy? He spoke with scorn, that "we hear of Mrs.
President so and so; and committees and secretaries of the
same sex." But if women can conduct their own business, by
means of Presidents and Secretaries of their own sex, can
he tell us why they should not? They will never make much
progress in any moral movement, while they depend upon men
to act for them. Do we shrink from reading the announcement
that Mrs. Somerville is made an honorary member of a scientific association? That Miss Herschel has made some discoveries, and is prepared to take her equal part in science?
Or that Miss Mitchell of Nantucket has lately discovered a
planet, long looked for? I cannot conceive why "honor to
whom honor is due" should not be rendered to a woman as well
as man; nor will it necessarily exalt her, or foster feminine pride. This propensity is found alike in male and female, and it should not be ministered to improperly, in
either sex.

In treating upon the affections, the lecturer held out
the idea, that as manifested in the sexes, they were opposite, if not somewhat antagonistic; and required a union, as
in chemistry, to form a perfect whole. The simile appeared
to me far from a correct illustration of the true union.
Minds that can assimilate, spirits that are congenial, attach themselves to each other. It is the union of similar,
not opposite, affections, which are necessary for the perfection of the marriage bond. There seemed a want of proper
delicacy in his representing man as being bold in the demonstration of the pure affection of love. In persons of re-
finement, true love seeks concealment in man, as well as in
woman. I will not enlarge upon the subject, although it
formed so great a part of his lecture. The contrast drawn
seemed a fallacy, as has much, very much that has been presented, in the sickly sentimental strains of the poet, from
age to age.

The question is often asked, "What does woman want,

more than she enjoys?" What is she seeking to obtain? Of
what rights is she deprived? What privileges are withheld
from her? I answer, she asks nothing as favor, but as
right, she wants to be acknowledged a moral, responsible being. She is seeking not to be governed by laws, in the
making of which she has no voice. She is deprived of almost
every right in civil society, and is a cypher in the nation,
except in the right of presenting a petition. In religious
society her disabilities, as already pointed out, have
greatly retarded her progress. Her exclusion from the pulpit or ministry—her duties marked out for her by her equal
brother man, subject to creeds, rules, and disciplines made
for her by him—this is unworthy her true dignity. In marriage, there is assumed superiority, on the part of the husband, and admitted inferiority, with a promise of obedience,
on the part of the wife. This subject calls loudly for examination, in order that the wrong may be redressed. Customs
suited to darker ages in Eastern countries, are not binding
upon enlightened society. The solemn covenant of marriage
may be entered into without these lordly assumptions, and
humiliating concessions and promises.

There are large Christian denominations who do not
recognise such degrading relations of husband and wife. They
ask no magisterial or ministerial aid to legalize or to
sanctify this union. But acknowledging themselves in the
presence of the Highest, and invoking his assistance, they
come under reciprocal obligations of fidelity and affection,
before suitable witnesses. Experience and observation go to
prove, that there may be as much harmony, to say the least,
in such a union and as great purity and permanency of affection, as can exist where the more common custom or form is
observed. The distinctive relations of husband and wife, of
father and mother of a family are sacredly preserved, without the assumption of authority on the one part, or the
promise of obedience on the other. There is nothing in such

a marriage degrading to woman. She does not compromise her dignity or self-respect; but enters married life upon equal ground, by the side of her husband. By proper education, she understands her duties, physical, intellectual and moral; and fulfilling these, she is a help meet, in the true sense of the word.

I tread upon delicate ground in alluding to the institutions of religious associations; but the subject is of so much importance, that all which relate[s] to the position of woman, should be examined, apart from the undue veneration which ancient usage receives.

> "Such dupes are men to custom, and so prone
> To reverence what is ancient, and can plead
> A course of long observance for its use,
> That even servitude, the worst of ills,
> Because delivered down from sire to son,
> Is kept and guarded as a sacred thing."

So with woman. She has so long been subject to the disabilities and restrictions, with which her progress has been embarrassed, that she has become enervated, her mind to some extent paralysed; and, like those still more degraded by personal bondage, she hugs her chains. Liberty is often presented in its true light, but it is liberty for man.

> "Whose freedom is by suffrance, and at will
> Of a superior—he is never free.
> Who lives, and is not weary of a life
> Exposed to manacles, deserves them well."

I would not, however, go so far, either as regards the abject slave or woman; for in both cases they may be so degraded by the crushing influences around them, that they may not be sensible of the blessing of Freedom. Liberty is not less a blessing, because oppression has so long darkened the mind that it cannot appreciate it. I would therefore urge, that woman be placed in such a situation in society, by the yielding of her rights, and have such opportunities

for growth and development, as shall raise her from this
low, enervated and paralysed condition, to a full appreciation of the blessing of entire freedom of mind.

It is with reluctance that I make the demand for the
political rights of woman, because this claim is so dis-
tasteful to the age. Woman shrinks, in the present state
of society, from taking any interest in politics. The
events of the French Revolution, and the claim for woman's
rights are held up to her as a warning. But let us not look
at the excesses of women alone, at that period; but remember
that the age was marked with extravagances and wickedness in
men as well as women. Indeed, political life abounds with
these excesses, and with shameful outrage. Who knows, but
that if woman acted her part in governmental affairs, there
might be an entire change in the turmoil of political life.
It becomes man to speak modestly of his ability to act without her. If woman's judgment were exercised, why might she
not aid in making the laws by which she is governed? Lord
Brougham remarked that the works of Harriet Martineau upon
Political Economy were not excelled by those of any political writer of the present time. The first few chapters of
her 'Society in America,' her views of a Republic, and of
Government generally, furnish evidence of woman's capacity
to embrace subjects of universal interest.

Far be it from me to encourage woman to vote, or to
take an active part in politics, in the present state of our
government. Her right to the elective franchise however, is
the same, and should be yielded to her, whether she exercise
that right or not. Would that man too, would have no participation in a government based upon the life-taking principle
—upon retaliation and the sword. It is unworthy a Christian nation. But when, in the diffusion of light and intelligence, a convention shall be called to make regulations
for self-government on Christian, non-resistant principles,
I can see no good reason, why woman should not participate

in such an assemblage, taking part equally with man.

Walker, of Cincinnati, in his Introduction to American
Law, says: "With regard to political rights, females form a
positive exception to the general doctrine of equality. They
have no part or lot in the formation or administration of
government. They cannot vote or hold office. We require
them to contribute their share in the ways of taxes, to the
support of government, but allow them no voice in its direction. We hold them amenable to the laws when made, but allow them no share in making them. This language, applied to
males, would be the exact definition of political slavery;
applied to females, custom does not teach us so to regard
it." Woman, however, is beginning so to regard it.

"The law of husband and wife, as you gather it from
the books, is a disgrace to any civilized nation. The theory of the law degrades the wife almost to the level of
slave. When a woman marries, we call her condition cover-
ture, and speak of her as a *femme covert*. The old writers
call the husband baron, and sometimes, in plain English,
lord. *** The merging of her name in that of her husband is
emblematic of the fate of all her legal rights. The torch
of Hymen serves but to light the pile, on which these rights
are offered up. The legal theory is, that marriage makes
the husband and wife one person, and that person is the *husband*. On this subject, reform is loudly called for. There
is no foundation in reason or expediency, for the absolute
and slavish subjection of the wife to the husband, which
forms the foundation of the present legal relations. Were
woman, in point of fact, the abject thing which the law, in
theory, considers her to be when married, she would not be
worthy the companionship of man."

I would ask if such a code of laws does not require
change? If such a condition of the wife in society does not
claim redress? On no good ground can reform be delayed.
Blackstone says, "The very being and legal existence of

woman is suspended during marriage —incorporated or con-
solidated into that of her husband, under whose protection
and cover she performs every thing." Hurlbut, in his Essays
upon Human Rights, says: "The laws touching the rights of
woman are at variance with the laws of the Creator. Rights
are human rights, and pertain to human beings, without distinction of sex. Laws should not be made for man or for woman, but for mankind. Man was not born to command, nor woman to obey. *** The law of France, Spain, and Holland—and
one of our own States, Louisiana, recognizes the wife's
right to property, more than the common law of England. ***
The laws depriving woman of the right of property [are] handed
down to us from dark and feudal times, and not consistent
with the wiser, better, purer spirit of the age. The wife
is a mere pensioner on the bounty of her husband. Her lost
rights are appropriated to himself. But justice and benevolence are abroad in our land, awakening the spirit of inquiry and innovation; and the Gothic fabric of the British
law will fall before it, save where it is based upon the
foundation of truth and justice."

   May these statements lead you to reflect upon this
subject, that you may know what woman's condition is in society—what her restrictions are, and seek to remove them.
In how many cases in our country, the husband and wife begin life together, and by equal industry and united effort
accumulate to themselves a comfortable home. In the event
of the death of the wife, the household remains undisturbed,
his farm or his workshop is not broken up, or in any way
molested. But when the husband dies, he either gives his
wife a *portion* of their joint accumulation, or the law ap-
portions to her a *share;* the homestead is broken up, and
she is dispossessed of that which she earned equally with
him; for what she lacked in physical strength, she made up
in constancy of labor and toil, day and evening. The sons
then coming into possession of the property, as has been

the custom until of latter time, speak of having to *keep*
their mother, when she in reality is aiding to keep them.
Where is the justice of this state of things? The change[s]
in the law of this State and of New York, in relation to
the property of the wife, go to a limited extent, toward
the redress of these wrongs; but they are far more extensive,
and involved much more, than I have time this evening to
point out.

On no good ground can the legal existence of the wife
be suspended during marriage, and her property surrendered
to her husband. In the intelligent ranks of society, the
wife may not, in point of fact, be so degraded as the law
would degrade her; because public sentiment is above the
law. Still, while the law stands, she is liable to the disabilities which it imposes. Among the ignorant classes of
society, woman is made to bear heavy burdens, and is degraded almost to the level of the slave.

There are many instances now in our city, where the
wife suffers much from the power of the husband to claim
all that she can earn with her own hands. In my intercourse
with the poorer class of people, I have known cases of extreme cruelty, from the hard earnings of the wife being thus
robbed by the husband, and no redress at law.

An article in one of the daily papers lately, presented the condition of needle women in England. There might
be a presentation of this class in our own country, which
would make the heart bleed. Public attention should be
turned to this subject, in order that avenues of more profitable employment may be opened to women. There are many
kinds of business which women, equally with men, may follow
with respectability and success. Their talents and energies
should be called forth, and their powers brought into the
highest exercise. The efforts of women in France are sometimes pointed to in ridicule and sarcasm, but depend upon
it, the opening of profitable employment to women in that

country, is doing much for the enfranchisement of the sex.
In England also, it is not an uncommon thing for a wife to
take up the business of her deceased husband and carry it
on with success.

Our respected British Consul stated to me a circumstance which occurred some years ago, of an editor of a political paper having died in England; it was proposed to his
wife, an able writer, to take the editorial chair. She accepted. The patronage of the paper was greatly increased,
and she, a short time since, retired from her labors with a
handsome fortune. In that country however, the opportunities are by no means general for woman's elevation.

In visiting the public school in London, a few years
since, I noticed that the boys were employed in linear drawing, and instructed upon the black board, in the higher
branches of arithmetic and mathematics; while the girls,
after a short exercise in the mere elements of arithmetic,
were seated, during the bright hours of the morning, *stitching wristbands*. I asked why there should be this difference made; why they too should not have the black board?
The answer was that they would not probably fill any station in society requiring such knowledge.

But the demand for a more extended education will not
cease until girls and boys have equal instruction, in all
the departments of useful knowledge. We have as yet no high
school for girls in this state. The normal school may be a
preparation for such an establishment. In the late convention for general education, it was cheering to hear the testimony borne to woman's capabilities for head teachers of
the public schools. A resolution there offered for equal
salaries to male and female teachers, when equally qualified,
as practised in Louisiana, I regret to say was checked in
its passage, by Bishop Potter—by him who has done so much
for the encouragement of education, and who gave his countenance and influence to that convention. Still, the fact of

such a resolution being offered, augurs a time coming for
woman which she may well hail. At the last examination of
the public schools in this city, one of the alumni delivered
an address on woman, not as is too common in eulogistic
strains, but directing the attention to the injustice done
to woman in her position in society, in a variety of ways.
The unequal wages she receives for her constant toil, &c.,
[present] facts calculated to arouse attention to the subject.

Women's property has been taxed, equally with that of
men's, to sustain colleges endowed by the states; but they
have not been permitted to enter those high seminaries of
learning. Within a few years, however, some colleges have
been instituted, where young women are admitted, nearly upon
equal terms with young men; and numbers are availing themselves of their long denied rights. This is among the
signs of the times, indicative of an advance for woman. The
book of knowledge is not opened to her in vain. Already is
she aiming to occupy important posts of honor and profit in
our country. We have three female editors in our state—
some in other states of the Union. Numbers are entering the
medical profession—one received a diploma last year; others
are preparing for alike result.

Let woman then go on—not asking as favor, but claiming as right, the removal of all the hindrances to her elevation in the scale of being—let her receive encouragement
for the proper cultivation of all her powers, so that she
may enter profitably into the active business of life; em-
ploying her own hands, in ministering to her necessities,
strengthening her physical being by proper exercise, and
observance of the laws of health. Let her not be ambitious
to display a fair hand, and to promenade the fashionable
streets of our city, but rather, coveting earnestly the best
gifts, let her strive to occupy such walks in society, as
will befit her true dignity in all the relations of life.

No fear that she will then transcend the proper limits of
female delicacy. True modesty will be as fully preserved,
in acting out those important vocations to which she may be
called, as in the nursery or at the fireside, ministering
to man's self-indulgence.

Then in the marriage union, the independence of the
husband and wife will be equal, their dependence mutual,
and their obligations reciprocal.

In conclusion, let me say, "Credit not the old fashioned absurdity, that woman's is a secondary lot, ministering to the necessities of her lord and master! It is a
higher destiny I would award you. If your immortality is
as complete, and your gift of mind as capable as ours, of
increase and elevation, I would put no wisdom of mind
against God's evident allotment. I would charge you to
water the undying bud, and give it healthy culture, and
open its beauty to the sun—and then you may hope, that
when your life is bound up with another, you will go on
equally, and in a fellowship that shall pervade every earthly interest."

[Philadelphia: T. B. Peterson, 1850.]

TO IMPROVE THE CONDITION OF OUR FELLOW BEINGS

SERMON, DELIVERED AT CHERRY STREET MEETING

PHILADELPHIA, DECEMBER 23, 1849

"As iron sharpeneth iron, so man sharpeneth the countenance of his friend." We are in constant observation of
this familiar comparison and although often misquoted our
experience confirms it in our intercourse with society, in
social life as well as in religious intercourse. [Sentence
illegible.] An obligation rests upon us to communicate
that which we have, as far as it is in our power; to do
good, to improve the condition of our fellow beings, in
society at large and in religious associations. We are
scarcely aware of the influence which we may exist one
over another for good, and it must be by the exercise of
our talents and moral power that this sharpening of the
countenance of our friends is attained. "To do good and
to communicate, forget not[,] for with such sacrifices God
is well pleased." In the present generations we have had
abundant evidence of the advantages that have occurred in
society by this intercourse one with another for higher
purposes and for greater good than mere animal gratifica-
tions and sensual enjoyments or the pleasures of the imaginations. The moral sentiments and spiritual feelings have
been appeased in a manner, to call these forth for the
best interests of man. How much my friends, is elicited
by this intercourse with our fellow beings. By this means
we may be brought to reflect upon the great, and high end
of our creation and our being. In reflecting upon what we

163

have already heard this morning, as to the true ground work
of all our religion, the revelation of God's truth to man,
and in securing this as sound doctrine, as the sufficient
basis for man's salvation, it behoves us to examine it and
try ourselves by this test whether we are producing fruits
which give evidence that we are acquainted with this ground
that we are building upon, for other foundation can no man
lay, than that which is already laid. If this is the foundation as we believe it is of the prophets and the apostles,
and of the great truths that Jesus preached, then are we
to look for the legitimate fruits of such ground. Among
the prophets, the evidence that was called for of their
allegiance to this truth was "Arise and shine for thy light
is come and the glory of the Lord is arisen upon thee,"
and in obedience to this light, this shining of truth, the
declaration was against Sectarian fasts, against Jewish
rites and ceremonies, as the sufficient worship of the
highest, and instead of these was portrayed the great duty
that "Ye loose the bonds of wickedness" as the acceptable
fast which God has chosen, "that ye undo the heavy burden
and let the oppressed go free and that ye break every yoke
and when thou seest the naked, that thou clothe him and that
thou hide not thyself from thine own flesh." These were the
evidences required, that the professors were building upon
the true, eternal foundation, that thou do justly love mercy
and walk humbly with thy God. And again when Jesus called
the attention of the people to the only true foundation, the
revelation of the father's will to their souls, what were the
fruits which he declared should ever receive a blessing? Why
that they should bring their deeds to the light, that it
should be manifest that they were wrought in God, that they
should let their works so shine, that men might see them and
come to acknowledge the God whom they worshipped, for it was
after the manner that was regarded as heresy. There was not
the necessity conformity to existing religious usages and

hence some evidence must be given of their acknowledgment
of God's omnipotence, there must be some fruits which show
that they were the called of God and were in the possession
of the true faith and hence they were called to let their
light shine; to be as a city set upon a hill that could not
be hid and that their good works might so appear, that man
might behold them and come to glorify the spiritual father,
who could be exalted in their midst, by producing the fruits
which he called for at their hands. When he called he gathered the people around him and he directed them to this divine government within themselves, this kingdom of God,
which cometh not by outward observation or observance. He
then declared that a blessing was to the merciful, to the
peacemakers, to the pure in heart and to those who hungered
and thirsted after righteousness. Here is a harmony as
much in the fruits that are called to give evidence of the
right foundation, as the true preaching from age to age as
to what this foundation is. We as certainly try ourselves
and those around us by these tests as could those in any
age of the world, for Jesus declared that the only rightful
test of Judgment and of Judging one another is by their
fruits Ye shall know them. Men do not gather figs of
thorns, nor of a bramble bush gather they grapes. Among
religious sects generally, there is a theoretical acknowledgment of the great truth of the divinity of God's teachings. There may be a difference as to the necessity of a
medium through which this teaching shall come; there may
be some leaning to their Moses, to their outward authorities, to their divine revelation through their ministers.
They not having aimed at this highest dispensation of all,
wherein they no more need that man should teach them but
when God shall be directly the teacher of his people himself. This I say is acknowledged among the different professors and I doubt not in great sincerity but after
making it they all in a general way fall into the fatal

error, that communion in their particular sect is the means
of carrying forward the work of salvation of righteousness,
of true faith, and acceptable worship. We hear the devotees
of the several religious professors expressing their full
faith that the bringing in of the people to what they call
Christian faith—which is in other words their acceptation
of it to their forms of worship whatever they may be[,] is
very essential and that after that is done,the work of the
soul's salvation is very nearly accomplished. These suppose
that this is the worship which God requires and that these
are the fruits that he asks for at the hands of his children.
Hence we see thousands up to this day, professing the Christian name, shutting themselves out from this intercourse
with society, which as iron sharpeneth iron would cause a
man to sharpen the countenance of his friends; imagining
that their faith may be far more rightfully shown by entering a monastery or convent or nunnery as the case may be.
We look upon this as an evidence of darkness and in one of
the sects great efforts have been made to enlighten the public so far that they shall not cloister themselves to the
extent that one sect has done. But let us look to it and
see whether there is not an [injuring] of the mind in Prot-
estantism as well as in Catholicism. Protestants may not
have monasteries erected for their special purpose, but
when we behold the various sects in their exclusiveness, in
regard to their faiths or manner of worship and see the effects of their preaching, we perceive that precisely the
same effect is produced as by entering a monastery, for
they are virtually shut out from that intercourse with
their fellow beings, to diffuse light, knowledge and instruction, which would sharpen the countenance of friends as iron
sharpeneth iron. The evil of this is that each sect comes
to believe that it is only by its particular ways of thinking and its peculiar performances that salvation is to be
attained and religious truth is to be understood. The

fathers of this people in the enlarged views which they
held, claimed for themselves the more universal appella-
tive of friends and mingled with their fellow beings of
every class of society; availing themselves of such opportunities as were continually occurring around them to gather the people to the truth and to the bringing forth of the
practical fruits of every day righteousness. In the beginning they were not sectarian; they showed by their
fruits that they believed that blessed were the merciful,
the peacemaker, the just and the upright, and as iron
sharpeneth iron so did they sharpen the countenances of
their contemporaries, by their intercourse with society and
spread true Christian principles before the nations. I
have sometimes thought that liberty, so far as it is enjoyed,
although we have mournfully to acknowledge that it is with
the exclusion of three millions of our fellow beings from
its blessings, yet so far as republican principles and
Christian democracy have spread in our country, that we are
to a considerable extent, at least, indebted to the faithfulness of the fathers of this people, who had the good of
man at heart, who felt that they could not be limited to
any particular sect, but who sent out and mingled with humanity and laboured for it, and their eyes being singled to
the light, they having no sectarian purposes to subserve,
their bodies became full of light, as when the bright shining of a candle doth give light to all around. This light
was indeed as a city set upon a hill that could not be hid.
Its influence was to all around and many were gathered to
this standard and many came to understand true Christian
principles apart from sectarian theology. We need, my
friends, in our day to extend our hearts, our [exertions]
beyond mere sectarian limits. We are in the same danger
that all other sects are, having our high partition walls,
imagining that we are a favoured people, that wisdom will
distinguish us that we must not mingle with the nations

around. And to some extent this is manifesting itself among
us, and the fruits are apparent in making, as was said a
few days ago, having a name to live and yet dead, making us a
body without life. The salt after having lost its savour
is henceforth good for nothing but to be thrown out and
trodden underfoot, and so it will be with our society if it
has lost its savour; for however beautiful and attractive
its outward habiliments may be, within there will be poverty and death. If there be any continued building on this
only true foundation, this building of God, it will lead us
to cast off the old clothing when it is no longer necessary,
it will cause us to leave behind that which has answered its
end—behold the old heavens and the old earth passing away.
And there will be created in their stead new heavens and a
new earth wherein dwelleth righteousness. Are the various
sects in our day labouring to promote righteousness and
peace? Are they showing by their fruits that the true fast
which God has chosen us is to break the bonds of wickedness,
to undo the heavy burdens and to let the oppressed go free
and to break every yoke? Are they bearing a testimony
against the great oppressions, the wars, the tumults, the
violence, that are in society? No, these sects are not
troubled with these things, they have sectarian business to
perform and they cannot attend to humanity. Depend on it,
such a sect, however high may be its profession, will have
Ichabod written upon its walls. The glory will be departed
and indeed has departed from many of these and the people
being sensible of the short comings of those with whom they
have been associated, are seeking a higher righteousness,
and asking who shall show us any good. And in order to
promote the good, and their own usefullness, they have been
compelled to leave their several religious orders and unite
themselves in some other way, to promote the great interests of society, and by so doing their own good. If we
look at the religious sects, there is scarcely one that has

not its exclusion of woman from any participation in its
public office of preaching, and they are nearly all perverting the Scriptures to prove an Apostolic prohibition of
woman's preaching. Abundant evidence is given from year to
year and almost from day to day that the people are not
satisfied with this state of things. For a long time it is
true the prophets were prophesying falsely and by this
means an isolated priesthood [has ruled] and it seems as
if the people loved to have it so, and were pinning their
faith upon ministers sleeves, but now the people are alive
to their duties and responsibilities. They are beginning
to see that those who are anointed preachers and priests
are not giving the evidence that Jesus did that the spirit
of the Lord was upon them, because he had anointed them" to
bind up the broken-hearted, to preach deliverance to the
captive and the opening of the prison to those who were
bound and to set at liberty them that were bruised." This
evidence not being manifested in their lives and conversa-
tions, there has been a distrust of the ministry, a distrust of the church itself and hence it has become to be
placed in its proper light, as a conventional arrangement
of society, answering a good and for a time, but being perverted from its original object by becoming sectarian, the
idea of conversation being more to bring to sect than to
Christianity. The people are beginning to think that they
may judge of themselves what is right and by this intercourse into which they are called, suffering a man to sharpen the countenance of his friends, they are using their
gifts which God has so bountifully bestowed, we may hope
for the regeneration of religious society. In our own day,
we may hope that the veneration so long misdirected will
come to be directed in its right channel and then those who
seek the improvement of their religious nature by gathering
together and sitting in the assemblies of the people will
find them to be improved not merely by preaching addressed

to their selfishness, but by preaching calling them to labor in the great field of humanity for the good of their
kind and by so doing they will experience in return that
richest of spiritual food, that blessed fullness of peace
which the world can never give, which misdirected veneration
can never attain and which can only be arrived at by going
upon this true foundation of which we have heard, in such a
manner as to build a fit building for the holiness of God's
spirit to dwell in. Then will our veneration be unto this
great master builder and we shall find him to be a God not
afar off but a father near at hand and in this beautiful
relation, this closeness of spiritual union, we shall come
to ascertain the great truth that God dwelleth in us, that
he is omnipresent, that he gives us power for every service
that he calls upon us to perform and acknowledging this,
the pure heart, the humble soul, walking humbly before him,
shall continually say "not unto us Oh! Lord, not unto us but
unto thy great and glorious name be all the praise, all the
victory, all the renown."

        [Sermons. MSS. Friends Historical
        Library, Swarthmore College.]

KEEP YOURSELVES FROM IDOLS

SERMON, DELIVERED AT CHERRY STREET MEETING,
PHILADELPHIA, MARCH 17, 1850

Are we engaged in prayer ——the silent quiet, communion, that is a profitable exercise of the soul; for true
prayer is the soul's sincere desire, uttered or unexpressed.
All of us may put up our petitions, according to our several needs and as they are offered in sincerity, so are they
accepted and the soul is straightened thereby. The prayer
of my heart has been in the short time we have been sitting
together this morning, that we may be kept from idols. I
remembered the exortation of the apostle to the brethren
"little children keep yourselves from idols." There is
quite as much need of a reiteration of this among professing Christians as in Heathen or Pagan lands. It is a question whether there be any more idolatry in carvings of wood
and stone——in the vain sacrifices offered by the unenlightened, than in the homage that is paid to form and ceremony,
to speculation and opinions, among those who claim to be
enlightened——those who are thanking their God, that while
all the Gods of the heathen are idols, their God is the
only true God, that while there are Gods many and Lords
many in the heathen world, that to them or to us there is
but one God, even the father, and one Lord Jesus Christ.
In the view that is entertained of these, the idea of God
and of Jesus Christ which prevails in Christendom——the offering of oblations and of Sunday worship which grows out
of this idea, a question is involved of serious inquiry,

171

whether indeed we are free from idolatry. If we of this
little company descended from our free thinking and free
speaking forefathers--we who claim our George Foxs for our
fathers, believe there is descended to us—or by any birthright any favorable circumstances of education, more clear
and enlightened views upon this subject, than have the professors of the Christian name around about us, then it becomes a serious and heart-searching inquiry, whether we are
faithful to the light that we have and are honest to our
convictions; For it is a fact now as formerly that light
enough is in the world but there is a want of moral courage
to acknowledge it, to come under its influence, to have our
faith enlightened by it. Men love darkness rather than
light because their deeds are evil. That which reproved
and makes manifest is light, and we have the light and why
should we shun it or shrink from the acknowledgement of it,
lest we should be made of no religious reputation around us.
Are we then worthy the name of disciples of Christ, unwilling as we are to drink the cup which Jesus drank, to be baptized with his baptism, unwilling to have our names cast
out as evil for the blessed truth's sake? Are we worthy
the name we profess? Are we not rather clinging to, and
giving sanction to the idolatry of the day, than being the
true reformers in the age in which we live, and therefore
worthy of the name of our fathers—worthy to have an Abraham or a George Fox for our father? Are we doing the works
of these reformers? Are we treading in their steps—that
is the steps of faithfulness to the light which governed
them—to the faith which was in Jesus, and which made him
so true to his father and our father—to his God and our
God? Other men have laboured in this enlightened pathway.
Are we entering into these labors or are we measuring our
piety, our devotion our Christianity by precisely the same
verbal and ceremonial standard that others are—even those
who we sometimes acknowledge we are called to testify against.

I often feel when gathered with my friends on a cloudy day and observe so many absentees, that we may be prone
to measure our zeal, our piety, our devotion, by the earnestness with which we gather together—making sacrifices
by exposing ourselves to the weather in order to come here.
Now while we acknowledge, and I do humbly acknowledge I
trust, all the benefits that may accrue to us through our
assembling together, and I was rejoiced on this day of the
week of last week to hear the various instrumentalities or
aids to our piety or devotion so clearly held up to view and
it has furnished a subject of profitable reflection to one
occasionally through the week, but in acknowledging all this
I can say at the same time that there is a great deal of
sectarian zeal manifested in habitually coming together
through all weathers on this day of the week, let the circumstances be what they may.

I conceive that there may easily be a zeal that is
not according to knowledge, and I doubt not that in this
many do err not knowing the scriptures, or the truth—not
reading intelligently, not understanding the truth aright.
I believe in this day particularly it behooves us to hold
out views of worship[,] of devotion[,] of piety entirely
disconnected with meeting or the Sabbath day observances.

There is a mighty effort in this day to impress,
these duties as they are regarded and make them the test of
the Christian character—of piety of devotion. We are not
aware, I fear how much we are in danger of being brought
under a yoke which neither we nor our fathers were able to
bear. For want of faithfulness to the light we have [not
the] moral courage to speak out our principles, and act in
accordance with them, it is not until within a few years that
liberal Pennsylvania—operated upon greatly by early Quaker
influence dared to make its appointments of fast days[,] of
prayer days[,] of thanksgiving days. Our early friends had
a bold testimony to bear against holy days, and some of

them carried it so far as to feel bound to perform their
business upon this day of the week. Of latter times these
rites, these observances, are being imposed upon us, if not
by legal enactments, by those high in authority, those whom
we are perhaps too much taught to venerate, for there is
great veneration for the government, for the powers that be,
more than is consistent with true Quakerism or true Christianity. Not only are these fasts and thanksgiving days
recommended to us, but we see even in the business relations
of society, how Sabbath laws and observances are creeping
in, and how few there are who dare take their stand; their
noble stand against these encroachments of Priestly power.
Depend upon it friends[,] we are in danger of being brought
under a Priestly Hierarchy. We may profess all the testimony against a hireling ministry and we may have a zeal
that would keep our young people from assembling with those
who do receive or who do preach under salary but it will be
but as a little feather in the scale[,] a drop in the buck-
et, if we are not at the same time so alive to these encroachments of sectarian zeal and of Priestcraft as to take
a noble and bold stand against everything of the kind, that
would limit our freedom or encroach upon our just privileges.

The liberty of conscience that has been guaranteed to
us is no mean privilege. The right of conscience is a noble
right and I would that we were so faithful in its exercise,
so honest in its practice, that we might show that we have
no fear of man which ever bringeth a snare, that we were
not seeking to please men, more than to please God. Beware
of idols not only in the matter of observance of days and
times, but of creeds and books; beware how we are brought to
worship creeds and how we bow down to the authority of a
book. The religion of Christendom has an abundance of
idolatry in it in this particular. It has brought forth
its Christ in a miracle and enrolled him in mystery, and
palmed him upon the ignorant believers, and made this ac-

ceptance of him as a test of the true believer. Let us not
fear to assert in the face of all Israel and the son that
our salvation has not the slightest dependance upon belief
in mystery, in miracles but that the more our religion is
in accordance with the true philosophy the nearer does it
approach the God of truth and reason. The more our religion
is from self-evident conviction, from intuition[,] and to the
obedient soul truth is received by intuition, the more we
live in accordance with the blessed precepts which truth
ever teaches to men, the higher will be the evidence and
the more certain the conviction we shall give, that we have
fellowship with the Father and the Son. Let our fellowship
with the Son be not a fellowship of faith in trinities and
atonements[,] in mysteries or in miracles, but let us look
at the beautiful life of Jesus, devoted to the truth; his
meat and his drink to do the will of his father, and to
finish his work, and he acknowledges that herein was he
born, and to this end and for this cause came he into the
world to bear witness to the truth. This witness had reference to the practical duties of life, teaching us to love
our neighbors as ourselves. Depend upon it friends, idolatrous Christendom is calling this mere morality, mere
works of righteousness. The religion of Jesus is denied;
his practical purity is not admitted as a necessary [de-
leted] to the church. There are other tests, other standards resorted to. It needs therefore that we should be so
honest as to acknowledge our dissent from all the creeds,
and from all this kind of worship. How few are there who
dare to speak of the bible, of sunday, of Jesus, and of
creeds as they really believe. This is the mournful view
I have taken at times, while at the same time I see that
there is a reaction even in the orthodox world. The children of a Lyman Beecher are made wiser than their fathers,
the children of the old calvanists are seeing beyond the
absurdity of their creeds. The doctrines of election and

reprobation are going to the winds, and it would be but
fighting the air to pursue them. But still there are
creeds and impositions, there are idols which ought to be
destroyed, and let us be willing to be the destructives in
this work; and show the world what harm has been done by
this undue veneration to forms and peculiarities. See how
in the hands of priestcraft the bible has been arrayed
against every improvement, every discovery in science or
morals. Even in natural science, no sooner as has there
been one step of progress than the bible has been brought
in away, and all the influence of the pulpit has been
brought to bear against its advancement. The victims of
this superstition have been made to deny with their lips
that which their heart has borne testimony to. Look at
Galileo and see whether we have no need to tremble at the
encroachment of the clergy. No sooner has practical righteousness been held up more clearly before the people than
in former days, for the purpose of advancing the beautiful
mission of peace on earth and good will to man and the removal of oppression from our land, then again the clergy
have come before us with bible in hand to prove the rightfulness of war, of slavery, and of the cursed aristocracies
which are crushing multitudes of the people. It is a subject which ought to cause the words of truth to burn within
us, to speak out boldly the truth of God as it is in Jesus.
We know on the single subject of capital punishment how
difficult it has been to enlighten the people because of
the efforts to prove from the bible that this was a divine
command. Not only upon this but again and again has slaveholding, that mightiest of oppressions, that deepest of
sins, been held up to view as a patriarchal institution.
And why? because the people have been superstitiously led
to look at the temple of the ancients of darker times for
their authority of action for the present day, because they
have been led away from God and the teaching of his people

himself, from the light of truth illuminating the understanding and conscience. Look to the record of past ages,
and make use of them which those very records never
sanctioned.   No my friends there is not a single text of
the bible which gives license to rest our practice upon the
practice or example of the ancients.   Let us receive
these records for all the good they may do[,] for all the
corroboration of truth that may be found in them, but oh!
let us discriminate, let us remember what even the writers
say of themselves that they are men of like passions with
ourselves.   Let us not with the undue veneration with which
we have been led to regard the book claim a divinity for
man that God never authorized.   Oh! that there were more
faith in the divinity of humanity[,] of the creation of God
and less faith in the divinity that priestcraft has set up,
to which too many have been bowing and which has now filled
Christendom with idolatry.   It needs not that I should go
on stating many particulars in which the bible has been
prostituted.   You know how ingeniously isolated passages
have been brought together and a creed interwoven and a
system based upon the false and wicked assumptions of innate or transmitted depravity of original sin[,] of human
depravity[,] in whatever way it may be defined.   This
scheme of salvation and plan of redemption as it has been
called has been pressed upon the people for their acceptance and how many are there who look further than this
interwoven belief? They are not examining for themselves,
and do not take the trouble to compare text with context,
and discover what a very different and opposite creed might
be, interwoven and drawn from the very same records.   Truth
is so in the world that we are not to be dependent upon any
record for our belief. Our Christianity must draw from the
very truth of God manifested to the souls of the children
of men.   There must be our faith and it must be an opera-
tive one, a faith acted out in life one unto another, in an

effort to remove the mighty evils which are crushing humanity. Let our creed be that faith in God which shall inspire us with love one unto another, and having this love
let us show our devotion and our worship by our every day
duties. Let our daily life be a prayer and our every day
actions be worship. Then my friends we need not hesitate
to speak of meeting-going, even while we acknowledge all
the aid that it may be as but a form, and speak of sabbath
observances as a superstition not becoming the enlightened
spirit of the age in which we live. Let us speak of the
bible as it really is and discriminate as we ought to do,
and not bow down to this idolatry which is one of the
greatest idols of the sectarian in the world. Let us when
we speak of the blessed son of God not wrap him in mysteries, but let him stand forth in his purity, in the brightness of his coming, acknowledging him in his walk among men
in all his purity and Glory. Let us aspire to similar purity—to similar glory. It is not too high an aspiration
for us, it is only because he has been clothed with kind of
God-like robes that people have made him something above
imitation. He is a blessed example as far as he was obedient to truth in his day, and made sacrifices for this truth
and was willing to give up all—to have not whereon to lay
his head so that he might be the means of enlightening the
people, so that he might be indeed the messiah of his age.
Let us not hesitate to aspire to be the messiah of our age,
to be the son of God in our day and as we do this are
obedient to the call, we may now work the work which will
cause the ears of everyone that hearest to tingle. We
should go on overturning all the machinations of priestcraft,
all the designs of the bigoted, sectarians and introduce in
the place thereof all the worship and devotion, all the
piety, based upon rational or divine principles. Every
truth of God, manifested to the souls of men is from a divine source. Let us acknowledge the divinity of this source

and be obedient to it, and bring forth fruits which shall
give evidence of the source whence they came. In other
words let our lights so shine that men may see our good
works and glorify our father which is in heaven. This is
the true glory and this is a heaven not afar off. It is a
heavenly state, a state of righteousness, peace and joy—
a state in which we may be strengthened to meet the trials
and vicissitudes of time in which as we enter we may see
what may have been our idols and how they may be broken;
whether they may have been the idols of sense, our devotion
to the things of the earth, devotion to our great wealth
and to the glory of this world, or whether our devotions
were to a mere sectarian theology, to a mere form of worship.
Let our prayer then be to the father of spirits to preserve
us from these.

[Sermons. MSS. Friends Historical
Library, Swarthmore College.]

WE HAVE FOOD WHILE OTHERS STARVE

SERMON, DELIVERED AT CHERRY STREET MEETING,
PHILADELPHIA, MARCH 31, 1850

Whenever I take my walks abroad
How many poor I see,
What shall I render to my God
For all his gifts to me.

Not more than others I deserve,
Yet God has given me more;
For I have food while others starve
Or beg from door to door.

How many children in the street
Half naked I behold,
While I am clothed from head to feet,
And covered from the cold.

While some poor creatures scarce can tell,
Where they may lay their head
I have a home wherein to dwell
And rest upon my bed.

While others early learn to swear
And curse, and lie, and steal,
Lord I am taught thy name to fear,
And do thy holy will.

Are these thy favours day by day
To me above the rest
Then let me love thee more than they
And try to serve thee best.

This poetic hymn composed by Watts and committed to
memory by many a child contains but the idea that it inculcated in the religious training of most of the children of
the age. It is the kind of praise and thanksgiving which
are offered from most of the pulpits not only in Christendom

but we may safely presume in the world. How far such
thanksgiving and such language is befitting us and in accordance with the more enlightened revelations of truth and
justice it is for us to consider. This morning as I took
my seat at our breakfast table with only my husband present,
I remarked that I did not know that we need pause long for
the spirit of thanksgiving and praise for blessings and enjoyments; but that I could not feel that it would be right
to return thanks for anything like peculiar blessings of
special favors, for indeed my heart at times smote me with
the feelings that there belonged to us at least our share
of the reproach and condemnation that things are as they
are. That there was a broad distinction in Society as so
truly portrayed by this simple yet sublime poet that "we
have food while others starve or beg from door to door."
I often feel it to be a profitable reflection to dwell on
this subject because it may lead to the laying of the axe
at the root of the corrupt tree, rather than leading to a
blind dependence upon an imagined providence to bring about
a different state of things without man's agency. I have
been instructed sometimes, in reading the early language of
John the Baptist, the forerunner of the blessed Jesus as
well perhaps as his own language "behold now the axe is
laid at the root of the trees and every tree that bringeth
not forth good fruit must be hewn down and cast into fire."
There is a great deal of true philosophy conveyed in this
assertion; for however we may rejoice at the alleviations
which are so generously and benevolently imparted to suffering humanity, and which to some extent are applied to existing evils, yet we must see as we look at the subject cor-
rectly that it is not until right shall take place, until
the axe shall be laid at the very root of these evils, that
they can be destroyed. I often rejoice and am and made
glad that there is so much of humanity in man; so much benevolence in his nature, that it has lead and still leads

to a great deal being done for the erring and viscious in
the name of benevolence and charity which belongs to them
in the name of justice. I rejoice that we are so constituted by our nature that we can and do accommodate ourselves to the circumstances in which we are placed; and
while we may be far from viewing those who are living in
self indulgence, luxury and excess as peculiarly blest of
God, or even as desirable to emulate, at the same time we
must admit that God in his wisdom, in his unbounded and il-
limitable benevolence, has abundantly crowned the earth
with blessings, and given unto man of this abundance, richly to enjoy, and it is desirable that all classes of Society partake of these rich blessings. While all this may be
admitted, there is a fatal want of faith and confidence, in
the power which God has gifted the creatures he has made,
to bring about such a state of Society as we acknowledge to
be desirable, but which in the erroneous teachings and
views which are instilled in our religious Education, we are
so prone to put off to some millenium day—some too frequently far distant future when by some miraculous providence the kingdom of this world shall become the kingdom of
our Lord and of his Christ. The fact is mournful that nearly all the preaching and praying, and the religious observances or beliefs of the world go to strengthen this idea
rather than impress upon men their individual and co-opera-
tive duty to do justice to their fellow-beings to exercise
mercy to all classes of society. We may remember the complaint uttered against Jesus was that he mingled with the
lowest classes of that age, the publicans and sinners of
his time. It was in vain that he assured them that men
might have different walks in life, one being called to one
work of reformation and another to another; that while John
came neigh neither eating nor drinking, the son of man
might come both eating, and drinking; yet both were liable
to have their motives called in question, and to be judged

by the zealous of their day——the accusers of the brethren
of their time. Of John they said "he hath a devil," of
Jesus they said "behold a glutton and a wine bibber; he sup-
peth with publicans and sinners." How beautifully Jesus
closed this with the language "wisdom is justified of all
her children." If we could so believe, and hail the virtuous efforts for the renovation of Society, and the improvement of man's condition in life——if we could bid Godspeed to every effort having for its object the redemption
of the race, then do I believe we should cease to indulge
the arrogant language, that "we are blest while others
starve, or beg from door to door." We should be led to
look how far in the free agency which so peculiarly marks
the character of man, we have abused it, and by means of unjust or improper distinction in Society——by Hierarchies, by
Aristocracies, and kingly nobilities, by the setting of man
above his fellow-man and making him his ruler, how far we
have been instrumental in bringing about these manifold
evils which now require all the wisdom with which man is
gifted, both by his nature, his divine reason, and his still
divine revelation, to discover the right means of——effecting
a speedy change, that year after year shall not consign its
thousands of starving people to an untimely grave.

        True religion, the religion of Jesus, if we understood
it aright, would lead us into the true philosophical spirit
of political economy, not in the partisan sense of the word,
by any means; but into such a true consideration of the
causes of these great evils as would lead into laying the
axe at the root of the corrupt tree of arbitrary power which
has been produced by the assumption of false claims of man
over his fellow-man.

        This cause has produced this most deplorable state of
things. Let our text then be all things whatsoever ye would
that men should do unto you do ye even so unto them. Likewise let the true principle of justice be ever exalted in

our midst; and let us be desirous to be armed with such a
power—and this power is ever present to give us the ability, if we seek it—as will enable us to do our individual
part in the work of human improvement and thereby be instru-
ments in bringing about a better state of things. This
will never impair in us the spirit of heartfelt thanksgiving and praise for the blessings that abound in life, even
while we see that perhaps our own superior power of acquiring or the more favorable circumstances in which we have
been placed, have secured to us a greater share of these
enjoyments. While we may be ready to say with the Psalmist
thou has cast my lines in pleasant places; we have a goodly
heritage; we shall at the same time feel a great responsibility resting upon us to better the outward condition of
our fellow beings. Thus whether it shall be confined to
the limited circles in which some are accustomed to move—
for there is all, this diversity of gifts even in acting
out these common duties of life— or whether it shall extend
to some embracing extensive ideas,yet it still will be recognized as one of the first duties to mark us as Christians
and brethren, as children of God.

    If there is any one thing more strongly inculcated
and enjoyed in the testimony of the ancients, both sacred
and profane as they are called, than another, it is the
duty of administering to the necessities of the suffering[,]
of giving aid to the weak and perishing. Righteous conduct,
right doing, good works, practical righteousness or whatever name we may apply to it, has been inculcated by the
good—the truly pious in all ages of the world. And this
goes to show the universality of God's love, to man it
goes to show that when we come to essential duties—when we
learn mere creeds, even the ceremonial observances of the
sectarian—there is then no difference found among the
children of man as to what belongs to the attributes of
God. Justice and right have ever been his fundamental

principles, mercy, and love, his darling attributes. These
have been stamped high above all sacrifices in every age,
[A short quotation not heard].

This Jesus applied to himself when he went about doing good. Was it not the body to which he ministered, to
the body only? by no means. While he relieved the sufferings of his fellow beings, he at the same time infused
his blessed gospel of glad tidings of great joy unto all
people, by directing them to that fount within themselves,
whence the pure water which springeth up into everlasting
life—that heavenly manna which might partake of—that
which cometh down from a heaven, from a source higher than
earth, and nourished the immortal soul. He then never
separated his spirit from his outward duties; and when the
Apostle following him would give the highest evidence of
love to God, he said "if thou seest a brother or sister
naked, destitute of daily food, give them not the things
needful to the body only"—mark the body.

Let not our religion be directed into a strain which
shall lead us into less sympathy for suffering and erring
humanity, and let mercy which must ever be coupled with
justice and love influence us, and we shall be instrumental
in relieving the afflicted mourners in Zion. We shall experience a reward, for true it is, that those who go forth
thus ministering to the wants and necessities of their fellow beings experience a rich return—their souls being as
a watered garden, as a spring that faileth not. They are
then prepared, and then only to administer the true spiritual food, and they go to the lowly mourners in Zion to
cheer them up. And while they know that they too have
their dark and cloudy days (for who of us has not, and it
is needful for the soul that there should be days of over-
cast as it is in outward nature) when they come into the
true philosophy, they will attempt to account physically
for that which many poor sufferer imagines to be the with-

drawal of spiritual sustenance and consolation. I believe
it to be our duty to lead the mourners to seek the spiritual
manna; and Oh! do I believe that it has been from the neglect or non observances of the laws of our being that great
depression is felt, and many have gone mourning on this way
believing it to be a special judgment or at least an immediate withdrawal of their beloved from their souls for
the sake of trying their faith. Oh! how is it that we bring
the highest down to our limited human understanding. Let us
understand cause and effect so far as we can by the study
of ourselves, spiritually and physically, and we will never
be abridged of anything that is truly spiritual or divine.
We may wish the mourning prophet Jeremiah has a right to
say "mine eyes are running down with water because the comforter that should relieve my soul is far from me." Again
may we adopt his language, and return multiplied blessings
and thanksgivings because "that when I was in the low dungeon thou heardest me." In quoting the language which
dwelt with me from the time of my taking my seat in this
meeting, I thought there might be many present ready to make
profitable reflections not in accordance with this language,
but in dissent; I quoted scarcely a word of it with approval
for I believe it to be based on long taught error.

I thought by bring[ing] out the few lines so familiar
to most of us, we might perhaps be led to religious contem-
plations as much as by quoting a text from the bible. I am
aware that very much is being done around us for the benefit of the suffering and erring; and we may well rejoice in
these efforts, the more as they seem to be now directed to
the early training, to the moral and intellectual culture
of those who have been so long neglected and suffered to
grow up as circumstances around them favored or otherwise;
who have been permitted to live in our midst, the living
subjects of vice, crime, temptations, and consequently sorrow. Feeling hearts have gone forth even to the outskirts

of our cities and mingled with those who seek to place them
in a position where their better nature and powers would be
called forth, and this fact is worthy of all praise. It is
greatly gratifying to behold this spirit in man, and I
would that every pulpit of this city were used this day to
commend these efforts, this extension of favor to those
without the pale of their Church. It is a mournful fact
that most of the preaching and praying is addressed to
those who are within the pale of the Church. We need a
church for humanity, a religion that shall reach the suffering and downtrodden; we need a Christianity that will lead
us to put our souls in the souls' stead of the oppressed and
explain the address alluded to. There is now going the
rounds of the papers an address which will produce a most
harmful influence upon society on the great subject of humanity, slavery, tending to direct the mind to it as a kind
of providential thing, scarcely admitting it to be evil.
O! I would that there were religion enough, Christianity
enough, humanity enough in the circumstances in which we
are placed—surrounded by three millions of suffering and
dumb—to see such means as are in our power to insure the
downfall of this foul and most iniquitous system. Oh! that
there were hearts to so feel for these suffering and dumb,
as to lead us to cry aloud and spare not, showing unto this
nation its transgression and the high professors of Christianity their short comings. If this were the case we
should not see and hear and read of the effort that [is]
made to sustain their giant, monstrous evil. We should
rather be led to look at our own garments, to see how far
they were cleansed from participating in its iniquities; to
feel that we must not build our house by unrighteousness,
nor our chambers by wrong, we must not use our neighbor's
services without wages and give him nought for his work.
"Here we should be brought to feel that the true fast which [the]
most high has chosen is to undo the bounds of wickedness,

and let the oppressed go free and to break every yoke.   Let
us rejoice and be glad that there is so much of the spirit
still moving about in society, that this reformation is
taught with a zeal and earnestness, with a Christian spirit
—that will never cease until Ethiopia shall lift up her
hands and the last day approaches when all shall rise, liberty be proclaimed throughout the land to all the inhabitants thereof. We may hope, and while there is the spirit
of true liberty in the heart it is impossible to reject it,
that while there is suffering, slavery and wrong—not only
these but the oppressions which we behold around us move
remotely allied to this iniquitous system of slavery, such
as the relations of those who are called the employers and
laborers —there will be a continual struggle to attain a
better state of things. We all ought to be laborers for it
is not God's design that some of us should live in luxury
and unbounded indulgence, while others are toiling morning,
noon, and night for bread. This ought never to be a subject
of thanksgiving or of praise, but blushing and confusion of
face, that such is the state of things around us that we
are ignorantly partaking to such an extent as tends to perpetuate evil rather than good. These are the subjects of
reflection with which my mind has been filled this day, and
I offer them to you under a sense of imperative duty believing that there might be other intelligent minds, not few
present, with whom they may be so received as to lead them
to other reflections which shall show the duties that belong to us as individuals, and the awful responsibilities
that attach to us to fulfill these duties; and in the fulfillment of them we shall experience that blessed reward,
that blessed return (for I would not use the word in the
sense in which it has so often been used) of that peace and
tranquility which knows no alloy and which flows as the
waves of the sea.

  [Sermons. MSS. Friends Historical
  Library, Swarthmore College.]

LUTHER'S WILL

REMARKS, DELIVERED AT A WOMAN'S RIGHTS MEETING,
WEST CHESTER, PENNSYLVANIA, JUNE 2, 1852

[Lucretia Mott thought it important that we should not disclaim the antagonisms that woman's present position rendered it necessary she should assume. Too long had wrongs and oppressions existed without an acknowledged wrong-doer and oppressor. It was not until the slaveholder was told, "Thou are the man," that a healthful agitation was brought about. Woman is told that the fault is in herself, in too willingly submitting to her inferior condition; but, like the slave, she is pressed down by laws in the making of which she has had no voice, and crushed by customs that have grown out of such laws. She cannot rise, therefore, while thus trampled in the dust. The oppressor does not see himself in that light until the oppressed cry for deliverance.]

[In commenting on the will just read (This was the will of Martin Luther which was offered as an example of what a husband might do for his wife at the time of his death) she further said:]

The extract from Luther's will which has been read, while it gives evidence of the appreciation of the services of his wife, to a certain extent, and manifests a generous disposition to reward her as a faithful wife, still only proves the degrading relation she bore to her husband. There is no recognition of her equal right to their joint earnings. While the wife is obligated to accept as a gift that which in justice belongs to her, however generous the boon, she is but an inferior dependent.

The law of our State and of New York, has within a few
years been so amended that the wife has some control over a
part of her property. Much yet remains to be done; and if woman
[will] "contend earnestly" for the right, man will co-operate
with her in adjusting all her claims. We have only to look
back a few years, to satisfy ourselves that the demands already made are met in a disposition to redress the grievances. When a delegation of women to the World's Anti-Slavery
Convention in 1840, could find no favor in London, what were
the reasons assigned for the exclusion? Not that the right
of representation was not as much woman's as man's, but that
"they would be ridiculed in the morning papers."

Daniel O'Connell felt the injustice done to those delegates, and in a letter on the subject to me, expressed his
deep regret, that owing to business engagements, he was not
able to attend the Convention and take part in the discussion.

Dr. Bowring advocated the admission of the delegates
at that time; and afterward in a letter to this country,
said: "How often have I regretted that the woman's question,
to me of singular interest, was launched with so little preparation, so little knowledge of the manner in which it had
been entangled, by the fears of some and the follies of others! But, bear up! for the coming of those women will form
an era in the future history of philanthropic daring. They
made a deep, if not a wide impression; and have created
apostles, if as yet they have not multitudes of followers.
The experiment was well worth making. It honored America—
it will instruct England. If in some matters of high civilization you are behind us, in this matter of courageous benevolence how far are you before us!"

Since that time women have fairly entered the field as
students of medicine and as physicians, as editors and lec-
tureres, engaged in schools of design, and in the taking of
daguerres, as well as in some other works of art, and in

holding Conventions in several of the States of our Union
for the advocacy of our entire claims. A National Society
has been formed; and the proceedings of these Conventions
and Society meetings have been fairly reported, and have received favorable notices in many of the papers of this country, as well as in the *Westminister Review* in England.

> [Recorded in *History of Woman Suffrage*,
> I, 359-60.]

DO NOT KEEP STILL

REMARKS, DELIVERED AT THE WOMAN'S RIGHTS CONVENTION,
SYRACUSE, NEW YORK, SEPTEMBER 8-9, 1852

[A petition was presented, during the Provisional
Government, before the last uprising of the people in
(France), for the rights of woman.* Some of the greatest
philosophers there present, saw that women were right in
their claim; they saw in it a new future for woman. The
reason of the failure of the Revolution of 1789, was that
they failed to be represented by one half of the intelligence of France—intelligence different but not inferior,
and for that very difference essential to form a complete
Republic. Woman had long suffered under a nightmare of oppression, without the power to state the cause of her suffering. Those only shunned or hated discussion, who, being
in the wrong, feared the light. The common remark in the
social circle is, "what do you want?" *Women* would not ask
that question, if they were not stupified with the gilded
pill of flattery, in place of rights.

It was said this morning, that woman could take her
rights in a quiet way, without making so much talk about it;
this is not the case, as is shown in the efforts already
made. In all reforms we have the assertion that agitation
is not best; that God in his own good time will bring about

---

*Since it is unclear from the text whether these re-
marks are paraphrased or quoted directly, the entire text is
placed in brackets.

the desired end; it had often been said, in the meetings of
which she was a member, that if Friends would keep still,
and not mix in the excitements of the day, Providence would
bring about all reforms. She was a believer in agitation—
in the wisdom of *not* keeping still. Jesus was an agitator;
he told the Scribes and Pharisees the practical carrying out
of the law of righteousness. She added, that the wife was
degraded in the marriage relation, in the false vow of obedience to her husband. Blackstone defines the law of marriage
to be that the husband and wife are one person, and that
person, the husband. Thus [woman is] degraded by law, by the
monopoly of the Church, and all the circumstances with which
she is surrounded. She must therefore boldly affirm her
rights. Lucy Stone, whom they all delighted to honor, had
to do battle for her rights, even in that college (Oberlin)
which was the first to open its portals for the equal education of women with men. Antoinette Brown, also a student in
that seminary, had to meet the prejudices against women's
preaching, and to show that no Apostolic or other Scriptural
prohibition could be found. Women must go on, in the exercise of their talents and powers. The first efforts were
feeble, but they would gain strength. Some women had resolved to study Law. We had already successful practitioners
of Medicine. The salaries of female Teachers are now from
five hundred to one thousand dollars per year. The teacher
of Grammar in the Girard College, a woman, is acknowledged
superior to most men. The number of female Editors is constantly increasing. Schools of Design, and other branches
of the Fine Arts, are offering employment to women. The U.S.
Mint employs three to four hundred women. Persevere then,
until no woman shall confess her own degradation, by saying
she has all the rights she wants.]

          [*Proceedings of the Convention,* Syracuse,
          N.Y.: J. E. Masters, 1852.]

INFINITE SOURCE OF GOOD

*REMARKS, DELIVERED AT THE FIFTEENTH ANNUAL MEETING
OF THE PENNSYLVANIA ANTI-SLAVERY SOCIETY, WEST
CHESTER, PENNSYLVANIA, OCTOBER 25-26, 1852*

We should attribute all good to the Inifinite Source
of good. The evils of the Fugitive Slave Law are infinite.
Ask the coloured people, whom it has scattered like sheep
upon the mountains, what can compensate them for their sufferings and terrors and losses. See how it has corrupted
the Northern people, and how easily men, at first shocked
at it, have become reconciled to it. This speculation is
incapable of demonstration. It opens a controversy without
end. Is it not better to speak of evil as evil, not deduc-
ing from it any consequences which do not strictly belong
to it? Does it not tend to weaken our abhorrence of wrong?
There is nothing easier than to quote texts of Scripture in
favour of any theory, as every sect supports its faith by
such texts. I am not willing to admit that Harriet Beecher
Stowe was moved to write Uncle Tom's Cabin by that law; if
she says so, I think she mistakes the influences which have
moved her. I believe, rather that it has been the moral
sentiments and truth promulgated by the *Liberator,* the *National Era,* and the public discussion of the subject, upon
her pure mind, exciting it to feel for the oppressed. If
you point to the progress of our cause, through persecution,
as evidence that the efforts of its enemies have helped it
on, I have as good a right to say that but for these impedi-
ments, Slavery would have been abolished before now. I hope
the Society will instruct the striking out of these passages

of the Report.

> [Other speakers intervene.
> Mott continues.]

[Mrs. Mott believed the Society had never pursued the measure of voting.] Our measures, as described in the Declaration of Sentiment adopted at the formation of the American Anti-Slavery Society, were to organize Anti-Slavery Societies, to send forth agents; to circulate books, tracts and periodicals; to seek to enlist the pulpit and the press in the cause of the suffering and the dumb; to aim at the purification of the churches from the guilt of Slavery; and to encourage the labour of freemen instead of slaves. Nothing was said of voting and probably nothing was thought of it. Whatever acts upon the parties and politics of the country is thus far *political action*. Our exhibition of the political and economical evils of Slavery and advantages of Freedom, our exposure of the aggressions of the slave power in through the government, are such.

> [*National Anti-Slavery Standard*,
> November 18, 1852.]

TO THE HEARTS OF TEMPERANCE REFORMERS

ADDRESS, DELIVERED AT THE WHOLE WORLD'S TEMPERANCE
CONVENTION, NEW YORK CITY, SEPTEMBER 1-2, 1853

You have had this cause presented in so many forms
and in so many ways that there seems indeed little necessity for any additional remarks. It has been presented in
its comic as well as in its tragic dress, and it has had
the harmony of sweet sounds to commend it to you. It has
had political appeals not a few, and moral appeals—would
that I could say more. I doubt not that our friend who
last spoke in his zeal for political action, and in what
were regarded as very able arguments to sustain it, somewhat unintentionally overlooked, or rather, in my view at
least, set too light an estimate on the moral aspects of
the case. Indeed, I have thought from time to time, that
in such an assemblage as this, if the subject could be held
up in its sublime moral aspect; if the hearts of temperance
reformers could have been appealed to, again and again, to
carry forward this enterprise on this ground, more than
they have done they need not fear, but that there would be
plenty of political action, just as fast as the moral sentiment is brought up to a condition to enact a law, for we
know very well that our government—that our statesmen—
that our politicians have enough of the retaliatory spirit;
that all these great reformatory movements are in accordance
with each other; and the moralist as well as the politician
may rejoice, that the cause has advanced so far, that their
retaliatory instrumentalities are used now on the side of

temperance rather than of intemperance, and rather than in
the granting of licences, and such other acts as governments,
laws and statesmen have been wont to perform. I have no
doubt but this will be the case.

They will find that in all these reforms there is work
enough for them to stir up the pure mind in themselves, and in
urging on the progress of the cause of truth——to hold up the
light higher and higher, and cause it to shine brighter and
brighter before more sustained action. It is interesting to
trace the progress of this cause from its earliest movement;
how it began by very little action, and how it has gone on by
faithfulness to greater and greater activity, until now this
entire teetotal ground has been attained. And we may remember,
too, how earnest, how vigilant, how constantly active, were the
temperance reformers. Our friend, in illustration of right in
political action, referred also to the practical case mentioned
by the blessed Jesus of Nazareth, in the treatment of the man
who was stripped, robbed, and left half-dead by the road-side.

The temperance men and temperance women have been endeavoring to carry out the principle of the good Samaritan,
and in proportion as they have taken that ground of benevolence and morality, have they succeeded in their efforts?
[Mrs. Mott proceeded (to) describe the early experience of
those who were engaged in the temperance movement. She had
herself been ashamed to enter the temperance meeting to raise
her voice in behalf of the poor drunkard, because she was an
abolitionist. It was feared, by the temperance friends, that
her presence would bring odium on their cause!]

[The various moral reformers were, however, becoming
more and more liberal in their views and sentiments, and
they discovered that there was not so much danger in blending several reforms together as was at first believed. And
still more recent events had made it imperative that those
exclusive notions should be annihilated. They now found
Lloyd Garrison and Elihu Burritt occupying the temperance

platform.]

[They could not restrain the natural course of such
principles as Peace, Temperance and Liberty from uniting
together. They were united in the same individuals, and
were of the same kindred. It had been the same with regard
to the movement for Women's Rights. It was supposed that
it would be an injury to the cause of temperance for those
who were engaged in that movement to be likewise prominent
in this. However, next week the women would have a meeting
of their own in the Tabernacle. The various leaders of the
different moral movements could now rejoice together and
mingle their power and spirits together in the great and
holy cause, without fear or outrage to the feelings of any.
She rejoiced at the fact that the children were all with
them in that cause. It was occasioned by their purity of
soul; and—were she speaking on a Theological instead of a
Temperance platform, she would say, it was from their inherent love of right—their *natural* love of right, for she
did not believe in the doctrine so long taught in the
churches of the inherent and natural corruption of the child.]

[The speaker appealed to the high moral sense of her
audience, to adopt the utmost liberality towards all other
movements; and, after condemning the custom of appealing to
scripture in support of slavery and intemperance, she concluded by referring to the vision of Peter, which was intended to teach the great Christian doctrine of equality:
that God was no respecter of persons, but that, in every
nation, they that feared him and worked righteousness, were
accepted of him.]

> [*The Whole World's Temperance Convention held
> at Metropolitan Hall in the City of New York,*
> September 1-2, 1853. N.Y.: Fowlers and Wells,
> Publishers, 1853.]

THE PRINCIPLES OF THE CO-EQUALITY OF WOMAN WITH MAN

REMARKS, DELIVERED AT THE WOMAN'S RIGHTS
CONVENTION, NEW YORK, SEPTEMBER 6-7, 1853

It may be well, at the outset, to declare distinctly
the objects of the present Convention. Its purpose is to
declare principles, not to descend into the consideration
of details: the principles, namely, of the co-equality of
woman with man, and her right to practice those arts of
life for which she is fitted by nature. Those are our
great principles, and the assertion of them is our only
present purpose. When they shall have been well recognized, then it will be quite time enough to speak of the
proper mode of carrying them into universal practice. Already, some of the rights of woman have been conceded to
her; but many yet remain, from the enjoyment of which she
is most unjustly restrained. But let us take courage; although we are met by ridicule, through the newspaper press,
magazines, and periodicals, let us rely on the inherent justice of our cause and our own exertions. The community [is]
already beginning to see that there are many occupations
which woman can fill with efficiency and propriety, that
were, until lately, closed against her. A generous feeling
has befriended woman to this extent; but now, when it is
perceived that she, and those who aid her, for the sake of
justice of her cause, claim for her the full exercise of her
faculties in the various walks of life to which men alone
are now admitted; when her high and just aim is perceived—
naturally, perhaps, there is a great deal of opposition to

203

to her, perhaps the more in proportion as she the more com-
pletely fits herself for pursuing those heretofore forbidden
paths. We are prepared for a great deal of religious prejudice and even hostility; that is, prejudice and hostility
claiming the name of religious. No wonder, for it is something new for woman to aim at the highest office—that which
places her in the pulpit. But already has her voice been
heard there, and to her credit.

We have obstacles to encounter, but let them not dis-
may us, for they are not insurmountable. In the Temperance
Reform, as well as in many others, it has been seen what
difficulties can be overcome by vigorous and systematic efforts, based on inherent truth and justice. We came here
full of hope, and prepared to prove that our cause is just.
Woman has long been the mere slave of social custom, the unreasoning victim of conventional cruelty. Her voice has
been suppressed, or fixed down to the slenderness of her
cambric needle. But I was pleased to hear her, on some late
occasions, use it in all the harmonious fullness with which
the Creator has endowed it; and here, I trust, she will make
it heard in the furthest corners of this hall.

I have not come prepared to open this Convention with
an address worthy of the principles we advocate, and I could
wish that the Chair were filled by some other. To one thing
I particularly request notice, namely, that the Convention
shall give its undivided attention to whatever subject shall
at the time be before it. Otherwise we shall be led into
devious paths, and the time that should be devoted to a defi-
nite aim will be wasted on irregular and useless subjects.
We are now organized and prepared for business. I introduce
to the Convention Lucy Stone.

                    [Lucy Stone speaks.
                     Mott continues.]

I think it well here to ask speakers to bear in mind,
as much as possible, the Resolutions that have been read, so

as, as far as possible, to make the remarks they shall offer
bear on these Resolutions. This is called a 'Woman's Rights
Convention,' but, I apprehend, the phrase, 'Human Rights'
would more appropriately express its principles and its aims,
as I am glad to find they have been set forth by the speakers here this morning. However, let us not be misunderstood.
This Convention does not arrogate to itself the power of
settling the propriety of a woman's choosing any particular
profession. The idea of the leaders of this movement is not
that women should be *obliged* to accept the privileges which
we demand should be open to her. There are, no doubt, many
women who have no inclination to mingle in the busy walks of
life; and many would, in all probability, feel conscientious
scruples against voting, or taking any office under the present constitution of this country, considering some of it[s]
provisions. That, however, supplies no objection to the co-
equality which we assert. This we mean to attain and keep.
The unwillingness of some to vote (assuming such to exist),
does not destroy the right of a class. Elizabeth Jones, in
a Convention at Waterloo, when asked what women wanted, replied, 'I want to vote, and be voted for.' In such circumstances, it is not beyond the reach of possibility, that the
law might be purged of its inconsistencies and its hardness
to be understood; and perhaps thus [come] within the assumed
feeble intellect of woman. So in theology. Even the liberal Dr. Channing maintained that its mysteries were too intri-
cate, its difficulties too numerous and formidable, for the
female mind to overcome them. Perhaps this science too might
be simplified until it came within our reach. I concur fully
in the wish that those who are against, as well as those who
are for us, will come here and speak their sentiments. I
hope and believe they will be courteously received, and earnestly desire that they may give themselves up to the guidance of
the truth which may be here elicited, no matter how much it
may jar with their preconceived opinions. In conclusion, I

hope there will be no long speeches, but that all that may
be said shall be terse, and directed plainly to the subjects before the Convention.

[Opening of the second day's proceedings.]

The uproar and confusion which attended the close of
our proceedings of last night, although much to be regretted, as indicating an unreasonable and unreasoning disposition on the part of some, to close their ears against
the truth, or rather, to drown its voice by vulgar clamor,
yet, when viewed aright, and, in some phases, present to us
matter of congratulation. I do suppose, that never, at any
meeting, was public propriety more outraged, than at ours
of last evening. I suppose, no transactions of a body as-
sembled to deliberate, were ever more outrageously invaded
by an attempt to turn them into a mere tumult; yet, though
voices were loud and angry, and the evil passions exhibited
themselves with much of that quality to affright, which us-
ually, if not always, attends their exhibition —not a
scream was heard from any woman, nor did any of the 'weaker
sex' exhibit the slightest terror, or even alarm, at the
violent manifestations which invaded the peace of our assemblage.

I felicitate the women on this exhibition of forti-
tude; of calm moral courage. Should not our opponents, if
they have any reason among them, reflect, that these exhi-
bitions are, in reality, some of the strongest arguments
that can be offered to support the claims which we stand
here to advocate? Do they not show, on the one hand, that
men, by whom such an overpowering superiority is arrogated,
can betimes demean themselves in such a way as to show that
they are wholly unfit for the lofty functions which they demand as their exclusive right? And, on the other hand, do
they not conclusively show, that women are possessed of, at
least, some of those qualities which assist in calmness of
deliberation, during times of excitement and even danger!

I think it was really a beautiful sight to see how calm the
women remained during last evening's excitement; their self-
possession, I consider something truly admirable. I know
that, in the tumult and noise, it would have been vain for
any woman to raise her voice in an attempt to check it. Indeed, I am satisfied, the outrage was predetermined, and I
regret that the aid of the police had to be called in to
quell it. Had there been here a company of women who were
taught to rely upon others, they would, doubtless, have
felt bound to scream for *their protectors*; but the self-
reliance displayed, which must have its basis in a consciousness of the truth and justice of our cause, and which kept
the members of the Convention unmoved, amid all the prevailing confusion, gives us matter of real congratulation. Let
us rejoice in this, my friends; and let us remember, that,
when we have a true cause——while our cause rests on the basis of right——we have nothing to fear, but may go on unmoved
by all these petty circumstances, by which we may be surrounded.

A request was made last night by some person, I don't
know who, or rather a challenge was offered, that three good
reasons should be given why women should vote. Perhaps, had
the person making this demand had this question put to him,
namely, 'What reasons are there why men should vote?' he
would have considered the reasons so self-evident as to make
any answer superfluous. Yet it would be found difficult, I
apprehend, to assign any reason, why men should vote, which
would not be found to be an equally good reason for extending the elective franchise to women. He asked, however,
why women should be allowed to take a part in the civil government of the country. This question will, I doubt not, be
answered to-day by some one more able than myself; and if
the person who asked it be present, and open to conviction,
he will hear reasons sufficient to convince him that women
have the right to vote. I only repeat the question now, as

one of the subjects claiming consideration to-day.

As to woman's occupying a high position in the social
state, the very scriptures, to which our antagonists point
in ill-founded triumph, as determining the matter against
us, supply instances in abundance of the high estimation in
which women were held. Nor is there any need of citing instances (so well are they known) of the part which woman
took in the propagation of the true faith, and the *minstra-
tion*, too. In that passage wherein mention is made of the
wives of deacons, (as the vernacular version gives it), a
reference to the original text, and a true rendering of it
will show that the real expression is, *the female* deacons.
This single fact is a sufficient commentary on the fairness
of some of the means employed to conceal the rights which
really belong to women.

A good deal of stress is laid on the command given to
women (as it is said) to be silent in the Church. The text
is to be found in 1st Corinthians, ch. xiv., v. 34 and 35.
But has this text the force and application which is demanded for it by our opponents? A calm and thorough investigation will show that it has not. It was one of those
ordinances, or recommendations, the character of which was
merely local, or confined to a certain place, and appropriate to a certain time. The same apostle who spoke thus,
gave directions as to women prophecying, preaching or praying, and attiring themselves. But all these injunctions
are as binding, and have as wide an application, as that
relating to woman's being silent. Are these now observed?
Manifestly not; and thus, in the admission made, that such
commands referred only to the customs of a time that has
long passed away. What were the real circumstances under
which the words, *'it is not permitted to them to speak,'*
were applied to woman? Circumstances of disagreement and
tumult in the Church, where many men spoke together, and
loudly, so that scarcely any voice could be distinctly

heard. In such circumstances it was but a reasonable counsel to women to hold their peace for the time. It is added
that *'if they will learn anything, let them ask their husbands at home,'* which was also the reasonable proceeding as
matters stood, and showed this, that women were enjoined to
have an interest in the affairs of the Church, and also to
take counsel on the same.

All such commands, (like that relating to attire,
which so plainly contemplates an oriental and ancient mode
of dress,) must, to be reasonably taken, be received only
as local, and suited to a particular time; and when these
conditions of locality and time are withdrawn, the command
ceases to have any cogency.

[Other speakers intervene;
Mott concludes the meeting.]

The time for adjournment having now arrived, I must
interfere to announce the fact. If the gentleman choose,
he can have the rest of his half hour, or twenty minutes, at
the evening session. I am sorry we cannot satisfy the gentleman by answering his objections as intelligently (to his
mind) as he seems to think he has stated them. However,
perhaps, even our dullness may be turned into an argument
to give us the liberty we demand; because, if we received
that liberty, it is possible we might use it in such a way
as, after the due time, to be able to answer so learned an
opponent as he is. He must remember it is hard for weak
woman to answer such solid arguments, and he must pity us
if we do not come up to his standard of excellence. If he
lay stress on his Scripture argument, that the wife must
obey the husband, it may in some cases come to cut the other way; as in mine, for example, because *my* husband wishes
me to vote, and therefore, according to the Scripture, the
gentleman must, even in his own reasoning, allow me the
right to vote. In one place, the gentleman said that woman
had already turned the world over; and that man must be

cautious not to allow her to do so again. Perhaps, if he
reconsidered these statements, he might be willing to re-
tract the latter; because, if she turned the world over
once, and put the wrong side up, he ought now to allow her
to turn it back, that she may bring the right side up again.

[Woman's Rights Convention. *Proceedings*.
The Broadway Tabernacle. New York, September
6, 7, 1853. N.Y.: Fowlers and Wells, 1853.]

THE LAWS IN RELATION TO WOMEN

*REMARKS, DELIVERED AT THE NATIONAL WOMEN'S RIGHTS
CONVENTION, CLEVELAND, OHIO, OCTOBER 5-7, 1853*

I would yield the floor to any one who has any thing
to say at this time, and would gladly do it. I approve of
the suggestion which has been made, that we should be limited as to time, for we are such imitators of men and customs around us, that perhaps we may forget that we are not
upon the floor of Congress, and so may inflict long speeches
upon the people.

I am glad you have had presented before you, in the
address you have just heard, a synopsis of the laws in relation to women, and the sentiments of some of the commentators upon those laws; and I want you to observe, (for it
stands in proof of what our brother said this afternoon,)
that there is a constant advance in truth, a constant uprising and appreciation of that which in the earlier days
of an enterprise was not anticipated. So in this movement;
Blackstone stated what was then regarded Law, (for it did
not then appear to be understood, although he too defined
it,) as a "means of sustaining justice and the right"—but
in giving a statement of what was Law and Gospel, Church
and State, have been thus united. But it is to be broken
up as regards woman, just as the religionists of our country
have attempted to break it up, and have succeeded in the
Church, as applicable to men. Our more modern expounders of
the Law, in many cases, present to the public the degraded
position of women in society, because of such enactments,

211

claiming to be, *Law*.   Of these are a Hulburt, in an essay
on Human Rights; and a Walker, I think, who first presented
the fact to the public—or to the reader, not so public as
I wish it was—that the Law has made the man and wife one
person, and that one person the husband! and Mr. Hulburt has
presented the condition of woman in a light which cannot
fail to be striking to those who will read his essays.

Look also at the Philosophers of the present time, and
their Revolutionists of the last upheaving in Europe. Why,
when woman went forth at the last effort to establish a republic through the provisional government in France, and
claimed to have equal representation with man, some of the
greatest statesmen acknowledged the justice of her request,
and responded to it, that she had sat in darkness long, that
this claim of women would have to be respected; that woman
had too long been suffering under a night-mare of oppression.
It was to me a striking comparison at the time I read it.
The only cause of the failure of the revolution of 1779, was
that it was represented by only one half of the intelligence,
of the race—an intelligence differing it is true, in some
of its peculiarities, but from the very difference calculated to form a truer republic. Victor Hugo in alluding to
this effort on the part of woman for the redress of the
wrongs and grievances under which she had suffered, says,
that as the last age was notable for the effort to gain
Men's Rights, so the present generation would aim to create
a revolution in public sentiment which should gain the independence of woman.

Now these steps are beginning to be followed out everywhere.   The Westminister Review, one of the cleverest journals in England, gave a very fair and interesting notice of
the first National Women's Convention in Worcester, and that
article has been republished in this country in pamphlet
form.   There have been repeated notices also in the best of
our own periodicals, encouraging women to go on and advocate

their claims.

But, we are told sometimes that we are satisfied; that it is not woman who is urging this movement, and that she really does not wish any change in society. Has the slave been oppressed so long that he cannot appreciate the blessings of Liberty? and has woman been so long crushed, enervated, paralyzed, prostrated by the influences by which she has been surrounded, that she too is ready to say she would not have any more rights if she could? Why she does not know her position, and whereof she affirms. A clergyman in Auburn, N.Y., soon after the Syracuse Convention, delivered a sermon pronouncing it an infidel convention —for you know that is the usual weapon of defence against whatever appears to conflict with accepted creeds. He said the ladies of *his* congregation, he was happy to state, were not sensible of any chains binding them, not sensible of any liberties taken from them. Now this is the common boast— there are persons in your own city who stated on being invited to come to this convention, that they had other engagements, they had to sew at the Home Missionary Society; and if they had not other engagements, they had all the rights they wanted, and did not care to come.

I heard not long since of some one who had several hundred acres of land left him by his father; a friend was speaking to him about the profitableness of his estate; he replied, the profits were not so great as might be supposed; the expenses of the family were large, for he had to *keep his mother* a good many years, and she lived to be ninety years old! He was asked if she were an active, industrious woman in her early days. O yes! in those days she was a very industrious woman. His Father and she commenced life poor, but gathered together this great estate by their united industry. How is it then that you can say that your expenses have been increased by having to keep your mother? He felt the rebuke much afterwards, and such was the impres-

sion it produced, and so great was the change in his views
that in his will he recognized no difference between his
sons and daughters. He saw the injustice of his past position, and was disposed to make some redress for the wrong
done his own mother in making her, in her old age, dependent
upon him.

Now, in this particular, there has been a great change
in our country. The doing away [with] the laws of primo-
geniture has opened the eyes of the people, to much evil on
all sides, for we cannot begin to look at and redress any
one of the wrongs done to mankind in the past, without being
carried further than we imagine, in our first attempt. It
was a true philosophy that Jesus uttered, when he said "He
that has been faithful over a little, shall be ruler over
more."

It is for the following generation to go on and make
yet other advance steps. Such advances are beautiful when
we come to look at them. Those of the past have given some
Theologians noble ideas; they have come to have more expand-
ed views and to rejoice in the belief of the continued advance of humanity. How much better the Theology which has
resulted from these great movements. They have led us to
read our Bibles better. Many cannot so read Christ, that
progress is going to break up the foundations of society.
Why, our own society which has been supposed to make greater
strides than others, especially for the rights of man——and
they have upon the questions of the ministry and the marriage covenant——has been affected by these advances. As regards the ministry, they did not see so clearly, that it
must embrace women also. They took only the ground that
ordination must not take the form of a human ceremony; that
it was God alone who could appoint to the ministry. Well,
they found that this God-ordination was manifest in their
women also. They began to look at their Bibles, and found
there that women were sent forth to minister to the people,

as in ancient times. When Deborah was Judge in Israel, when
the Captain would not lead the army, and a woman had the
glory of the conquest made. Again, when they were in exigency, they went to Huldah, and she counselled them.

It is not Christianity but priestcraft that has subjected woman as we find her. The Church and State have been
united, and it is well for us to see it so. We have had to
bear the denunciations of these revered (irreverend) clergymen, as in New York, of late. But if we look to their authority to see how they expound the text, quite likely we
shall find a new reading. Why, when John Chambers returned
to Philadelphia, from the World's Temperance Convention at
New York, he gave notice that he would give an address, and
state the rights of woman as defined by the Bible. Great
allowance has been made by some of the speakers in this Convention, on account of his ignorance, and certainly this was
charitable. But I heard this discourse. I heard him bring
up what is called the Apostolic prohibition, and the old
Eastern idea of the subjection of wives; but he kept out of
view some of the best ideas in the scriptures.

Blame is often attached to the position in which woman
is found. I blame her not so much as I pity her. So cir-
cumscribed have been her limits, that she does not realize
the misery of her condition. Such dupes are men to custom,
that even servitude, the worst of ills comes to be thought a
good, till down from sire to son it is kept and guarded as a
sacred thing. Woman's existence is maintained by sufferance.
The veneration of man has been misdirected, the pulpit has
been prostituted, the Bible has been ill-used. It has been
turned over and over as in every reform. The temperance
people have had to feel its supposed denunciations. Then
the anti-slavery, and now this reform has met, and still continues to meet, passage after passage of the Bible, never intended to be so used. Instead of taking the truths of the
Bible in corroberation of the right, the practice has been,

to turn over its pages to find example and authority for the
wrong, for the existing abuses of society. For the usage of
drinking wine the example of the sensualist Solomon is always appealed to. In reference to our reform, even admitting that Paul did mean preach, when he used that term, he
did not say that the recommendation of that time, was to be
applicable to the churches of all after time. We have here,
I had liked to have said, the *Reverend* Antionette Brown. She
is familiar enough with these passages to present some of
them to you; for it is important when the Bible is thus appealed to, and thus perverted, that it should be read with
another pair of spectacles. We have been so long pinning
our faith on other peoples' sleeves that we ought to begin
examining these things daily, ourselves, to see whether
they *are* so; and we should find on comparing text with text,
that a very different construction might be put upon them.
Some of our early Quakers, not seeing how far they were to
be carried, became Greek and Hebrew scholars, and they
found that the text would bear other translations as well
as other constructions. All Bible commentators agree that
the Church of Corinth, when the Apostle wrote, was in a
state of great confusion. They fell into discussion and
controversy; and in order to quiet this state of things, and
bring the Church to greater propriety, the command was given
out that women should keep silence, and it was not permitted
them to speak, except by asking questions at home. In the
same epistle to the same Church, Paul gave express directions how women shall prophesy, which he defines to be
preaching, "speaking to men" for "exhortation and comfort."
He recognized them in prophesying and praying. The word
translated *servant,* is applied to a man in one part of the
scripture, and in another it is translated minister.
Now that same word you will find might be applied to Phebe,
a Deaconess. That text was quoted in the sermon of John
Chambers, and he interlarded it with a good deal of his

ideas, that wom[e]n should not be goers abroad, and read
among other things "that their wives were to be teachers."
But the "wives" properly translated would be "Deaconesses."

It is not so Apostolic to make the wife subject to the
husband as many have supposed. It has been done by Law, and
public opinion since that time. There has been a great deal
said about sending Missionaries over to the East to convert
women who are immolating themselves on the funeral pile of
their husbands. I know this may be a very good work, but I
would ask you to look at it. How many women are there now
immolated upon the shrine of superstition and priestcraft,
in our very midst, in the assumption that man only has a
right to the pulpit, and that if a woman enters it she dis-
obeys God; making woman believe in the misdirection of her
vocation, and that it is of Divine authority that she should
be thus bound. Believe it not, my sisters. In this same
epistle the word "prophesying" should be "preaching"—
"preaching Godliness, &c." On the occasion of the very
first miracle which it is said Christ wrought, a woman went
before him and said, "whatsoever he biddeth you do, that
do." The woman of Samaria said, 'come and see the man who
told me all the things that ever I did."

These things are worthy of note. I do not want to
dwell too much upon scripture authority. We too often bind
ourselves by authorities rather than by the truth. We are
infidel to truth, in seeking examples to overthrow it. The
very first act of note that is mentioned when the disciples
and apostles went forth after Jesus was removed from them,
was the bringing up of an ancient prophesy, to prove that
they were right in the position they then assumed. On the
occasion when men and women were gathered together on the
holy day of Pentecost, when every man heard and saw those
wonderful works which are recorded, then Peter stood forth
—some one has said that Peter made a great mistake in
quoting the prophet Joel—but, he stated that "the time is

come, this day is fulfilled the prophesy, when it is said I
will pour out my spirit upon all flesh, and your sons and
your daughters shall prophesy" &c.——the language of the
Bible is beautiful in its repetition——"upon my servants and
my hand-maidens I will pour out my spirit and they shall
prophesy."   Now can any thing be clearer than that?

It has sometimes been said that if women were associated with men in their efforts, there would not be as much
immorality as now exists, in Congress, for instance, and
other places. But we ought, I think, to claim no more for
woman than for man; we ought to put woman on a par with man,
not invest her with power, or claim for her superiority over
her brother. If we do, she is just as likely to become a
tyrant as man is; as with Catherine the Second. It is always unsafe to invest man with power over his fellow being.
"Call no man master"——that is the true doctrine. But, be
sure there would then be better rule than now; the elements
which belong to woman as such and to man as such, would be
beautifully and harmoniously blended. It is to be hoped
there would be less of war, injustice and intolerance in
the world than now. Things are tending fast that way, and
I hope we shall all be prepared to act. These Conventions
ought to give encouragement to the steps of advancement.
Now that women are capable of reading and beginning to be
their own painters and historians, you see how much is
brought out from history. I heard a lecture last year
which astonished me with its number of remarkable women,
not only in medicine, but in the law and jurisprudence,
further back than the twelfth century——all this is encouraging women to go forward in this movement. Why only lately a woman stood forth in England, or France, and plead her
own cause and gained it.

And the more her powers are cultivated, the more woman will see the light in which she has been regarded, and
when she comes to unite herself in the most holy marriage

relation, she will not submit to the authority the church
now binds upon her. Women are bound by the church on one
hand, and acknowledge subjection to the laws and to the husband under the church and the law, on the other part. I
cannot bear to hear woman blamed. She is taught that she
must promise that she will be obedient to her husband. I
know some ministers now who make a little change in this respect. A minister said to me the other day, that he did not
make the parties promise to obey. He used the word "duti-
ful," for the wife; "well then," I said, "you will make it
apply to the husband also, will you not?" He replied perhaps he would hereafter.

I alluded to my own society making no difference between man and woman in the ministry and the duties of the
marriage covenant. It seemed to be a great step for those
early reformers, William Penn and George Fox, moving as they
did in fashionable society, amid the universal veneration
for power in that country. It was a great step for them to
take—making the marriage relation entirely reciprocal—
asking no priest to legalize their union, but declaring
their own marriage, and themselves invoking the Divine aid.

When woman shall be properly trained, and her spiritual powers developed, she will find in entering the marriage
union nothing necessarily degrading to her. The independence of the husband and wife should be equal, and the dependence reciprocal. But Oh! how different now! The so-
called church, and the state together, have made her a perfect slave. Talk of the barbarous ages! Why the barbarous
ages are now! Even now, she may be yoked with the beasts of
burden in the field. In France, she loads herself most
heavily with the baggage of passengers. The Irishwoman now
goes about barefoot, the husband with shoes and stockings;
—she with her child in her arms, he carrying nothing. I
have seen these cases again and again in a little travel of
a few months in the old world; and what might those see who

go throughout the continent. Woman is not considered there
as out of her sphere in pitching hay upon the stack; when
the coach stops for relays of horses, the coachman does not
leave the box, but a woman comes out and takes the four
horses, leads them away, and returns with the other four
from the stable. Talk of the barbarous ages! They are now!

Notwithstanding all these things, women in this country will not come to our conventions to hear Women's Rights.
They may be the mere toys and playthings of society, and do
not therefore feel these things. They can amuse their husbands, and brothers, and fathers by beautiful notes of music
or by the dance, and I do not say that these things are not
very well when practiced at home instead of in public places,
and not continued till late hours of the nights. When we
consider the character of the romance, the sickly sentimental yellow covered literature that she reads, we cannot expect that she will be much. Then in other cases, she has
too much to do to be a fine show. These are the extremes.
We want woman to come forth and walk in a higher sphere than
either of these. Let her come forth and fill it, and she
will certainly show forth the beauty of higher aims in life.
Why, today, a woman at one of your most respectable hotels,
dressed in a fashionable manner, saw one of our women in the
street dressed in a Bloomer costume. She tho't it "an in-
sult to decency," and expressed herself very indignantly.
But how was she dressed hereself? Why, laced so tight that
she could scarcely breathe, and her clothes so long that
when she went out into the dusty streets her garments formed
a kind of broom to gather up the dust. *This* is beautiful!
This is fashionable!

But blessed be the advance of the age, for it is
teaching woman in principles of physiology. Many are going
forth teaching this science to ears annointed to hear, and
finding eyes skillful to see, and souls wise to so observe
the laws of health, that they may not be subject to disease,

or require so much of miserable medical treatment. Then
again many are availing themselves of the profitable occupations of society, in the way of mercantile business. In
Philadelphia it is no uncommon thing to see women behind
the counter. To be sure if they are only employed the
merchant can rob them of half their wages. But they are becoming capitalists, and setting up their own stores. In
some of the works of the Artizan, in Jewelry, in Daguerreo-
typing, and in many other departments, women are coming forward and showing themselves apt scholars; that they can do
something besides stitching wristbands and making samplers.
In early days, how many hours were employed in making emery
strawberries, in foolish fancy work, and in overworked samplers. Women are now beginning to learn that men can do
without so much stitching. Indeed, so greatly is Discovery
progressing, that machines are already doing a large portion
of this work. A woman in the Crystal Palace sits by a sewing machine to show the visitors how one woman, in a day,
can perform the work of thirty or forty women in the same
time! On the Island of Nantucket—for I was born on that
Island—I can remember how our mothers were employed, while
our fathers were at sea. The mothers with their children
round them—'twas not customary to have nurses then—kept
small groceries and sold provisions, that they might make
something in the absence of their husbands. At that time
it required some money and more courage to get to Boston—
they were obliged to go to that city, make their trades,
exchange their oils and candles for dry goods, and all the
varieties of a country store, set their own price, keep
their own accounts; and with all this, have very little
help in the family, to which they must discharge their duties. Look at the heads of those women; they can mingle
with men; they are not triflers; they have intelligent subjects of conversation.

    This then is what we ask for woman, that she may be

so prepared for life's duties, that she can fill her walk in
life respectably, and show that she can be something more
than a slave, on the one hand, or a toy, or an effeminate
being on the other. She is giving the proof of this. She
is doing this today. Go on then and encourage her, O! my
brothers. I have no idea that there is on the part of man,
or the race, such a disposition to love the wrong, as many
suppose. We have been so much accustomed to false Theology,
that we might think the whole race were really fallen, if
we did not *know* better. Why, this very afternoon, I heard
quoted in the Temperance Convention—but there is no such
passage in the Bible, "The heart of man is prone to evil,
and that continually." Now we know that man is prone to
good, and that continually. Job stated that "man was prone
to *trouble,* as the sparks to fly upwards." But how has
Theology perverted it! Man is prone to *evil*! Why the very
evils there are in society around us, are greatly mitigated
by the goodness of heart, that is natural in man. His *inherent* love of justice, right, mercy, and goodness, are ever
operating upon him, and leading him to act aright. Why is
it that good works have such great success all over the
world? Translate that sermon on the Mount into all langu-
ages, and the response to it, is world wide. Why is it that
HARRIET BEECHER STOWE has had such success throughout the
wide world? Because her work reaches the sense of right in
the universal human heart.

   Did ELIZABETH FRY, of England, neglect her family?
No! After rearing her eight or ten children, she went forth
and did the things that HOWARD did, and greater. See
DOROTHEA DIX, and what a ministering angel she has been!
Look at the licentiousness of our own city of Penn, and see
how MYRA TOWNSEND went forth and established a reformatory
house for her sisters; see how she gathered them there and
improved their situations, and awakened in them a desire
for a better life. The other day I had a letter from a

young married woman, who told me she had heard a woman say
that when she had eleven children, she had less trouble
with them, than when she had but four, for as the older ones
grew older, they were a help to her in caring for the younger. She wrote to me putting five or six questions to me on
the subject of woman's rights. She was going to deliver a
lecture in Pennsylvania. She had had advantages that we did
not have in our day. She had been a little accustomed to
speak in public, and tho' she had the care of her little
children, and with her own hands had to make the bread for
a family of twenty, yet she was ready to do what she could.
She had hard work to do where she lectured, for many of her
auditors were ignorant Dutch women. [Mrs. Mott apologized
for having occupied so much time and gave way to the next
speaker.]

Second Morning Session

We ought to thank Dr. Nevin [previous speaker] for
his kindly fears, lest we women should be brought out into
the rough conflicts of life, and overwhelmed by infidelity.
I thank him, but at the same time, I must say that if we
have been able this afternoon to sit uninjured by the hard
conflict in which he has been engaged, if we can maintain
our patience at seeing him so laboriously build a man of
straw, and then throw it down and destroy it, I think we
may be suffered to go into the world and bear many others
unharmed.

Again, I would ask in all seriousness, by what right
does Orthodoxy give the invidious name of Infidel, affix
the stigma of infidelity, to those who dissent from its
cherished opinions? What right have the advocates of moral

reform, the Woman's Rights movement, the Abolitionists, the
temperance advocates, or others, to call in question any
man's religious opinions? It is the assumption of bigots.
I do not want now to speak invidiously, and say sectarian
bigots, but I mean the same kind of bigotry which Jesus rebuked so sharply, when he called certain men "blind leaders
of the blind."

Now we hold Jesus up as an example when we perceive
the assumption of clergymen that all who venture to dissent from a given interpretation must necessarily be infidels; and thus denounce them as infidel. For it was only
by inference that one clergyman this afternoon made Joseph
Barker deny the Son of God. By inference in the same way,
he might be made to deny everything that is good, and
praiseworthy and true.

I want that we should consider these things upon this
platform. I am not troubled with difficulties about the
Bible. My education has been such, that I look to the
Source whence all the inspiration of the Bible comes. I
love the truths of the Bible. I love the Bible because it
contains so many truths; but I never was educated to love
the errors of the Bible; therefore it does not startle me
to hear Joseph Barker point to some of those errors. And
I can listen to the ingenious interpretation of the Bible,
given by Antoinette Brown, and am glad to hear those who
are so skilled in the outward, when I perceive that they
are beginning to turn the Bible to so good an account. It
gives evidence that the cause is making very good progress.
Why, my friend Nevin has had to hear the temperance cause
denounced as infidel, and proved so by Solomon; and he has,
no doubt, seen the minister in the pulpit, turning over
the pages of the Bible to find examples for the wrong.
But the Bible will never sustain him in making this use
of its pages, instead of using it rationally, and selecting
such portions of it as would tend to corroborate the right;

and these are plentiful; for notwithstanding the teaching
of Theology, and men's arts in the religious world, men
have ever responded to righteousness and truth, when it
has been advocated by the servants of God, so that we need
not fear to bring truth to an intelligent examination of
the Bible. It is a far less dangerous assertion to say
that God is unchangeable, than that man is infallible.

[National Women's Rights Convention.
Proceedings. Cleveland: Gray
Beardsley, Spear and Co., 1854.]

AN ENCOURAGING VIEW AS TO WHAT
HAS ALREADY BEEN EFFECTED

REMARKS, DELIVERED AT THE SEVENTH NATIONAL WOMAN'S
RIGHTS CONVENTION, NEW YORK, NOVEMBER 25-26, 1856

At this late hour it will not be proper for me to add
many words, even were it necessary. You have heard all, it
seems to me, that can be said upon the subject, and if I
would add anything it would be rather to offer an encouraging view as to what has already been effected, and to inspire the hope that the time is not far distant when those
wrongs and evils, under which woman is suffering—so clearly
depicted at this and at former Conventions—will be so obvious to the thinking men of the American People, that they
will be ready to redress them. And although woman may not
yet be so awakaned to the consideration of the subjects as
to be sensible of the blessing of entire freedom, she will,
I doubt not, as she comes to reflect on the subject more and
more, see herself in her true light. It only needs that we
should look back a few years to see the progress that has
been made. Even in England, in 1840, when a few women went
over as delegates to the World's Anti-Slavery Convention,
although the call had been made so universal, yet they were
afraid to welcome women to a seat in that Convention, lest
they should be ridiculed in the morning papers. Daniel
O'Connell, Dr. Bowring, William Howitt, and some able and
strong men of that time, it is true, came forth and approved
the claim of women to a seat; and O'Connell showed that,
even then, women exercised the right to vote as holders of
bank-stock, and as members of the East India Company, and

some other institutions of that country. Their youthful
queen, too, had just then ascended the throne, thus showing
how very inconsistent it was to make objections to the
claim of equal rights for women. Dr. Bowring at that time,
or soon after, wrote a letter to the friends in this country, saying that he had feared that the women question was
launched among them without sufficient preparation; but the
coming of these women would form an era in the history of
philanthropic bravery; that they had left a deep if not a
wide impression; that they had created apostles, if as yet
they had not many followers. Well, the result, as shown
from the facts presented to you this evening, the petitions
to Parliament, for the redress of the wrongs of women, the
willingness to receive, to so great an extent, such a memorial, all go to show a change that has taken place in the
minds of many there. Some of you must know that among the
English authors, when Maria Edgeworth wrote, within the day
and generation of some of the older ones of us, she was not
willing to let her own name appear as an author, but her
first works, and those of her sister, were put forth in the
name of her father, because it was not considered decorous
then for a woman to appear as an author. It was supposed
to be without the sphere of woman. And you know how since
that time woman has advanced in the literary field. You
know that when the work entitled "Jane Eyre" appeared, with
a fictitious name, it was said to be a work of too great
power for any woman—that it must have been written by a
man. It proved, however, to have been written by a woman.

So we have seen already, in the few years' efforts
that have been made in this Woman's Rights Reform how colleges for women, schools of design, and other institutions,
heretofore unknown, have sprung up, opening to woman new
fields, and extending and elevating her sphere.

I was glad this morning when that young man came
forth with his objections against our claim, based upon the

Bible; and although it would not be proper to go into a
theological discussion of the question, it is of the greatest importance that religiously-minded women, those who
have been accustomed to regard this volume as their rule
of faith and practice, should be led to examine these Scriptures, and see whether these things are as our opponents
claim. And if they will read that book intelligently, not
with the eye of the theologian, nor with a blind faith in
what their ministers have taught them, but with a reliance
upon their own judgment, they will discover that the Scriptures cannot be wielded against us. They will find that
from the earliest days of which the Scriptures give account,
honorable women have risen, notwithstanding the obstacles
of the times in which they lived, to a high degree of emi-
nence. They were the Deborahs, the Huldahs, the Annas, and
others, in olden times, who filled conspicuous places, and
to whom the honorable men of the age resorted for counsel
in times of exigency. Deborah assured one of the captains
of the host that he was not to succeed, for the honor of
the battle was to be given to a woman. She was a prophetess; and if you will read you will find that prophetesses
were recognized as well as prophets from the earliest days.
And in later times, Anna and the woman of Samaria, and others were employed to speak to the men of the city, to all
those who looked for redemption in Jerusalem. And women
were recognized in the very first noble act that was brought
to view after the disciples came together, which was a realization of the old prophecy, that the time should come when
women as well as men should prophesy. And even Paul, though
he is quoted so much as an authority for bringing women under subjection, even he gave special directions to woman how
she should attire herself when she did publically pray or
prophesy; and in the seeming prohibition of woman's speaking
in church, there is no mention of preaching, of praying, or
of prophesying. There is something said, to be sure, about

the subjection to the husband, but it was also said that it
was spoken in a mystery in reference to the Church, evident-
ly not intending thereby to apply it literally. In the meta-
phors of that age you know there is great liberty taken on
other subjects; why not on that? Even though Paul should
approve of many things, being himself under the influence of
the Jewish customs of that age, with regard to woman, I
would ask of those who most religiously bind themselves to
the authority of Scripture, whether they find any Scripture
text from the beginning to the end of the Bible that makes
it incumbent upon them to receive any recommendation given
by Paul to the women of the Church of this day, unless it be
in the great principles of virtue, of justice and of love,
which are unvarying in all ages of the world? No; when theologians quote Paul as against us, they should be careful
lest they prove too much; for, if the recommendations of
Paul were to be applied now, no woman would be allowed to
enter into a second marriage after having lost her first husband. Paul says he thinks they should not marry again, and
at the same time says, he thinks he has the Spirit of the
Lord. But this prohibition of Paul is not applied now, and
hence theologians do not bring it up against us, as they do
some other prohibitions in regard to women.

    And I would ask that young theologian, who quoted the
Bible against us, what he thinks of the direction concerning
holding his peace when he is in his pulpit, when anything is
revealed to him that sitteth by, allowing that person to utter his thoughts, so that all may speak, and all be edified?
With the exception of the Quakers, and perhaps the Method-
ists, there is always one singled out as the "oracle of God"
to the congregation; and this recommendation of Paul is entirely ignored. So also with the direction to wash one another's feet, and many other things.

    It would be well for people to remember that this
readiness to bring up the Bible against this reform has been

equally manifested in regard to every other reform. I would
not undervalue the efficacy of these Scriptures to any that
may profit thereby, but I would ask that all should read
them so intelligently as to discriminate between that which
belonged to the age exclusively in which it was written, and
that which is applicable to the time in which we live. Very
great changes occur in history, very great advances are made,
and we must make this discrimination in everything.

The young man who spoke here this morning asked whether it was not a new idea this claim of equality for women,
this claim in her behalf of the inalienable right to life,
liberty and the pursuit of happiness. Strange as it may appear, the great statesmen and politicians of the age do not
seem to be aware of the application of the principles they
are constantly upholding. The very men who signed the Declaration of Independence, many of them educated under English
aristocratic institutions, did not seem to know how far
those principles would carry them. Some of them at that
time were very much opposed to educating the working-classes,
for fear it would raise them above their proper level. And
more recently, many who professed so great a reverence for
these republican principles, were strongly opposed to a universal popular education, in place of the charity schools
that disgraced the age.

There has been a great advance as regards the education of women. Many of our grandmothers did not know how to
write their own names, it being then regarded as unnecessary
for woman to learn to write. Now she has so far come up to
the level of the intelligence of society as to rise above
the mere drudgery of life, and demand something more.

Catharine Beecher in her first public work expressed
the belief that time was coming when woman would not be satisfied with her present low aims; and when she returned from
the precincts of education she would no longer be satisfied
with seeking a little reading, and working devices on muslin

and lace, but, her powers being called out, she would be
seeking immortal minds, wherever she could fasten impressions that should never be effaced. She did not anticipate
the fastening of impressions on immortal minds in public
conventions. No; she revolted at such an idea, because she
had been educated by her father to believe that the pulpit
and the public platform was no place for woman. But a few
months ago I received a note from her, inviting me to attend
at a large public school, where she was going to deliver an
address to men and women; showing that her own mind has
undergone a change upon the subject, in the general advancement of public opinion.

The religious veneration of woman has been so misdirected by her religious training, that she needs to be
taught to judge for herself. She will find, when she does
so, that the Scriptures have been perverted, and that the
customs of society are not always founded in truth and justice. Nor will her veneration for the good, the true, and
the divine, be lessened when she learns to respect the divinity of her own nature; nor will she be ashamed of this
new Gospel of truth, or afraid to declare it before the people. She will behold a vision of a new heaven and a new
earth, wherein dwelleth righteousness; and entering in, she
will find all that will supply the wants of her spiritual
nature. She will find the inspiration that was in Paul, and
in all the servants of the Most High, in olden times, is not
withheld now, even from woman, but that she will be prepared
to go forth upon the mission whereunto she may be called.

Believe me, my sisters, the time is come for you to
avail yourselves of all the avenues that are opened to you.
I would that woman would wake up to a sense of the long-con-
tinued degradation and wrong that has been heaped upon her!
Like the poor slave at the South, too many of our sex are
insensible of their wrongs, and incapable of fully appreci-
ating the blessings of freedom. I therefore submit, in

reference to this subject, the following resolution:

> Resolved, That as the poor slave's alleged
> contentment with his servile and cruel bond-
> age, only proves the depth of his degradation;
> so the assertion of woman that she has all
> the rights she wants, only proves how far the
> restrictions and disabilities to which she
> has been subjected have rendered her insensi-
> ble to the blessings of true liberty.

[Woman's Rights Convention. *Proceedings*.
N.Y.: Edward O. Jenkins, 1856.]

RELIGIOUS INSTINCT IN THE CONSTITUTION OF MAN

SERMON, DELIVERED AT YARDLEYSVILLE, BUCKS
COUNTY, PENNSYLVANIA, SEPTEMBER 26, 1858

"The kingdom of God is within us," and Christianity
will not have performed its office in the earth until its
professors have learned to respect the rights and privileges
of conscience, by a toleration without limit, a faith without contention. This is the testimony of one of the modern
writers. And have we not evidence, both from our own religious records, and those of all the worshippers of all ages,
that there has been this divine teaching acknowledged, in
some way or another—that there is a religious instinct in
the constitution of man, and that, according to the circumstances of his birth, of his education, of his exercise of
his free agency, has this religious essence grown, and
brought forth similar fruits, in every age of the world,
among all peoples? This has been likened, by various figures, emblems, parables, to things without us and around us.
It has been variously interpreted, variously explained; for
no nation has a spiritual language, exclusively such. We
must therefore speak of our spiritual experiences in language having reference to spiritual things. And we find
this has been the case, especially in the records of the
Jews, the scriptures of Israel, and what are called "Christian scriptures." They abound in emblems and parables.

This divine illumination is called "the spirit." It
is said that "God breathed into man life," a spirit, his
"own image," which is spiritual, and he became a *living* soul.

235

The after writers acknowledge this divine spirit——"Thou
gavest also thy good spirit to instruct us."

An idea has prevailed that the immortality of this
spirit was not understood till about eighteen hundred years
ago; but if we read the old scriptures intelligently, we
shall find the acknowledgment of its eternity, as well as
its divine nature. "Then shall the dust return to the earth
as it was, and the spirit shall return to God who gave it."
And these same writers, even though they were very much
clouded, and the clearness of their views obscured by tradition, so that when Jesus came among them, he said. "they
made the word of God of none effect by their traditions;"
yet, the far-seeing among them acknowledged that these ob-
scurities must pass away, and that the time should come
when the divine light should be more clearly understood,
"when thou shalt hear a voice behind thee saying, 'This is
the way, walk ye in it.'" And it is spoken of sometimes as
the "still small voice." It is spoken of again as a new
covenant that should be made; "I will write my law in their
hearts," the law of justice, mercy, forgiveness, that they
should have no more need of the old proverb, "The fathers
have eaten sour grapes, and the children's teeth are set on
edge." "But if a man be just, and do that which is lawful
and right," "in his righteousness that he hath done he shall
live." On the other hand, "when the righteous turneth away
from his righteousness and committeth iniquity, in the wickedness that he doeth shall he die."

So we see that the teachings of this divine spirit
have been the same in all ages. It has led to truth, to
goodness, to justice, to love. Love was as much held up
among these old writers, these old religious teachers, and
as clearly set forth, as in the later day. Their testimony
fell upon ears that heard not, upon eyes that saw not, because they had closed their eyes, shut their ears, and hard-
ened their hearts. They had substituted something else for

this divine light; this word, which, in a still earlier day,
Moses declared to his people was "nigh unto them, in the
mouth, and in the heart." The truths of inspiration are the
way of life, and he that walketh in the right shall grow
stronger and stronger. These were the teachings of "the
light" to walk up-rightly; to act righteously; to be just;
to be faithful. "With the merciful, thou wilt show thyself
upright; with the pure, thou wilt show thyself pure." Believe not, then, that all these great principles were only
known in the day of the advent of the Messiah to the Jews——
these beautiful effects of doing right.

We should come to understand the divinity of this spirit, and its teachings to us now. I believe there is a growing understanding of it. It has been likened unto leaven,
which was hid in the meal, "till the whole was leavened";
and also to the little seed that was sowed in the field,
which became "the greatest among herbs." The word of God is
life-giving, fruitful; and as it is received, it produces
its own generation, sometimes called re-generation. Another
beautiful figure is sometimes employed, the change in the
physical being. We have first the little child; then the
young man; then the strong man in the Lord. All these
things we must read and accept intelligently, rationally.
Too long has the religious element been upheld to the veneration of man through some mystery whereby he could understand the growth of his own divine nature. Why, it needs no
miracles. They belong to darker times than ours. It is
when we are wide awake, and capable of reading, reflecting,
and receiving this ingrafted word, that we come to know the
anointing that teacheth all things. And we shall not need
that any man teach us. We shall come away from these false
dependencies. We shall come to the source——the immediate
access which we have made to the source of all truth; to the
source of all good. I know this is merely regarded as the
Quaker doctrine, the *ignis fatuus* of the Quakers, and it is

every where spoken against. We know how it was treated in
the early days of the Quakers. We know how the Son of God
was received when he preached; and it was because his teachings led him to non-conformity with the rituals of the day.
He was led to bear his testimony against the doctrines of
the Scribes and Pharisees of his time.

All ecclesiastical history goes to assure us, that
when there has been a sectarian standard raised, and a mere
verbal theology and ceremonial performances instituted, good
works have invariably been lowered. We all know how bitter
the sectarian spirit has become—how hatred and antipathy
have grown up among the people, and among people making the
highest profession of the name of Jesus, who become horrified,
shocked, if any shall deny what they are pleased to consider
his divinity; and yet, if any speak of the fruits of obedience to the law of justice and of goodness in the soul, they
brand it as mere morality, mere human benevolence, and not
the religion by which salvation is wrought. This is the tendency of sects, and it needeth a prophet to come forth declaring your circumcisions, your false lights, to be of no
avail. This has been the uniform condition of acceptance,
the working of righteousness—doing justly, loving mercy,
and walking humbly before God—and not in oblations and sacrifices.

And so, down to the present time, we see the same tendency and the same results. We need prophets among us, bold
non-conformists, to come forth and say, Verily, your baptisms
are not the right tests; your communions are not the proper
evidence of your intimate union with the Father and with the
Son. What are your Sabbath-day observances but conventional
rites? Verily, your silent meetings, your plain attire,
your peculiar language—are they the rightful tests of your
sound faith, your pure worship? No more than that of any
other denomination. We may take every denomination, and
where we find them setting up their forms as an evidence of

worship, above the pure acts of devotion to God, manifested
by love to the people—to the common children of God, the
world over—wherever this is to be found, there is need of
the right testimony to be borne; there is need that we
should say, he is not a true Christian who is one outwardly.
We need higher evidences, therefore, than now exist. Christianity will not have performed its work in the earth, until
its followers have learned to respect the rights and privileges of conscience, by a toleration without limit, a faith
without contention.

What have we to do with granting to another a point, a
belief, a doctrine? It is assumption. It leads to despotism. It has led to crucifixion; and it leads in the same
direction now, as far as the customs of the times will admit.
The name is cast out now, just so much as ever. And why is
it? Because there is a verbal creed set up. Because there
are doctrines fixed upon as being the essential requirements
of believers. They assume that the scriptures are the word
of God instead of taking them and ascertaining the uniform
testimonies to righteousness and truth, as found in the various pages, and discriminating between these and the practices of those ancients, many of whom were semi-civilized,
many of whom regarded their God as the God of war. The
scriptures should be read intelligently, so that we should
not be going back to the example of those ancients as our
authority for the present day. They do not justify that. I
would not shock the religious feelings of any, but I would
ask them to read their scriptures again, and see if they can
find any authority for sustaining their actions, and especially such as have done injury to their fellow-beings and
themselves. Especially are they appealed to for sanctioning
the use of wines and strong drinks, as our authority for the
far-extending influence of these for evil among the children
of men. So has it been the practice to cite the example of
olden times in approval of the abomination of American

slavery, as being a patriarchal institution. It is time
that we should no longer err. We do err, not knowing the
scriptures nor the power of God, when we resort to this Bible to find authority for anything that is wrong. We have
a divine teaching to which we should adhere. The great
principles of justice, love and truth are divinely implanted
in the hearts of men. If we pay proper heed unto these, we
shall have no occasion to go to the ancient practices to
find authority for our actions in the present day.

     We cannot help our opinions in these matters; this is
impossible. They grow up with us, and depend on circumstances, on our education, and immediate influences. We are
justified in our skepticisms. It is our religious duty to
be skeptical of the plans of salvation. The veneration of
believers has been held to them by not allowing them to
think. They have been afraid to exercise the test of enlightened reason which God has given them lest they should
be called infidels—should be branded with infidelity. It
is time the theology of the day had passed away. And it
has, to a great extent. It is modified. As an instance,
we might refer to the New School Presbyterians, arraying
themselves against the old Calvinistic doctrines. Others
might be enumerated. The people now are ceasing to believe
what their verbal creed teaches them. If there was a freedom and independence among them, such as the truth would
give, they would be less trammelled. "If the truth shall
make you free, ye shall be free indeed." How few are made
free by the truth! They are hampered by their undue adherence to the gloomy appendages of the church. I would not
set a high opinion on the Catholic Church, the Episcopalian,
Presbyterian, Methodist, Quaker, or any other. They all
have their elements of goodness, and they all have their
elements of bondage; and if we yield obedience to them, we
become subject to them, and are brought under bondage. If
we acknowledge this truth, and bow to it, we shall dare to

show our dissent. We will let them alone, treating them
with a toleration without limit, a faith without contention,
with regard to their opinions.

The doctrines of Christianity are perverted in order
to sustain the doctrine of total depravity. We take not to
ourselves that which belongs to ourselves. The proper sense
of the divine nature of man, in all its relations, first the
animal, next the intellectual, and then the spiritual, is
not properly understood. This is a beautiful trinity in the
human being. We shall find "the glory of the natural to be
one, and the glory of the spiritual another." While the
general faith of Christians is to denounce the animal, and
to build up a kind of new birth on this degradation, we are
erring, we are not acknowledging the divinity of all man's
instincts as we ought; and hence it is I deem it necessary
to speak forth, and be branded with heresy. And believing
this, and asserting it before the people, I cannot feel that
I am advocating a mere Quaker dogma. It is not a mere Quaker doctrine. In this latter day, we find it being regarded
more and more by every sect, and by those who attach themselves to no religious denomination. They acknowledge this
when it can be regarded free from the gloom of sect.

When we thus appeal to the teachings of the divine
spirit, we shall find it to exist in every human breast.
This is the revealed religion, and it is time that it was
claimed as such. It is time that that which is regarded as
mere morality should be preached as the everlasting, divine
truth of God; and as it is shining in the hearts and minds
of the children of men, and they come to receive it, they
will behold its glory, and it will be the glory of the only
spiritually begotten of the Father, dwelling in them as full
of grace and of truth. They overlook it because of it[s]
simplicity.

There is an acknowledgment of the regenerating power
of the eternal, so far as we may call it regeneration by application to natural things, without basing it on the

assumption that the first birth is evil. Jesus said, "Except a man be born again, he cannot see the kingdom of God."
But he spoke to those dark Jews, who did, no doubt, need to
be born again, to die out of their old forms and ceremonies.
Well did he answer Nicodemus, who thought this was such a
miracle, "That which is born of the flesh is flesh; and that
which is born of the spirit is spirit. Marvel not that I
said unto thee, 'Ye must be born again.'"

We may all admit, that if we receive the divine spirit,
in its operations in our soul, there will be no mistake; it
will be found a reprover of evil; and if we obey it, it will
be regenerating in its nature. It will make us understand
that which is spiritual, and to discriminate between that
which is spiritual, without underrating the natural. If we
suffer the propensities to have the mastery over us, we must
reap the consequences. Look at slavery in our country; look
at war. Whence come wars? "Come they not hence, even of
our lusts that war in your members?" If we attempt to govern ourselves and our feelings by these low principles, they,
of course, will lead to evil, to wrong, to wickedness. The
apostle says, "the natural man receiveth not the things of
the Spirit of God; neither can he know them, because they
are spiritually discerned." The natural man hath natural
powers and abilities; the intellectual man hath powers differing from these; and the spiritual man knoweth not the
propensities of the natural.

We are not to be regarded as denying the Scriptures,
because we have not so read them, and so learned Christianity, as have many of the authors of the theological opinions
of the day. Men are too much wedded to these opinions. Women in particular have pinned their faith to ministers'
sleeves. They dare not rely on their own God-given powers
of discernment. It is time that ye had looked to these
scriptures, and studied them rationally for yourselves, and
not follow the teaching which interprets them in support of

the wrong, instead of the right. Women in the earliest days
associated with men in carrying forward the great principles
of truth, as advocated by that remarkable son of God. A
Deborah arose, and Huldah, a prophetess. It was a woman who
announced to the people of Samaria the advent of Christ:
"Come see a man which told me all things whatsoever I did."
And this induced the men to go forth "out of the city, unto
him." And they said unto the woman, now "we have heard him
ourselves, and know that this is indeed the Christ." And
the very first act of the day of Pentecost was to declare
that the time would come when the spirit should be poured
out upon women. Phoebe was a minister of Christ. Priestcraft has rendered the word so as to apply to man instead of
woman. The degradation of the women of that day had its effect.

People should judge more intelligently than to take
the practices of former times, and make them a test for
practical Christianity of this day. "The kingdom of God is
within us"; the "word is nigh in the heart, and in the
mouth." If any are so faithless as still to need outward
corroborative testimony, they will find it in all ages, and
from the earliest times, as recorded in the Bible. And this
is the value of the scriptures among us. We have no right
to go to them now to establish a creed or form. We cannot
control our opinions; we cannot believe as we will: therefore belief is no virtue. We have not the power to control
our being; it is by the circumstances around us, by our
power of receiving, that we come to see, and to know, and
believe; therefore we must make a different use of the Bible,
in order to make it to us a book that is invaluable.

Goodness has been goodness in all ages of the world,
justice, justice, and uprightness, uprightness. "I will
make all my goodness pass before thee." This was a beautiful answer to Moses. This is the way that God manifests
himself to his children. It has been so in every age. It

is emphatically the case in the present day, which is marked
by the advances that have been made in this generation. It
is this which should be held up as an evidence that Christianity is being better understood; that the veneration of
the people is being drawn away from undue observances of
Sabbath days, of the worship of churches; that they are
coming to judge in themselves what is right, when they are
disposed to do this. How plentifully are the testimonies
of scriptures found to be in favor of the right, in all
ages!

The fast, then, that God has chosen is easily recognized: "To loose the bonds of wickedness, to undo the heavy
burdens, and to let the oppressed go free, and that ye break
every yoke." Jesus did not say, Blessed is the believer in
the trinity: blessed is the believer in the popular scheme
of salvation; blessed the believer in a mysterious divinity
attached to himself. He said nothing of the kind. He
called them to judge of himself by his works: "If I do the
right works, believe me, and the Father also, for I come
from the Father." "Blessed," he said, "are the merciful;
blessed the pure in heart; blessed the meek" —not the
"meek" that bow before sect. We must know a meekness that
will make us "as bold as a lion," that we may proclaim
righteousness, and reclaim this generation from its sins,
and denounce this meekness before sect. Jesus declared
this by his life of goodness, of active righteousness, of
pure morality, of sympathy for the poor. It is for the
love of his principles that we should place him on the high
pedestal that those who delight to worship him ceremonially
want to do.

It is not strange that there should be atheism in the
world, while such false ideas of God are inculcated in the
hearts of the people. We cannot in any way come to the worship of God, by any of these fancied attributes, without
humanizing him. Therefore, we must come to know him by our

merciful acts, our pure, our upright conduct, our every-day
righteousness, our goodness. We must come to be with him
by declaring "woe unto the transgressor." We must not make
compromises with injustice. If the mission of Jesus was so
emphatically to bring "peace on earth and good will to men"
we must endeavor to carry it out, and not place it away in
the distance, in the "millennium." Why, the millennium is
here; they kingdom of God has come. This is what we want to
preach. Oh that the fruits of this divine spirit should appear, which are love, peace, joy, goodness, truth; the spirit that is first gentle, pure, full of mercy, full of good
fruits. Here is no disparagement of good works.

    We forget the practical parts of the Bible, in our
zeal for preaching up a religion that is to do nothing. And
so we must let war go on "until the millennium comes." In
the olden time, they knew that war was wrong, and hence the
far-seeing proclaimed the day when "they shall beat their
swords into ploughshares, and their spears into pruning-
hooks; nation shall not lift up sword against nation, neither shall they learn war any more." They looked forward and
prophetically proclaimed the day when the "King cometh, who
is just, and having salvation." "And I will cut off the
chariot from Ephraim, and the horse from Jerusalem, and the
battle-bow shall be cut off; and he shall speak peace unto
the heathen; and his domination shall be from sea even to
sea, and from the river even to the ends of the earth." If
we are believers in this, and believe in the Messiah that
came with such a beautiful announcement, it is time that we
should love the name of Christ; should part with war, and
leave nations to settle their disputes in some way that will
put an end to the barbarism of war. It is abominable that
we should retain it—that we should still have recourse to
arms.

    But the efforts for the dominion of peace are greater
now than ever before. The very first message transmitted

to us across the Atlantic, by means of the mightiest instrument of men, the offspring of the divine, intellectual intelligence of man, wrought in our day, was a prophetic view
of greater peace on a earth. There is something so beautiful in this universal instinct of men for the right, that I
am pained to know that people of intelligence, professing
Christianity, should vouchsafe their assent to the duration
of any of the relics of the dark ages. Let us do away with
these things. We need the faith that works by love, and
purifies the heart. And sorrowful is it that the hearts of
men should be turned from right by the temptations that so
easily beset them, and lead them to do injustice to their
fellow-man, binding him down to slavery. Ah! the chains of
human bondage! They should make every one to blush and
hang his head. Mournful is it that they should countenance
the Sabbath day, and then, tomorrow, recognize a system
by which their fellow-men are sold at the auction-block to
the highest bidder. We should bear our testimony against
the nefarious claim of the right to property in man; and
the worst of this is, that we should hear this institution
claimed as sanctioned by the Bible. It is the grossest
perversion of the Bible, and many ministers have thus turned
over its pages so unworthily, to find testimonies in favor
of slavery. "Wo unto him that useth his neighbor's service
without wages, and giveth him not for his work." This is
what we want to quote. And we are all guilty of the blood
of our brother. The crime is national. We are all involved
in it; and how can we go forth and profess to believe the
faith of the Son of God, with all these great wrongs and
evils clinging to us, and we upholding them? Have we nothing to do with it? Every one has a responsibility in it.
We are called to bear our testimony against sin, of whatever form, in whatever way presented. And how are we doing
it? By partaking of the fruits of the slave's toil? Our
garments are all stained with the blood of the slave. Let

us, then, be clean-handed. Seek to be so; and if we find
the monstrous evil so interwoven with what we have to do,
politically, commercially, by manufacturing interests, by
our domestic relations, then so much the more need is there
for our laboring. Every church in the earth should be
roused; every people, every profession and interest. We
find democratic, republican America clinging to slavery;
and it will be found the last stronghold of the sin in the
civilized world. "He that doeth truth cometh to the light";
but we have rejected the light of Christ. We are told that
the Lord, in his own time, is going to put an end to this
thing. How, except in some way or other to defend the
right? "Break ye the hands of wickedness"; "Proclaim liberty throughout all the land, unto all the inhabitants thereof." And because ye have not done so, ye shall fall victims to the plagues that are around you. Here is where we
need faith, to know that we must reap the reward of our doings.

I have nothing to do with preaching to you about what
we shall be hereafter. We even now, by our obedience, come
unto the kingdom which is righteousness, peace, and joy in
the Holy Spirit. We know something of an inheritance into
that higher life where there is that communion with the
Father, so that we can understand, as far as is given us to
understand, that we may elevate ourselves above that which
is mortal to that which is immortal.

We need, therefore, this faith, which will make us
believe and know, that if we do the wrong, we must receive
for the wrong that we are doing; for there is no respect of
persons with God. He "rewardeth every man according to his
works" and according to the fruits of his doings. God's
laws are eternal, and I wish there were more conscientious
believers in the immutable laws of God. When such a man as
George Combe comes forth, teaching the everlasting laws of
truth to the children of men, he is called a mere

materialist. I would not exchange the true test for all the
theology that ever existed. All the theological assemblies
and gatherings united could not give such benefit to the
world as the truths and writings of George Combe, and others
who have a profound veneration for the laws of God.

It is impossible to hold any nation in slavery, when
their minds shall be enlightened sufficiently to appreciate
the blessings of liberty. When the sacred principles of
truth come to be evolved to the understanding of the children of men, how will all your theologists sink before them!
The rightful test, then, of the Christian character will be
peace, and love, and justice, and a claim of greater equality among men. There will no longer be the lordly heel of a
government trampling upon the children of men—no longer a
high-bred aristocracy, exercising their exclusiveness—no
longer an aspiring priesthood, bringing all under its spiritual domination. It is time these things were understood;
time that we should show how simple the religion of Jesus
is. This was the highest theology uttered by Jesus; "By
their fruits ye shall know them." The good man, out of the
good treasure of his heart, bringeth forth that which is
good; and the evil bringeth forth that which is evil. The
soil must be good, and the seed received must be cared for,
so that it may produce its own. And what will it produce?
Overlook not the truth of God. There is nothing that requires that ye should underrate your natural powers. Let
them grow with your growth and become strengthened, and you
will be made advocates of the right.

This is really a notable age, and we have to hail it
that we have not to wait for a far-distant day for the kingdom of God to come. There is an advancement, and its influence is felt so much that the minister begins to be ashamed
to turn over the leaves of the Bible to prove the wrong,
rather than to find therein advocacy of the right. The
young people ever hear truth gladly; in their hearts, there

is an instinctive revolting from wrong. Did not the love
of power abide to such an extent among us, there would be
an instinctive revolt against slavery and wrong doing. And
see how the reformer can stand before the Bible and say,
Ye tell us that ye treat the slave kindly; but I say unto
you, hold no slaves at all. Do justice to the colored man.
Do away with your infernal prejudices; they are infernal.
This impure spirit, this wrong that ye indulge in, is not
from above; it is earthly, sensual, devilish. A grave
charge rests upon ye who countenance the wickedness of
American slavery.

Public sentiment is changing. What, though, the political horizon may lower, believe me, the time is near,—the
kingdom of God, of justice and mercy, is entering, that
will be for the salvation of the slave. Believe me, that
the labors of a Beecher, a Chapin, A Furness, a Garrison,
and many other advocates of the right and true of our day,
preceded by those of a Hicks, a Clarkson, a Wilberforce,
and their confederates of former days, have not been in
vain. God ever blesses the rightful laborer. "In the
morning sow thy seed, and in the evening withhold not thy
hand; for thou knowest not whether shall prosper, either
this or that, or whether they shall both be alike good."
So having thus gone forth, we see how it is renovating, how
it is purifying the church from its corruptions.

The temperance movement is likewise prospering. It
has given evidence of great advancement in this day. War,
too, is falling from its original foothold in the earth.
There is greater delight manifested in right doing. The
power of moral-suasion is becoming better understood. These
are good indications, and, with many others, they point to
a happier and better state of things, the fruits of the
ushering in of the great and glorious gospel, that which
was to level distinctions, caused the highways to be
straightened, and institute equality among men. Let that

so be brought about that the reformers shall say to the poor,
"Come up hither! come up higher!" thus awarding justice to
these, and recognizing their rights, and their equality with
themselves. The day is coming, it has come; "the kingdom of
God is at hand."

The people flock more to hear moral discourses than to
hear the preaching from the pulpit. This would not be the
case were the preaching of the pulpit like that of Jesus.
There is quick understanding in the fear of the Lord among
the people, and I will trust the people. I have confidence
in their intuitive sense of the right, of the good. It is
this great heart of the people we are to preach unto, to
proclaim liberty and truth, justice and right unto; and let
it be done.

The immediate teaching of God's holy spirit, inspiring
love for the brethren, inspiring a desire for the promotion
of good, is your mission. Oh, it is your heavenly call;
obey it, and look not for any thing marvellous. Obey it, my
young friends! Come ye unto the harvest, and labor truly.
There is need of preachers against the excesses of the age.
There is need of preachers against the existing monopolies
and banking institutions, by which the rich are made richer,
and the poor poorer. Thou, oh man of God, flee these things,
and follow that which is right! It is contrary to the spirit
of this Republic that any should be so rich. Let this
blessed Christian equality prevail. Let us have a Republic
that shall be marked by its Christian principles; and by its
Christian, I mean its universally *right* principles. These
are eternal; divine in their origin, and eternal in their
nature. Let us have faith in these, and then let us believe
that the "kingdom of God is within us," and that Christianity will not have performed its office in the earth, until
the believers have learned to respect its rights and privileges, by a toleration without limit, a faith without contention. That faith will fill the heart with holy joy.

Thanksgiving will come up from such a heart, and there will
be an entering into the joy of the Lord, acknowledging that
he is good; that his mercy is everlasting; and that his truth
endureth through all ages.

[*Liberator*, October 29, 1858.]

ONE STANDARD OF GOODNESS AND TRUTH

SERMON, DELIVERED AT BRISTOL,
PENNSYLVANIA, JUNE 6, 1860

"Righteousness exalteth a nation, but sin is a reproach to any people."

It appears to have been a great comfort to one of old,
that he could say, "I have preached righteousness in the
great congregation; lo, I have not refrained my lips, O
Lord, thou knowest"; and it is interesting to learn among
these declarations of the ancient prophets, that there
seemed to be but one standard of goodness and truth. The
Scriptures derive advantage from the fact that we find
therein so uniform a testimony to the right; that is, among
those who are not bound by sect, or devoted to forms and
ceremonies. "Your new moons and appointed feasts, your
Sabbaths, even the solemn meeting," were classed as abomina-
tions, and for the reason that they executed not judgment
and justice and mercy in the land. The injunction was
"Learn to do well; seek judgment, relieve the oppressed,
judge the fatherless, plead for the widow." If they put
away their iniquities, and did that which was right, then
they should find acceptance. This is the testimony from
age to age, as we find it recorded; and it is time we should
discriminate between those scriptures that conflict with
righteous principles, and such as emanate from a spiritual
understanding of the requirements of truth. These requisitions of the holy spirit in the mind of man have been the
same in all ages, and it needs no learned disquisitions to

lead men to understand them. The people know the truth. The
time has come when it is not needed that man should teach
his brother, saying, "Know the Lord." It is this assurance
that all men understand the truth and the right —justice,
mercy, love, which inspire confidence that we may speak so
as to meet a response in the hearts of the hearers; and the
more we appeal to the inner consciousness and perception of
truth as received by intuition, by divine instinct in the
soul, and not through forms, ceremonies, and dogmas, the
more will there be amendment in the conduct of life. Our
appeals would be more effectual, were religion stripped of
the dark theologies that encumber it, and its operations
will prove more availing when presented to the hearers and
to the thinkers free from the gloomy dogmas of sects.

The true gospel is not identical with any scheme or
theological plan of salvation, however plausibly such a
scheme may be drawn from isolated passages of Scripture, ingeniously woven; it is through the intelligence of the age,
the progress of civilization and individual thinking, that
the right of judgment has been so far attained, that there
is great daring of thought, of belief and expression, and
much shortening of the creeds. A great deal that was de-
moralizing in its tendency has been separated from them.
Still, what remains is so tenaciously held as the only
touchstone of religious character, that there is a propor-
tionate lessening of the effect of sound morals, and a
lowering of the true standard. While we should feel a
largeness of heart towards all religious denominations,
at the same time, if we are true to God and the divine
principle of his blessed Son, we must ever hold up the
blessing to the merciful, the pure, the upright; regarding honesty, goodness, every-day works of usefulness
and love, as paramount to all the peace and enjoyment that
would follow an adherence to any of the abstract proposi-
tions of faith, that are held as the touchstone of sound

Christianity. We must be as Jesus was, a non-conformist.
That peace which "passeth understanding" comes from obedience to truth, not to sect, for great hardness of heart often proceeds from this; it leads not to love, but to persecution and bitterness. Unless the faith of the sectarian is
worked by a love, not of its own inclosure, to gather in the
outcast and the oppressed, it is not efficient conversion.
The apostle Paul believed he was acting in good conscience
when he was a great persecutor, and no doubt many of the
persecutors that perform their vile acts towards men, believe they are doing God's service; but their acts are wicked nevertheless. Many go so far as to say that if a man
does what he *believes* to be right, he is exempt from guilt.
This is a mistake. We have far too much charity for any
wrong-doer. What is wrong in itself, is wrong for any one
to do. The truth must be spoken, and the dark conscience
enlightened.

Many persons have become so inured to slavery as not
to discern its sinfulness. It has been said that "no one in
his inmost heart ever believed slavery to be right." We
know there is this instinct in man, else it would never
have been proclaimed that all men are born equal, and endowed by their Creator with the inalienable right to life,
liberty, and the pursuit of happiness. Many have so seared
their minds that the light of the glorious gospel, which is
the image of God, does not and cannot shine it upon them.
Hence it is that in this day there should be an earnestness
in advocating right doing. The people should be so enlightened as to distinguish between mere creeds and forms, and
practical goodness.

It is irrational to deny the sinfulness of slavery.
"Wo unto him that buildeth his house by unrighteousness, and
his chambers by wrong; that useth his neighbor's service
without wages, and giveth him not for his work." Wo unto
those who are partakers of other men's sins. "Wo unto them

that will not 'cry aloud,' spare not, lift up the voice like
a trumpet, and show the people their transgressions." These
old sayings show that the requirements of truth are the same
in all ages —to do right to give freedom to the oppressed,
the wronged, and the suffering. Those who have appealed in
behalf of these, have not appealed in vain. Progress attends
the work; but nothing can be effected by sitting still, and
keeping aloof from the arena of activity; it is by labor, by
many crosses, many sacrifices —brother giving up brother
unto death, and even submitting to martyrdom —that beneficent results are accomplished. And what do we ask now? That
slavery shall be held up in every congregation, and before
all sects, as a greater sin than erroneous thinking; a greater sin than Sabbath breaking. If any of you are seen on Sabbath day with your thimble on, performing some piece of
needlework, the feelings of your neighbors are shocked on
beholding the sight; and yet these very people may be indif-
ferent to great sins, regarding them with comparative uncon-
cern, and even complacency. This is what I mean in saying
that the standard of religious observance is placed higher
than the standard of goodness, of uprightness, and of human
freedom. To some, the sin of slaveholding is not so horri-
fying as certain deviations from established observances.
While the sticklers for these gather together and exhibit
great marks of piety, in some instances they are guilty of
small acts of unkindness, of meanness and oppression towards
their neighbors. It is not enough to be generous, to give
alms; the enlarged soul, the true philanthropist, is compelled by Christian principle to look beyond bestowing the
scanty pittance to the mere beggar of the day, to the duty
of considering the causes and sources of poverty. We must
consider how much we have done towards causing it.

     The feeling of opposition to war, that has been grow-
ing in the minds of men, is not confined to the Society of
Friends; people of various denominations have examined this

subject, and presented it in its true light. Faith in the
efficacy of moral influences has increased, and the possibility of settling disputes without recourse to arms is being regarded more and more favorably. Still, the spirit of
war exists, and it is surprising that those who look up to
the Son and adore his sacred name should forget that the anthem of his advent upon the earth was "Peace on earth, and
good will to men." Is this reformation going on? We should
see how far we are attending to the practice by which nations become demoralized. In looking abroad we discover a
revival of the brutal spirit of barbarous ages, to determine
what may be done by single combat; and in our own land we
find repetitions of these wicked experiments. Are those who
disapprove of these things careful to use their influence in
the family circle with their children, that they may not be
carried away by this brutal spirit? Mind acting upon mind
is of much greater power than brute force contending against
brute force. We have been in the dark long enough. The
likeness we bear to Jesus is more essential than our notions
of him.

The temperance reformation has accomplished almost a
revolution in our age, but the movement seems now to be
somewhat retarded by running too much into political and
masonic channels. Much may be effected by the young men
and the young women. How commendable that benevolence which
lifts the poor victim from the gutter of degradation, to
place him on the rock of temperance, and put a song of to-
tal-abstinence in his mouth. This oft-times leads to something higher. I desire that all may be first pure, then
actively engaged; that all, in their various religious denominations, and those not belonging to any, may see what
their duty is, and neither shun nor disregard it. Let not
those be forgotten that are beyond the reach of religious
inclosures, for they, the lowly and the outcast, need our
aid. Especial attention should ever be paid to that which

will exalt the condition of those that are downcast. If we
perform our whole duty, we shall give heed to these things,
in the spirit of a broad, all-embracing philanthropy, the
tendency of which is to equalize society. We should act the
part of true philosophers. Some are afraid to hear the
word "philosophy" in connection with Christianity. But
there is a divine "philosophy" which it should be our aim to
reach, and when we have attained to this, we shall see a
beautiful equality around us.

The efforts that are making for the elevation of woman, the enlargement of her mind, the cultivation of her
reasoning powers, and various ameliorating influences are
preparing her to occupy a higher position than she has hitherto filled. She must come to judge within herself what is
right, and absolve herself from that sectarian rule which
sets a limit to the divinity within her. Whatever is a bar-
rier to the development of her inherent, God-given powers,
and to the improvement of her standing and character, whether it be ecclesiastical law or civil law, must be met and
opposed. It is of more moment that she should be true and
faithful to herself than to her sect.

The more we are disposed to enter this reforming theatre of the world, the greater will be the promise of improvement of the social system, and the nearer the approach
to the true end of human existence. There is much to be
done. If we have entire faith in the efficiency of right
doing, we shall find strength for it. What is needed is
confidence in the possibility of coming into the kingdom *now*.
A great deal of time and effort has been spent in the sphere
of poetic fancy, picturing the glory and joy of a kingdom
hereafter; but what is chiefly required of us is to come into the divine government *now*—and to be pure even as God is
pure.

So far from preaching up human depravity, my practice
is to advocate native goodness. It was a beautiful condi-

tion—the little child. Had we faith in little children,
treating them aright, giving them a guarded education, we
might see in the next generation far greater purity than is
found at present.

It is essential that we have faith in uprightness, in
justice, love, and truth, for these are among the highest
evidences of true Christianity. I care not for charges of
verbal infidelity; the infidelity I should dread, is to be
faithless to the right, to moral principle, to the divine
impulses of the soul, to a confidence in the possible realization of the millennium now. We know what we are at present; if we are doing right, acting in accordance with sacred
principles, we all know how peaceful and happy we are. And
we know how we are brought into torment by violating the
right. We should have assurance that if we *resolve* to do
right, we *can* do it.

All we can do, one for another, is to bring each to
know the light of truth in the soul. It is pure, holy, un-
mistakable, and no *ignis fatuus*. Feeling and believing this
I would call you all to it. And we should come to recognize
the great principles of justice, humanity, and kindness,
holiness in all its parts, in the full belief that the establishing of the dominion of these in the earth is the divine
purpose of the Eternal, in sending this essence, or, as some
term it, in sending His Son into the world. What I mean by
the "Son of God" is that divine word which is quick and
powerful, which is a discerner of the thoughts and intents
of the heart; and if any shall speak of it as the "Christ of
God," let them so speak, and lay no stumbling-block in a
brother's way; but have faith in it, never fearing; it will
be sufficient for its own work. So believing, I can commend
you, my friends, to God, and to the word of His grace, as
sufficient to give an inheritance to those that are sanctified; and when we have finished our works here on   earth,
and are about to be removed from before the eyes of men, I

doubt not but there will be a blessed earnest of that which
shall appear hereafter, whatever it may be—that there will
be an entrance into that which is glorious and eternal.

"To the Christ that was never crucified; to the Christ
that was never slain; to the Christ that cannot die, I commend you with my own soul." Quoted from Elias Hicks.

[Reprinted in *Life and Letters of James
and Lucretia Mott,* ed. Anna Davis Hallowell.
Boston: Houghton, Mifflin and Co., 1884.]

I AM NO ADVOCATE OF PASSIVITY

*REMARKS, DELIVERED AT THE TWENTY-FOURTH
ANNUAL MEETING OF THE PENNSYLVANIA ANTI-
SLAVERY SOCIETY, OCTOBER 25-26, 1860*

[Lucretia Mott was glad that the resolution does not
sanction the measures resorted to by John Brown, as in con-
tradistinction to those approved by this Society, and by
the American organization of which it is a part. Mrs. Mott
read from the Declaration of Sentiments what she said were
her views, and what were at the same time the authorized
doctrines of this Society.]

"Our principles lead us to reject and to intreat the
oppressed to reject all carnal weapons, relying solely on
those which are mighty through God to the pulling down of
strongholds." We did not countenance force, and it did not
become those—Friends and others—who go to the polls to
elect a commander-in-chief of the army and navy, whose business it would be to use that army and navy, if needed, to
keep the slaves of the South in their chains, and secure to
the masters the undisturbed enjoyment of their system—it
did not become such to find fault with us because we praise
John Brown for his heroism. For it is not John Brown the
soldier that we praise; it is John Brown the moral hero;
John Brown the noble confessor and patient martyr whom we
honor, and whom we think it proper to honor in this day when
men are carried away by the corrupt and pro-slavery clamor
against him. Our weapons were drawn only from the armory of
Truth; they were those of faith and hope and love. They

were those of moral indignation strongly expressed against wrong. Robert Purvis has said that I was "the most beligerent Non-Resistant he ever saw." I accept the character he gives me; and I glory in it. I have no idea, because I am a Non-Resistant, of submitting tamely to injustice inflicted either on me or on the slave. I will oppose it with all the moral powers with which I am endowed. I am no advocate of passivity. Quakerism, as I understand it, does not mean quietism. The early Friends were agitators; disturbers of the peace; and were more obnoxious in their day to charges which are now so freely made than we are. [Mrs. Mott concluded by expressing her pleasure that the resolution committed the Society to nothing inconsistent with the high moral grounds it had ever occupied. O'Connell had said that no revolution was worth the cost of a single drop of human blood. John Brown had well illustrated in his own case the superiority of moral power to physical power; of the sword of the spirit to the sword of the flesh.

[*National Anti-Slavery Standard,* November 3, 1860.]

NO GREATER JOY THAN TO SEE THESE CHILDREN
WALKING IN THE ANTI-SLAVERY PATH

SPEECH, DELIVERED TO THE AMERICAN ANTI-SLAVERY SOCIETY AT ITS THIRD DECADE MEETING, PHILADELPHIA, DECEMBER 3-4, 1863

When I see these young men and strong coming forward with acknowledgments of their indebtedness to the cause, and rejoicing that they have been among its later advocates; and when I look around upon this platform, and see here a LUCY STONE, an ELIZABETH JONES, and a THEODORE TILTON, all laboring so effectively in the field, I feel that we older ones may indeed retire, and thank God that he who has blessed us all our lives long is now blessing the lads; for there is surely no greater joy than to see these children walking in the anti-slavery path.

I feared yesterday that we were dwelling too much upon the past. We were so deeply interested in the earliest movements of this Anti-Slavery Society, that we did not go back, except by mere incidental mention, to BENJAMIN LAY and RALPH SANDIFORD, who dwelt in caves and dens of the earth, of whom the world was not worthy, to ELIAS HICKS, THOMAS CLARKSON, and all those earlier laborers; we did not go back as far as that. I feared, however, that we were not enough leaving the things that were behind, and pressing forward toward those that were before. Although I did not entirely agree with our friend FOSTER, and was glad that he was answered as he was—for I have so large hope that I always take encouraging views of things when I can— yet I felt that there were duties to be performed in our case in regard to freedmen as well as in regard to those

still held as slaves in our land. It is of little consequence to us now what we have suffered in the past, what
obloquy, reproach and contumely we have endured in our religious societies, and in other relations in society. We
might, as women, dwell somewhat upon our own restrictions,
as connected with this Anti-Slavery movement. When persons
interested in the cause were invited to send delegates to
the London Convention of 1840, and some of those delegates
were women, it was found out in time for them to send forth
a note declaring that women were not included in the term
"persons," but only men; and therefore, when we arrived in
London, we were excluded from the platform. Yet, let me
say, in justice to the Abolitionists there, that we were
treated with all courtesy, and with a good deal of flattery
in lieu of our rights. But all those things we may pass by.

Last evening, when we were listening, some of us, to
the eloquent and earnest appeals made by HENRY WARD BEECHER,
we saw in the assemblage some who, a few years ago, rushed
from their seats in the church, because they could not bear
to hear WILLIAM FURNESS speak so plainly on the subject of
slavery, and who warned friends from abroad that they must
not come to our houses because we were Abolitionists. When
Madame PULSKY and her friends came, and were asked to go
with men on a visit to the Penitentiary, and the carriage
was at the door, word came that they were discouraged from
coming, because we were Abolitionists! When I see those
men coming forward now, and joining in the applause for the
thorough anti-slavery sentiments of HENRY WARD BEECHER and
others, so far from blaming them, or setting them at nought,
I would rather welcome them at this eleventh hour, and I
hope they may receive their full penny, if they work diligently to the end. I have felt sometimes almost with the
Apostle, willing to be accursed of my brethren for this
cause's sake; but willing afterwards, when they come forward and mingle with us, to give them the right hand and

invite them upon the platform, and glad to hear them, if
they have anything to say on the right side. When I saw
these things last evening, I remembered the remark of RAY
POTTER, one of the signers of the Declaration, who, in a
speech in Rhode Island, said that Abolitionists had the
great Temple of Liberty to rear, and must do all the rough
and hard work; but when it was near the top, he said, then
would come forth people to lay their little fingers upon it,
and say, "We have got it up!" I could not but remember
this last evening, and also a few weeks ago, when I rejoiced
to see the crowds listening to the words that proceeded out
of the mouths of PHILLIPS BROOKS and others upon this very
platform. When I heard some of the members of the Freedmen's Association, in this meeting, talking about the objections that were met and answered again and again by the Abolitionists years ago, of the duties connected with the liberation of the slave which we must perform, I felt that,
after all, we were but unprofitable servants, and had not
done as we ought to have done in regard to doing away with
that deep-rooted prejudice which is the concomitant of
slavery, and which we know can never be removed while slavery exists. Some of us women can perhaps more fully sympa-
thize with the slave, because the prejudice against him is
somewhat akin to that against our sex; and we ought to have
been more faithful than we have been so that when we hear
the words applied to us, "Come, ye blessed of my Father,"
we might be ready to ask, "When saw we thee   ahungered, or
athirst, or in prison, and ministered unto thee?" It seems
to me, therefore, as has been recommended here today, that
we should keep on our armor. It may not be necessary to
multiply our periodicals, and scatter them, as we have done
heretofore, with good effect. When our friends were talking
of what was done, and how we were received in the beginning,
and when Church and State were, as our friend GARRISON
showed so clearly, arrayed against us, I remembered that

then, just as in olden times, the common people heard us
gladly. In truth, the original good heart of the people—
excuse my theology—cannot resist the wisdom and the power
with which Truth speaks to their understanding; and therefore it was that we were gladly received among them. Many
have come and made their acknowledgments, that when we were
mobbed, when Pennsylvania Hall was burned, they were in the
wrong, they were in the mob; but now they say, "Whereas I
was blind, now I see, and I am willing now to be faithful
to what I see." Let us welcome them, hail them in their
coming, and gladly receive them. And with all these coad-
jutors, the work will go on, emancipation will be proclaimed,
and we may be just as confident and earnest as we were before our friend FOSTER reproved us. I think we may rejoice
and take courage. I like a little addition to the rejoicing
of good old Simeon: "Now lettest thou thy servant depart in
peace, for mine eyes have seen of thy salvation"; for the
whole salvation has not come, but we have seen of the salvation.

> [*Proceedings of the American Anti-
> Slavery Society at its Third Decade*,
> N.Y.: Arno Press, 1969.]

THE MOTHERS SHOULD DEPART AND
GIVE PLACE TO THE CHILDREN

*REMARKS, DELIVERED AT THE ELEVENTH NATIONAL WOMAN'S
RIGHTS CONVENTION, NEW YORK, MAY 10, 1866*

I am sorry to come before you with so impaired a voice, and with a face so scarred;* but I rejoice that as we who have long labored in the cause become less able to do the work, the younger ones, the Tiltons and the Harpers, come forward to fill our places. It is no loss, but the proper order of things, that the mothers should depart and give place to the children. It is now more than twenty years since this Woman's Rights movement began in this country. We were allowed to read, if we could not understand much; and could read that Blackstone defined the law, "that the husband and wife were one person, and that person the husband"; and we labored therefore to change the law, so as to recognize the wife as a person with civil rights.

It has been said this morning that every appeal that has been made to the legislatures of the several States, has been favorably received, and answered by changing the laws for the benefit of woman. I can but hope, comparing such an audience as this with the handful who met with Elizabeth Cady Stanton, in the first Convention, in a little Wesleyan church at Seneca Falls, and seeing Henry Ward Beecher for the first time on our platform, and speaking

---

*Mrs. Mott had a severe cold and hoarseness, and her face was bruised from a fall from a street car.

267

such noble words for woman, I can but hope that it will not
be as our friend Frances D. Gage expressed her fear it
would, that the degradation which centuries had created
among us, would require centuries to remove; but that, as
in the great anti-slavery movement, in regard to which the
most ardent Abolitionists never anticipated that we should
live to see the work accomplished, and yet a great work has
been wrought, for which we all feel increased veneration
for that power which not by might, but by His Eternal Spirit,
will work the change in this equally important enterprise,
to free woman from her enslavement; for it is an enslavement,
although not equal to the degradation of the poor black
slaves, and although I have never liked to use the word
"slavery," as applied to the oppression of woman, while we
had a legalized slavery in our country. But the oppression
of woman has been such, and continues to be such, by law,
by custom, by a perverted Christianity, by church influence.
This very church is an indication, from the darkness of its
appearance as we entered it this morning, that they love
darkness here rather than light, I will not say "because
their deeds are evil," but because they are ignorant
and know not what they do. They profess to follow the apostle Paul; but they understand him not, they know not the
Scriptures nor the power of the gospel, which is indeed glad
tidings and good news to the human race: glad tidings of
great joy unto all people.

We are beginning to realize this in regard to the millions who have been slaves in our land. And this is an
earnest to us that the good time is not distant, that light
and civilization have advanced. As our President said, we
have in our army such minds as Spencer, and Mill, and I
would add Buckle, and many others, who are consecrating
their talents to the great cause of womanhood, and freedom,
and right. So we find women as artists, in all its branches,
everywhere; and even in a Catholic country Rosa Bonheur

receives the cross of Honor (or something of that sort, about
which you know more than I do); for I am now only one of the
fossil remains, asking you in my imperfect way, to sit here
a little longer with your work. Remember that the apostles
sat all night, in their beginning, and that the Abolitionists
when we were crowded into an upper chamber, were glad to continue hour after hour preparing our resolutions.

Another thought was suggested to me this morning. If
it were true, as we were told, as it was not true, that the
slave was satisfied with his condition of slavery, it only
proved the depth of his degradation, for liberty was no less
a blessing to him because he was ignorant of it. So when
woman asserts again and again that she has as many rights as
she wants, it only gives evidence of the depth of her degradation; and when the rights which we demand shall be conceded to her, they will prove no less a blessing than if her
ignorance had never led her to deny or to dispute the propriety of asking for the redress of the grievances under
which she labored.

When, in 1848, the women of France went to the Provisional government and asked that they might be represented
under the new order of society, the most intelligent and enlightened statesmen of that country came forward and said
that the only reason why France did not succeed in the former Revolution of 1789 was that she represented then only
half the republic; that woman was as necessary to form a
complete republic as man; that although she differed from man,
that very difference was essential to form a complete republic.

Woman has been laboring for years under the present
condition of society, which like a great nightmare, crushes
her down, so that she is unable to tell the cause of her
suffering. When some of us in 1840 were sent forth as delegates to the World's Convention at London, and were denied
the right of acceptance because we were women, O'Connell and

William Howitt came forth and pleaded our cause; and a short
time after, Sir John Bowring said that the coming of those
women to England would form an era in the history of philanthropic doings, and would create a deep if not a wide impression there. I like to allude to these things to show
what progress we are making. Education has done much for
us. We now have women as physicians, and in various departments of society. A little while ago when the daughters of
Edgworth put out their volumes, they were afraid to publish
them over their own names, and borrowed the name of their
father. And when Lady Morgan wrote her history, in her introduction she mournfully says that "man tells woman that
obsurity is her true glory, insignificance her distinction,
ignorance her law, and passive obedience the perfection of
her nature," and proceeds to state the effect of this erroneous and vicious teaching on the mind and powers of woman.

Young women of America, I want you to make yourselves
acquainted with the history of the Woman's Rights movement,
from the days of Mary Wollstonecraft. All honor to Mary
Wollstonecraft. Her name was cast out as evil, even as that
of Jesus was cast out as evil, and as those of the apostles
were cast out as evil; but her name shall yet go forth and
stand as the pioneer of this movement. I want to note the
progress of this cause, and know now that Woman's redemption
is at hand, yea, even at the doors.

        [Woman's Rights Convention.
        Proceedings. N.Y.: Robert J.
        Johnston, 1866.]

WORSHIP IN SPIRIT AND IN TRUTH

*DISCOURSE, DELIVERED AT FRIENDS MEETING, FIFTEENTH
STREET, NEW YORK CITY, NOVEMBER 11, 1866*

"The Lord is in his holy temple, let all the earth
keep silence before him." Those who can thus, in silence,
feel after and find Him who is not far from every one of us
—for, as saith the apostle, "in Him, we live, and move, and
have our being" —those need not make the harmony of sweet
sounds to attune the heart to praise, melody, and thanksgiving; but, in this nearness of approach unto Him, they
can feel with the psalmist, that they love His law, and it
is their meditation both day and night. Now, this is a reality: it is no fancied mount of transfiguration, but it is
an experience in which the desire is often felt: "Lord,
evermore give us this bread." The worship in spirit and in
truth is the worship that is called for at our hands. It is
a great privilege we have, it is true, to enter His courts
with thanksgiving, and into His gates with praise, to acknowledge that the Lord is good, His mercy everlasting, and
His truth enduring to all generations. But the worship
which is required of us, is the active use of all our God-
given powers, all our facilities, our intellectual as well
as our nobler spiritual gifts. All these consecrated to God,
to truth, to righteousness, to humanity, and acts in accordance with such consecration, constitute the worship which is
needed, and very different from mere Sunday-worship paid in
oral prayer, in sacred song, or in silent bowing of the head.

271

We are too apt to confound these means to an end, legitimate, acceptable, noble as they are, with the end itself.
We are too apt to mistake sabbath-observance and Sunday-
worship for that which the Father is seeking from us all—
for the obedience which is called for.

We have just heard the inquiry made [by a preceding
speaker] as to what must be the state of mind "in the trying hour." I asked myself, What is that trying hour? Many
put it off, supposing it to be when the head is laid upon
the pillow of death, perhaps, or to a fancied day of judgment. But we need to understand, "the trying hour" to be
every hour when our consciences are awakened to a sense of
our situation—a sense of our unworthiness, it may be need-
ing repentance of sins, or with present duties imposed upon
us, when the trying hour is the struggle whether we shall
do our duty. Some men's sins, the apostle says, go before-
hand to judgment and some they follow after. Many understand this as going before death and after death, but it
seems to me that it is before they are committed: when we
are tempted, we are brought to judgment, to consideration,
to reflection, as to how far we shall yield or give up, or
come to a right decision as to our course of life.

We need to bring our experience, our religious faith,
duties, and worship more down (or up, I would say) to our
every-day life, more to our real existence. We need to pray
for strength; for, the great efficacy of prayer is not to
pray for partial favors, which would be perhaps in violation of the very laws we have transpressed, and which bring
upon us their proper penalty, not to pray for special favors
which we have no right to ask, but to pray that strength may
be given us to do what is required of us, to stand fast, to
have a conscience void of offense toward God and toward man.
We may not have sins to repent when brought together, if
we are every day desirous to be found thus doing our duty,
and invoking the Divine Power to aid us in this great desire

of our hearts. We know we are human, we feel our weaknesses,
and we feel the spirit of thanksgiving and praise for all
his mercies, which are new every morning. When we are thus
brought together, and can sit down, and can feel one with
another, and enter into our own hearts' communion, and know
his divine presence, notwithstanding our infirmities, our
human weaknesses —these are profitable considerations for
us individually. But I often feel that we have need to
press on the consideration of the people the great duties
of life, which belong to them, collectively, and which, as
individuals, we are bound to exert ourselves to promote, in
order that the Kingdom of God may be, in reality, near at
hand, nigh even at the doors. There is great instruction in
the records of the past in finding how the great seers, the
anointed of God, in every age, were always looking for a
higher and better state of things, a kind of millenium, and
often prophesying that this state should come, when peace
should reign, when the government of the Divine and the
Eternal should be extended from sea to sea, and from the
rivers unto the ends of the earth; and this we find described in the Scriptures in various ways; and each writer
in his turn has called upon the people around to do their
part to bring in this kingdom—to hasten the time, when in
the figurative language of Scripture, the lion and the lamb
shall lie down together, when all violence shall cease, all
wars, all injuries one of another, when there shall be regard one for another in every way, when loving our neighbor
as ourselves shall be more prevalent in the earth. And this
millenium was not completed at the advent of the Messiah to
the Jews: it seemed barely begun in the darkness in which he
found them, borne down by unmeaning ceremonies, useless
forms and sacrifices, which were never called for from on
high, but which were only suited or adapted by Moses and
others to the weakness and low condition of the people with
whom they dwelt and labored. In this dark state the great

truths uttered by Jesus often seemed to fall to the ground;
and he lamented over them: "Are ye yet without understanding?" "Shall the Son of man, when he cometh, find faith in
the earth?" Some of these mournful interrogatories show
how he deplored the condition of things which he found
among his own people: and yet he was ever hopeful of a better state of things, as was his forerunner: "He that cometh
after me is mightier than I; he shall baptize with the Holy
Spirit and with fire." And so Jesus, using terms figurative
of the truth, in his language, said, "The bread that I give
you, cometh down from Heaven; if ye eat my flesh (that is,
take the truth which I proclaim to you, receive the word
which is thus spoken to you) ye shall have everlasting life;
for, my flesh and my blood are meat and drink indeed." He
found that they were very outward in their reception, their
understanding of it, accustomed as they were to hieroglyphs,
symbols, figurative language: "Are ye yet without understanding?" "Know ye not that the flesh profiteth nothing?" "The
words which I speak unto you, they are spirit and life. Let
him that is athirst come unto me and drink." What did it
mean? I know that theology makes this all outward, all
suited to an outward atonement, to a vicarious sacrifice, to
the general orthodoxical idea of salvation by Christ.

   I think, however, the spiritually-minded, the clear
intelligent reader and thinker, may understand this in a far
wider sense, and it is time that this theological gospel of
despair had passed away. Even the disciples, outward and
ignorant as they were, said: "Thus spake he of the spirit
which they who believe in him shall receive." And so with
the apostles: Jesus called them continually to the freedom
which the truth would give—the liberty which was of God,
and which was to be bestowed by obedience, by doing right,
by doing the will of the Father, and in this way, his gospel
was indeed, "glad tidings of great joy to all people."

   The gloomy ascetic, whether Quaker or Catholic, makes

it just so revolting and repulsive to the young. Therefore,
if we attempt to preach the religion of Jesus, salvation by
Christ, we have need to understand it better, or we shall
never know what these "glad tidings of great joy" really
mean. We must learn to exhibit by our very countenances
that we have attained to this state.

True religion makes not men gloomy. Penances, asceticism, old sacrifices, "daily crosses"—all belong to a more
gloomy religion than that of the benign and beautiful spirit
of Jesus. (The term "daily cross" occurs only once in the
New Testament—in the Bible, I believe.) We know well there
are sacrifices to make in our life, in the pursuit of our
duty, the attempt to uplift the lowly, to spread the gospel
of glad tidings of great joy unto all people. We know that
the right hand and the right eye (to use again a figure of
speech) have to be parted with at times; but always we feel
the conviction that we enter into life thereby and its rich
experiences.

It was no new doctrine that Jesus preached. When
asked what it was he preached, he declared that it was not
new. "The peace that passeth understanding" had long before
been spoken of. Even the disposition to return good for
evil had been recommended long before his day. We make a
great mistake and limit the Holy One of Israel, when we date
the commencement of true religion eighteen hundred years
ago. There have been evidences of it in every age, and even
now in all the nations under the sun, in a form more gross
or refined, according to the circumstances of the times, of
the age, of the nations, we find recognitions of the Divine
and the Eternal, the Creator of us all, and in some form,
ceremony or worship offered unto Him. The native Indians of
our forests have their worship; and having witnessed some of
their strawberry festivals and dances, and religious operations, I have thought that there was, perhaps, as much reasonableness and rational worship in it as in passing around

the little bread and wine; or, I might name, perhaps, some
of the peculiarities of our own people, for all sects, all
denominations have their tendency to worship in the letter
rather than in the spirit—with an outward rather than an
inward salvation.

The apostolic in every age, the-sent-of-the-Father,
are ever calling for a higher righteousness, a better development of the human race, a more earnest seeking to equalize
the condition of men. And now, when the call is, "Behold
the kingdom of God is at hand," it is a disgrace on our profession of Christianity—the present unequal condition in
Christendom—these vast distinctions that exist in Europe,
even in England, between the rich and the poor. The lordly
aristocracy, the kingly government, the aspiring priesthood
there, and your own tenement houses here—all things go to
show how little we have really advanced; and yet, with other
views of the subject, how much, how great is the progress.
I more frequently have cause to rejoice in the evidences of
the progress of real Christianity, real truth, righteousness,
and goodness, than to be pained by evidences of anything
like a retrograde movement. I never look back to the past
as the Golden Age, but always forward to it, as coming; and
I really believe it to be nigh, even at the door, though not
perhaps by man's calculation. And, indeed, one (may I say
apostle?) of our own day, our great and good Elias Hicks,
dared not to leave much record of his own [experience] and
religious views of things, because he saw the generations to
come must be in advance of him, must go on unto perfection,
must see and act further than he had done—that difficulties
would be overcome, that the trammels of superstition and
tradition would be removed: but not entirely, he said, for
wars would never cease among men until the professors of
Christianity had learned to read the Bible more intelligently, more as they would other books, and come to a right judgment as regards the acts there required. Something on this

wise he has left; and I am glad he has; because there is a
tendency, having begun well, and run well for a time, to
suffer ourselves to be hindered from obeying the truth, and
go back again to the weak and beggarly elements of theology.
Hence I am glad that there is enough left for some of us,
the older ones, to recur to as being the faith for which we
struggled thirty years ago, and by which we conquered, as I
believe. I want that we should hold fast to this inward
guidance, this inward teaching, without wavering.

Another of the seers of our age (and I like sometimes
to quote those not of our own household) an anointed one,
delcared: "Mighty powers are at work in the world and who
shall stay them? God's word has gone forth, and it shall
not return unto him void. A new comprehension of Christian
spirit, a new reverence for humanity, a new feeling of
brotherhood and of all men's relation to the common Father.
This [is] among the signs of our times." This was declared before the late struggle, and the late events for the removal
of the bonds of slavery from millions of our fellow-beings.
We see that this reverence for humanity has done its work
in so far, and we can believe that it is going on if we are
faithful; if we can understand the Christian spirit and act
it out, we shall be instrumental in hastening the day when
the kingdoms of this world shall become the kingdom of our
Lord and his Christ. The day may be hastened: it is man's
instrumentality that is needed. We acknowledge a mighty
power far above all human effort, and indeed independent, as
I regard it, of the battlefield, that has brought about the
marvelous work and wonder of our day; but it was not without
many having to make sacrifices, to suffer their names to be
cast out as evil, and having to go forth as with their staff
in their hands and passing through this Jordan before we
could reach the promised land. How should one have faced a
thousand and two, put ten thousand to flight, had not the
Lord been on the side of justice, mercy, and truth? This

has been manifested, and in so many ways that I now have
great hope that the time will not be long, before the great
barbarism of war will be placed in its true light before the
people, and they will easily learn that where the disposition exists to resort to means for the redress of grievances
(either national or individual) other than physical force,
the way will be found. The prayer we need is for strength
to our feeble human efforts, and it is granted, blessed be
his name: "Whatsoever ye ask believing, ye shall receive."
Have faith, then. This idea, if we can only receive it
aright, not applying it to outward events but to inward confidence in the sufficiency of the mighty power of God, the
sufficiency of the attributes with which we are furnished;
if we will only carry them to him and do his work, and not
look to man for praise, for help; if we will come out of our
sectarian inclosure, and bind not ourselves to any theories
or speculations, but go on in fullness of faith —the desired end will be truly attained.

        The great historian, probably the greatest historian
in our day, Buckle, has very erroneously, it seems to me,
attributed the advancement of the world so far in civilization, more to the intellectual development of man, than to
his spiritual and moral growth and advancement. It seems to
that he mistook the mere sectarian effort of days past (which
he said died out in a generation and produced no great effect
upon the world) for the moral effort at human progress. Let
us see what has really been the progress since the great law
of love of right, of regard to man, was proclaimed more
clearly and extensively by Jesus of Nazareth. Let us see
what has been the progress since that time, despite the
checks given, as I deem many of them, by the organization of
the sects; that is, by erroneous theories involved in those
sects. Notwithstanding all these, there has been such progress in human society that now the writers of the present
day may well claim that there is a better understanding of

God dwelling with man, the Holy Spirit being with us, and of
man's regard to his fellow-being. The efforts that are made
for education, for improvement, morality, and the great numbers in all parts of Christendom, in various parts of the
world, enlisted in behalf of improving the condition of society—all go to disprove the idea, which I fear, when put
forth by such a historian, would have an undue influence,
and warp the judgment of many of his readers, and lead to a
lighter estimate of moral effort than really belongs to it.
He asked, what new law since the days of Jesus of Nazareth?
We might as well ask, what new law in science? There is no
new law in truth: we want no new law. It is no new doctrine
which I preach, said Jesus. But we want a better carrying
out of the law, a better life, a better recognition of the
Divine, and of the great duties of life springing from the
right worship of the Divine, and the Eternal. I allude to
this simply, because I know that when a writer becomes popular we are apt to receive his say-so without much criticism
or instruction; and I believe we have intelligence, judgment,
and capacity to read and understand; and I rejoice that woman is so elevated; and I would not ask more evidence of the
great moral advancement in society, than the estimate that
is set upon woman in our day; and she can read, and reflect,
—and judge understandingly of what she reads. Let us rejoice in these things. I would not disparage—far be it
from me—any intellectual advancement: I regard it all divine. We are as responsible for our intellectual as for
the highest gifts of God's holy spirit to the soul: "First
that which is natural, afterwards that which is spiritual."
It is theology, not the Scriptures, that has degraded the
natural; the intelligent reading of the Scriptures will not
disparage man. A gloomy theology has done this to the full
extent, lowered the estimate of good works, and dethroned
reason in so far that it is almost dangerous to hold up reason to its rightful place, lest it should be charged to the

French atheists. Why, my friends, we are responsible, divinely so, for our reason and its right cultivation; and I
am glad to perceive that the people are not afraid to think,
and that scepticism has become a religious duty—scepticism
as to the schemes of salvation, the plans of redemption,
that are abounding in the religious world; that this kind of
doubt, and unbelief are coming to be a real belief, and that
a better theology will follow—has followed. The old Calvinistic scheme is very much exploded—very much given up. The
Thirty-nine Articles are called in question by their own
subscribers; and the creeds of many Dissenters are set at
naught; and the formula of religion is changing: less and
less value is set on ceremonies. We find that which, generations ago, was the holy eucharist is now the simple memorial
bread and wine—a very simple thing it has become. Even
with this idea, many, I believe, if they were faithful, would
find that they go to the table unworthily, and would feel
bound to withdraw from it. The fear of man proves a snare
to many; and we do not make as much progress as we should by
reason of this fear of sect, of man, of non-conformity. We
need non-conformity in our age, and I believe it will come;
as heterodoxy has come, as heresy has come, so I believe
there will be non-conformity enough to set a right estimate,
and no more than a just estimate, upon days, and times, and
places of worship.

These subjects occupied my mind in the few moments
that we were sitting together this morning, and I felt too
that we were gathered, as our brother expressed it, with an
idea and feeling of worship which would perhaps supersede
all discourse of such common things of life, would raise
the mind up to an elevation where we might be brought together in spirit, and the prayer in spirit individually
reach the Father of spirits, who would be found to be very
near us—not a God far off, but a God near at hand; and that
his holy attributes of love, justice, right, and truth would

be manifested in us, and that we should be drawn together as
heart to heart, and, with the heart, the language of praise
and thanksgiving might ascend. And I trust even now it will
be found, that these every-day duties of life presented to
us, and this great worship of obedience in common things, in
regard to the poor and the lowly, and in all the relations
of society, will not make us less prayerful; and that there
will be such obedience and faithfulness even among the young
that they will also come into this Kingdom, in their very
youth, and find it all beautiful within, as one of the old
writers has said; "The King's daughter is all glorious within." There are many now rather doubting whether the feelings they have are indeed all that they are to look for—
whether it is he that shall come or look we for another. My
young friends, you have both seen him, and it is he that
talketh with you, and if you receive him in the hour of his
coming, in simplicity and lowliness, in the little duties
presented to you, perhaps among your young companions, ye
shall see greater things than these; ye shall go on until
ye can acknowledge that this is indeed he that shall come
into the world; and great will be your blessing; great will
be your peace; and when that peace which passeth understanding shall be yours, then will the language of praise ascend;
and you will be made to rejoice evermore, and, in all
things, to give thanks.

[*The Friend*. Reported by Andrew
J. Graham, December 1866.]

THE NECESSITY OF OUR CAUSE

SPEECH, DELIVERED AT THE MEETING OF THE
PENNSYLVANIA ANTI-SLAVERY SOCIETY,
PHILADELPHIA, NOVEMBER 22, 1866

I hardly feel satisfied with the statement of our friend, Edward M. Davis, of the action of the Executive Committee. We have all been surprised at the marvelous progress which has been made. We have witnessed the growth of the political parties in this country; for I believe both parties have grown and are coming round right as regards according the right to the ballot to the freedman. But on the other hand we have watched the accounts that have been furnished—some in the daily papers, and some in letters and communications directly to us, and in personal visits, of the cruelty that has been practiced at the South; and those accounts have come to us with the expressed desire that we should keep on and not resign our organization. They have told us that the time has not yet come, while the slave in so many instances is only nominally and legally free, while in fact the almost unlimited power of this oppressor continues; and that in many parts of our Southland large numbers of families of slaves are still actually held in bondage, and their labor extorted from them by the lash, as formerly; that while, so far as the law is concerned, they may no longer be publically bought and sold, yet they have been actually sold and transferred from place to place.

All these facts show the necessity of our cause, and the continued existence of the Anti-Slavery Society, not-

withstanding the legal abolition of the accursed system. All
this has kept us on the watch, and has kept our interest
alive in the great cause. Although there has not been much
done in the way of public meetings, in sending forth agents
and lecturers, we have not been idle. Early in the summer
we circulated some forty or fifty circulars to our friends.
There must have been some irregularity in the mails—for we
received fewer responses than usual; but there are some of
our friends here to whom we sent them, and we hope they will
make amends for the shortcoming of the past.

     I felt that it was due that we should say something
more with regard to what had been done; and I have therefore
mentioned these facts to show the mighty work that is still
before us, to secure manhood to the long bound and long en-
slaved. From the time of the proclamation of emancipation
up to to-day, what a wonderful change has been wrought in
the public mind! The hearts of the benevolent, the good and
the pure, not particularly of those who have been associated
in our anti-slavery organization heretofore, but all over
the country, young men and strong, young women and active,
have been reached, and they have felt it their duty to consecrate themselves and their all, for the time being, to the
education of those poor, wronged, stricken, needy slaves.
They have gone these three or four years, again and again,
returning during the unhealthy months, but, with scarcely an
exception, returning to the work with willing hearts, with
no disposition to relax their efforts. And the result of
their labors have been cheering, in the readiness to learn
which has been manifested. Last evening we had letters read
in our Friend's Freedmens Association, from the pupils of
those who had labored but a short time there, and who had
therefore had but a few month's instruction; and it was wonderful to see the progress they had made, not only in their
handwriting, but in their composition.

     But this is only one evidence of the great and marvel-

lous uprising of this people. The political progress of the
nation is wonderful. Even while we mourn that so much wrong
yet exists, we are all astonished and wonder at the advance
in our land so far above our most sanguine calculations; for
the most sanguine anticipations of the Abolitionists never
reached what has been realized within a year or two. I want,
therefore, in the beginning of our anti-slavery meeting,
that we should be affected in our hearts so much as to offer
the silent thanksgiving of praise to Him who is greater than
we, whose power is mightier than all, in that so much has
been effected through us more than we could hope for.

[*National Anti-Slavery Standard*,
December 1, 1866.]

THE ARGUMENT THAT WOMEN DO NOT WANT TO VOTE

ADDRESS, DELIVERED TO THE AMERICAN EQUAL RIGHTS
ASSOCIATION, NEW YORK, MAY 9-10, 1867

The argument that has been made that women do not want
to vote is like that which we had to meet in the early days
of the Anti-Slavery enterprise that the slaves did not want
to be free. I remember that in one of our earliest Woman's
Rights Conventions, in Syracuse, the reply was made to this
argument, that woman was not much to be blamed, because the
power of the government and of the church, that was vested
in man by the laws, made it impossible for woman to rise,
just as it was impossible for the slave to rise while the
chains were around him, and while the slaveholder's foot was
upon his neck. The common and civil law of England made woman a cypher, and blotted out her civil existence upon her
marriage. Blackstone, in his commentaries, says that the
law made the husband and wife one person, and that person
the husband. This being the power of the husband over the
wife, as established by law, that despotism followed which
must ever be exercised, when power is vested in one over
another, be it man or woman, to the great injury of the
victim. The law had crushed woman; and the Church, support-
ing the law, had assumed that the bible forbade woman from
using her rights. And if she asked to be a religious teacher, the perversion of the words of Paul was presented to
keep her back. When she became a wife, the Church stepped
in, and asserted the authority of the husband, and made the

wife acknowledge her inferiority and promise obedience to
him. That extends down to the present time. That is the
law of marriage now among the great body of religious professors in the land; and it is well for woman to know it.
Until she can be brought to a sense of her natural and inalienable rights, to go forth and defend herself against
these chains of society, she will be kept in this low state.

The resolution which was offered in Syracuse, as nearly as I remember it, was that as the assertion that the
slave did not want his freedom, and would not take it if offered to him, only proved the depth of his degradation, so
the assertion that woman had all the rights she wanted only
gave evidence how far the influences of the law and customs,
and the perverted application of the Scriptures, had encir-
cled and crushed her. This was fifteen or twenty years ago.
Times are altered since. In the Temperance reformation, and
in the great reformatory movements of our age, woman's powers
have been called into action. They are beginning to see that
another state of things is possible for them, and they are
beginning to demand their rights. Why should this church be
granted for such a meeting as this, but for the progress of
the cause? Why are so many women present, ready to respond
to the most ultra and most radical sentiments here, but that
woman has grown, and is able to assume her rights?

In regard to the remark of Mrs. Gage that by the want
of the consecration of marriages by the Church, the sacred
and holy ordinance of marriage is prostituted, I wish to say
that it does not follow that marriages unattended by religious ceremonies are therefore not true marriages. It is
now two hundred years since George Fox took the ground, far
in advance of the age in which he lived, that the parties
themselves were sufficient for the marriage union; that marriage did not necessarily require either to be sanctified by
the minister or legalized by the magistrate; but that the
parties themselves, acknowledging the religious obligation

of so sacred a union, were sufficient. And in that Society,
the parties were at liberty to appoint their own time and
place, and to invite such of their friends and neighbors as
they wished to be present; then in acknowledgment of the
divine presence, their obligations to each other were announced, entirely reciprocal, with no assumption of authority on the one hand or promise of obedience on the other;
but entire reciprocity, and a pledge of fidelity and affection until death should separate them. For two hundred
years, the marriages in the Society of Friends thus conduct-
ed, have been held as sacred, the union has been as harmonious, and the management of the children as free from complaint, as any other marriages in the community. The Parliament of England, after a time, saw fit to legalize such marriages; and so in our own country do the laws of the several
States.

In many of the States the laws have been so modified
that the wife now stands in a very different position as regards the right of property and other rights, from that which
she occupied fifteen or twenty years ago. You see the same
advance in the literary world. I remember when Maria Edgeworth and her sister first published their works, that they
were afraid to publish their own name, and borrowed the name
of their father. So Frances Power Cobbe was not able to
write under her own name, and she issued her "Intuitive
Morals" without a name; and her father was so much pleased
with the work, without knowing it was his daughter's, that
it led to an acknowledgement after a while.

The objection has been made to me—"Here you assume
equality and independence. Now, I feel dependent on my husband for everything." Women in our Society do not feel dependent for anything. They are independent themselves; and
in the true relation of marriage the husband and wife will
be equal. Let woman be properly educated: let her physically,
intellectually and morally be properly developed; and then,

in the marriage relation, in spite of law and custom and
religious errors, the independence of the husband and wife
will be equal.

    I was delighted with the remarks made in our Anti-
Slavery meeting by our friend Durant, that the conscience,
and the sense of right in man, was the basis of law.   The
idea seemed rather new; but it occurred to me that our
friend Burleigh told us that twenty years ago. We were
told, too, that when the work of the Anti-Slavery Society
should be finished, there would still be work to do. And
although Wendell Phillips is sensitive with regard to the
introduction of this question upon the Anti-Slavery platform, adhering so strictly to the Constitution of that Society that he does not want anything attached to it of the
other great reforms of the day which do not legitimately
belong to it, I think we shall find that he will continue
to be as able an advocate for woman as he has been, and
that he really does not lower our standard in any respect.

    [*Proceedings of the First Anniversary
    of the American Equal Rights Association*.
    N.Y.: Robert J. Johnston, Printer, 1867.]

I AM NOT HERE AS A REPRESENTATIVE OF ANY SECT

REMARKS, DELIVERED AT A MEETING
HELD IN BOSTON, MAY 30, 1867

Our President announced me as a representative of the
Quaker Sect, or the Society of Friends. I must do our
friends at home the justice to say that I am not here as a
representative of any sect. I am not delegated by any portion, or by any conference or consultation of Friends in
any way. I am here, as some say, "on my own hook." And if
I can be heard, in my feebleness, it will not be to present
to your view, as our first speaker has done for Universalism, the various phases of the Society of Friends —the
Orthodox portion, the Hicksite portion, the Progressive
Friends, or any of these —because I think people generally
are more interested in these divisions of their own denominations than outsiders, or than the other sects are. And I
do not know whether it is so profitable a use of the time
to enter into the little differences which have caused divisions among religious denominations, as to take a more
general view of the advantages and disadvantages of religious organizations.

I had not understood, in coming here, the precise nature of the meeting; I did not know how Radical the Convention was expected to be. One speaker, who has just sat down,
has deprecated the idea of dissent from all congregational
association; but it seems to me that a convention on so
broad a basis as I had understood this to be, should learn

better than to deprecate any religious dissent or "come-
outer-ism" from organization, and that there should be understood among us the charity, the toleration (if I may use
that "proud, self-sufficient word," as some one has called
it), to bear all things, and to recognize the march of the
religious sentiment in all ages. And I have regretted,
since I sat here, that our friend, known to so many, and
probably to all of you here —William Lloyd Garrison —who
is not in the country, is not able to be here. He is the
representative of no religious (as such) or sectarian organization, although the Anti-Slavery Society, by its advancement of right and justice, has found itself eminently a religious organization, I think.

The movements of the present age are striking and
deeply interesting. The fact of a Jew being called to a
Unitarian pulpit in Cincinnati recently, and the fact of a
Jewish sermon being published in one of the papers in Philadelphia, and being commented upon with favor since that time
—these facts, as well as other evidences, go to show the
enlarged ideas and enlarged spirit of the religious world —
or at least of Christendom —in this country, and in England.
Look at the divisions and subdivisions, and the free inquir-
ies now in the Church of England. First a few individuals
here and there came out, and then there came others, and
great scholars among them. And this was also noticeable
among the Unitarians; and these were so liberal that for
years, I believe, no Unitarian association in this country
has ventured to reprint their Radical works. Following
these, there were the seven essays, with their products
startling the church, and an examination was made on a
charge of excommunication. Following these, was Bishop
Colenso, going still further, and making the others almost
admitted to be Orthodox, since he went so much further than
they. Thus I see in the English church great confusion,
from the dissenting spirit. The various dissenting churches

in England and in this country (I will not take the time to
enumerate them), have been coming forward in recognition of
the religious ideas that are implanted in all human hearts,
the universal religious elements of our constitution. As
culture, and education, and civilization advance, these associations are gradually coming out of the old superstitious,
traditional ideas in which they have been educated; and although the articles of faith remain the same; although the
articles of the church, or the various creeds, in their verbal standing, may remain untouched, and it would appear that
they were indeed the same; some of them Orthodox, as they
are termed (we all claim to be Orthodox, I suppose), and
some of them old and very strange notions, yet if you hear
them explained now —though people admit that they believe
what the creed really says —they put very different inter-
pretations upon it. Still although these persons do shorten
the creeds every time, each still remains Orthodox just as
much after the shortening as before. And we have now had
movements through the Unitarians and Universalists, and, more
especially perhaps, through the Spiritualist; for although I
have never attended their meetings, and know but little of
them, except what other persons have told, yet I understand
that they have effected more against the dogmas of the time,
than other congregational organizations have as yet done. I
know our Friends are very jealous of any association with
Unitarians or Universalists, or even with the Progressive
Friends. And therefore I say that I am here representing
myself, and not the Friends, although I am much attached to
the organizations to which I belong. And I shall hope that
in the discussion which may follow, there may be the broadest recognition of existing sects and denominations; that
there shall not be a con-sociation and continuance with existing denominations; but on the other hand that there shall
be such a recognition of the come-outer element, if I may so
call it (I do not know what to call it), a dissent from

organization.

I believe, as fully as that the command was given to
Abraham, that the command is now to many, "Leave now the
kindred of thy father's house, and go into the land that I
shall show thee." As George Fox was drawn away from all organizations of his time, and had to retire alone, and there
be instructed from a higher power than himself, from the divine word; and claim that as the highest authority for action; no Bibles, no human authorities, no ministers, no pulpits, no anything that should take the place of this divine,
inward, everday teacher, so simple in its instruction —as
he, I say, was thus called out from all his kindred, and
from his father's house, and brought unto the land that was
therefore shown unto him; so I say there is an increased
number now of this description. I remember especially one
whose book I have read with very great interest, who even
from Spain, came out in advance of the friends of progress
and of the most liberal Unitarians in England and in this
country —Blanco White. I regret that those who were called
to the reformation in the land were not satisfied with being
destructives. Immediately they went to again constructing.
Our friend, I think, before me, deprecated the idea of the
destruction of religious organization. I do not know that
it is to be deprecated. I know that there can not be any
movement, any fellowship of anybody together without some
form or some rules of government. But in a republic like
this, if I understand self-government aright (I wish there
was some better nomenclature; we have the term self-government, and we have the same term to represent self-government
in a republic), we have yet to learn something that shall
recognize independence of the mind, and the truth that maketh free, and that by which if we are made free we are free
indeed. I have as full faith in the religious experience
and devotion of those who have withdrawn from all religious
association going occasionally to hear the liberal preaching

around them. Now I cannot say that these are not just as
religious in their devotion as the most sectarian observer
of forms. Many of these believe it to be better to come out
more openly in the matter of prayer. They believe it a very
wise recommendation of Jesus Christ of Nazareth, that divine
Son of God, "When thou prayest, enter into thy closet, and
when thou hast shut the door, there pray in secret, and thy
Father, which seeth in secret, shall reward thee openly."

I say I represent myself. I am a kind of outlaw in my
own society. It is a universal custom for us to rise in
time of prayer. It is considered out of order for any to
keep their seats. I have not felt free to do this for many
years, and have been subjected to reproach and contumely by
those with whom I have been associated. It is very difficult for us to be non-conformists with those with whom we
associate. It seems to me that we show this infidelity (if
I may so speak), this denial, in our indisposition to follow
in some of the acts of conformity more than in any other way.
It is of little matter to me what the creed shall be as regards trinity and unity, as regards what has been explained
here as Universalism, or in a more limited way. We know so
very little of the after life, that I am glad that the intelligence of the age is leading us to apply our religion
more to this life, and to every day practice and everyday
necessity, and uprightness and goodness, and to enter into
our heaven here.

I was interested a few weeks ago, at the opening of a
new Unitarian house of worship in Germantown. One of the
speakers said that they had got a "regular built church."
It had a font, and table, and pulpit, &c., and he did not
like the idea that churches should be converted into lecture
rooms. Now it seems to me that it is a great progress, that
a church may be used sometimes for lectures. I want our
friends to be liberal enough; and I should be glad to see a
more general disposition to have a church or place of

worship a freer place of gathering. And when our friend was
speaking in Germantown, a large portion of the people present were Friends, and large numbers that had been admitted
into that society were unaccustomed to the baptismal font;
and it seemed to me that he was behind the age in speaking
in the way he did. But I notice that the father of the
young Mr. Neal who was to be ordained, in turning over the
pages of his Bible, chanced to open to the passage in the
last of John the divine, that had always been rather a favorite one, where it speaks of the new Jerusalem that cometh
down from God out of heaven, and he read that in that new
Jerusalem there was no temple found. Now if that be the
case, why may we not suppose that some of these regular
radical supporter[s] have entered this new Jerusalem. But
how are we to judge of them, and how are we to judge whether
these persons who love their baptismal font and communion
table, love the Lord Jesus Christ? How are we to judge
whether they do or do not, except by their everyday practice and good works. We must hold these up, and with this
view.

     I do not wish, as a single individual, to commit the
society to which I belong, in any wise. But I would desire
that the convention may result in so enlarged a charity and
so enlarged an idea of religion, and of the proper cultivation of the religious nature and element in man, as to be
able to bear all things, and to be able to have that extended charity that is not offended, and does not deprecate
going on before, and to have charity for those who are behind, and also for those who go on before.

     May we then in thus coming together learn charity and
if we want an organization, let us not suppose that it must
necessarily be an organization similar to any in existence,
that are recognized as churches. I do not mean the Quakers;
but we can have an organization, and have it understood that
there shall not be a regular minister who shall be obliged

every appointed day to have a sermon prepared, and a prayer, perhaps, whether in the spirit or not. I often pity your ministers who have to come forth with their prepared sermons every Sunday. Why not carry out the precept that when anything shall be revealed to him that standeth by, let the first hold his peace.

I remember some thirty years ago, that on being introduced to Dr. Burleigh (we do not like to say "Reverend" among Quakers), by Dr. Channing, I asked him why there should be a monopoly in excluding woman from the pulpit. He said, "It is something that never entered my mind." I believe a large portion of the people never thought of the thing. But believe me, my friends, when I tell you that this monopoly will have to be broken up, and that there will be a ministry among us of a freer character than that which has been known heretofore.

Now, I do not know how far I have presented what was required by the platform this morning, but these are the thoughts which were in my mind, and which I have attempted to give forth, without any preparation.

[*Free Religion: Report of Addresses at
a Meeting Held in Boston, May 30, 1867.*
Boston: Adams and Co., 1867.]

WHEN THE HEART IS ATTUNED TO PRAYER

DISCOURSE, DELIVERED AT THE SECOND UNITARIAN
CHURCH, BROOKLYN, NEW YORK, NOVEMBER 24, 1867

When the heart is attuned to prayer, by the melody of
sweet sounds, or, it may be, by silent introversion, it
seems sometimes almost as if words were a desecration. Still,
we have need to stir up the pure mind, one in another, by
way of remembrance, to endeavor to provoke one another to
love and to good works. And in yielding to the invitation
to gather with you here this morning, it was in accordance
with a desire previously felt that I might have such an opportunity to gather with those accustomed to gather here;
not supposing, however, that there would be the general
notice or invitation extended which I found in the papers.
And in coming now and mingling with you I have felt somewhat of the desire of the condition that existed in the
first coming together of the disciples after their Beloved
had left them; when they were so moved by the divinity of
His presence and the inspiration of His faith and of their
faith, of His God and their God, that—the record states—
they spake one to another so that each man heard in his own
tongue in which he was born, whether Parthian or Mede—and
so on. It is not needful that I should go on.

Now I can suppose this. I can believe it to have been
done without mystery or without miracle—and, therefore, I
seek no supernatural aid, but the Divine aid, which is natural, which is the Divine gift of God to man equally with

his intellectual powers; seeking only this aid I feel that
we may now speak one to another so that every man may hear
in his own tongue in which he is born. To us, coming together here this morning, with all our variety of sentiments
and of use, as to worship, there is, after all, notwithstanding this diversity—there is a language through which
we can address one another that is universal in its application. And we find this to be the case from the hearty response that is returned to truth when read—to righteousness,
to justice and mercy, and all the attributes of the Deity
with which we have any right to see the acquaintance. We
find that there is this appreciation of the right. Why, to
these same beatitudes which have ju~t been read, who is
there that would not respond? Into what language can they
be translated, free of the incumbrances of theology, in which
there would not be a recognition of their divinity?

I believe that there would be none. And knowing that
it is customary, in presenting what is called "a sermon" to
the people, that there should be a text taken from the Scriptures, and, not being accustomed to bind myself to such a
form or such an arrangement in preaching, I had not selected
any particular passage of the Bible; but, after sitting down
with you here a text arose from the Apocrypha, the truths of
which there found are to me just as canonical as any other
part of the Scriptures. Indeed, coming down to a later time
in the full faith that the revelation of God is as clear, as
plain, and His inspiration as universal now as in any former
time, I can, with as much veneration for the truth, cite occasionally the good words of more modern inspiration—of
that which proceedeth from those who have been enlightened
in our generation and day, equally so with those who have
been enlightened in any other time. And this does not lessen our regard for the Scriptures, but increases, rather, an
intelligent appreciation of Scripture; though not for it to

be made the idol of Christendom, as it seems to me it is, to
some extent. Indeed, long before that time, long before the
advent of Christendom, we find from the researches that
have been made elsewhere, that they disclose a divinity as
pure, a revelation of God as sacred as the revelation found
here. And this research is most valuable to us in that it
furnishes corroborative testimony to the eternal inspiration
of God, to the Divine teaching of His Holy Spirit, which is
coming to be, I rejoice to believe, more the acknowledged
faith of Christendom. Beginning, it may be, with the despised name of Unitarian and of Quaker (but 'Quaker,' I must
say first, as George Fox and his co-workers, preceded what
is called the Unitarian beginning), I rejoice to believe
that this universal gift of God is now presented not only by
those in a clearer light, as the advance has gone on, but a
Bishop Colenso comes forward; the learned and distinguished
ones of the dissenting denominations are beginning to assert
this as transcending all other authorities, including the
Church arrangement of the Thirty-nine Articles—that the authority of this truth is beginning to be declared as paramount, however all those may be aids to piety, to devotion,
and a confirmation of our faith.

Well, the passage is this—"For thine incorruptible
Spirit searcheth all things" (or proveth all things); "therefore chastenest thou them, by little and little, that offend,
and warnest them by putting them in remembrance wherein they
have offended, that leaving their wickedness they may return
to thee, O Lord." This I consider to be the prevailing language of the Divine Spirit, this the voice of the Word of
Truth which we may so speak of and declare that every man
may hear in his own tongue wherein he is born, whether
Presbyterian, Unitarian, Methodist, or Episcopalian—Catholic or Protestant —Dissenters, or what are called Infidels
—though I would rather not use any term that might not seem
sufficiently respectful to the free-thinker, for I believe

free-thinking to be a religious duty; and a scepticism of
the religious plans that prevail—however those may be held
in religious veneration —I believe that such proving all
things, such trying all things, and holding fast only to
that which is good, is the great religious duty of our age.
The superstitions of the past must give way to this incorruptible spirit which searcheth all things. Our own conscience and the Divine Spirit's teaching are always harmonious;
and this Divine illumination is as freely given to man as
his reason, or as are many of his natural powers. Let us
believe this, my friends! Why, it is a Trinity of a great
deal more consequence to us than any theological trinity
that may be taught; and far nearer, because it may become
self-evident; while a trinity that is contrary to reason can
never become self-evident to the natural man, or to the com-
ponent parts of his nature. And this faith is in accordance
with this Divine teaching, this supreme teaching of the
Apostle. First, that which is natural, or animal, and after,
that which is spiritual. "The natural man receiveth not the
things of the Spirit of God, for they are foolishness unto
him; neither can he know them"—Why? Not because the natural man is weak, but—"because they are spiritually discerned." Let us believe this, and then we shall find God's
ways to be explicable and not inexplicable. God's ways are
not "past finding out." The more we apply this to the revelation of God's truth, the more we shall discover the invariable nature of this law; and it will modify the prayers
that are put to Him, which are often an abomination. The
Apostle said, Ye asked and received not, because ye asked
amiss. Let us bring our kingdom of heaven here—down, for
it has been placed up so high that even your ministers cannot speak of God without the uplifted eye. But the Quaker
cannot do that, because that which is known of Him is revealed within: and so of the "engrafted word which is able
to save the soul." Why, the young are setting up or

imagining some wonderful operation because the persecuting
Saul needed a light above the brightness of the sun to see
that it was indeed Jesus whom he persecuted. Believe me, my
younger friends, when you would ask, where is He? and, Who
is He? Thou hast both seen Him and it is He that talketh
with thee. It is so simple, so beautiful, and I think so
plainly in accordance with His teaching—if they would not
overlook this Spirit dwelling in them.

And this, it seems to me, is my mission to you. It
was my mission in Boston last spring, where I mingled with a
large company who imagined in some measure that they had
outgrown religious organization. How my heart yearned for
them. The congregation came together and heard with patience the simple words that I uttered, and though feeling
as on the brink of the grave, I, on arriving here, with this
feeling in my heart, the more readily come to you and mingle
with you. But with reluctance, knowing that at this hour of
the day there is in Philadelphia such an objection to have
women come into the pulpit. And not only on this account,
but from the education I have received and which by conviction has become an adoption, and as a testimony in favor of
a free gospel ministry, a testimony in favor of an acknowledgment of the Divine Spirit teaching women and men equally
to declare that which God hath done for their souls, and to
incite their brethren to say, "The Lord, He is God"; and believing that George Fox and his contemporaries in their day
did a mighty work towards breaking down the monopoly of the
pulpit, until I am glad to see there are no longer in your
churches the high enclosures for single persons, as in the
churches of England, but that all is widening and spreading,
until encouragement is given, that the time is coming when
the ministry will be more extended, and when there will be
a different understanding to that by which one person ministers year after year to the same people. I am glad to see
an effort made to this end in your radical journals. I know

that this is very different [from] the learned and beautiful
discourses that are delivered from this place, yet I think
if men and women practiced more to give utterance to their
thoughts they might learn to do it with more effect. All
this, however, may be merely educational with me.

The special mission which brought me to you, which
took me to Boston, was to call upon those who seemed to see
beyond the dry theology of the day—why, even one of your
own writers has said that the consecration of the Sabbath
intimates the desecration of the other days of the week—
and seeing all this and the more enlightened views, as I
think, which are presented from time to time by a certain
class of thinkers, views that are well worth receiving,
though they may be slow to find entrance into the minds and
hearts of the orthodox, because a liberal faith is always
everywhere spoken against by the more thoughtless among
them—seeing all this my mission is to call upon you. Why
not judge ye for yourselves what is right? Yet after all,
the fear of man is so strong that too often the believer
suffers himself to believe in the truth. I know that stigma cast upon the Quakers because they could not receive the
peculiar theology of the day, as the English Quakers have
received it, and now, that generation having passed, and a
people having been raised up who know not Joseph, they are
now beginning to go back again to the weak and beggarly elements of theology. This is painful to see because I believe
Truth to be ever progressive. As Jesus used to say so frequently: "If the truth make ye free, then are ye free indeed." This is no new doctrine, as He affirmed: and so let
us believe it, my friends. I have been accustomed from
early life to receive these truths as I found them, the
reading of the Bible often being more to me than my daily
food, and yet never read as a religious ceremony, but in
asking for the truth and finding it. "Blessed are the poor
in spirit, for"—though I dwell in the high and holy place—

"theirs is the kingdom of heaven. Blessed are the pure in
heart, for they shall see God. Blessed are the merciful for
they shall obtain mercy." To the pure, thou wilt show thyself pure. To the merciful, thou wilt show thyself merciful.
To the upright, thou wilt show thyself upright. By many it
has been said that peace has its origin with Jesus. By no
means. Why the apostle had to quote the old testament itself. "If thine enemy hunger, feed him; if he thirst, give
him drink, for in so doing thou shalt heap coals of fire on
his head."

My friends, let us see how universal this truth is,
how universal its requirements, how the entering of sacred
temples is as nothing compared with walking uprightly and
speaking the truth in the heart. "I am weary of your Sabbaths, of your solemn assemblies, because ye grind the face
of the poor, saith the Lord." The requirements of truth
have ever been similar in all ages, and as nations have been
prepared by circumstances to receive it, they have ever
found it requiring "righteousness and true holiness." I
want this age to be more zealous of good fruits, of everyday righteousness and true holiness, in business, in all the
transactions of life. Hearing last night some of your politicians talking together about the corruption in this State
and in Pennsylvania, I said, Why is it that your religion is
not brought into politics? Why is it that your religious
worship has regard to Sabbath day devotion rather than an
everyday truth? Why is it that you are not uplifting the
poor and the lowly. In the paper yesterday I saw that call
to give to the Lord the best hour of today. Ought you not
to give it to him every day? Man's instincts are all favorable to this. Talk of the native wickedness of man! Why
there would not be half the wickedness in Albany or in Har-
risburg that there is, if theology had not taught people
there, that human nature was more prone to wickedness than
to goodness. We are expected to be pure because God is pure;

to give up our lives for the brethren even as Christ gave
up His life for the brethren. This doctrine leads us to be
content with a lower state of morals than we desire to be.
We need that the standard of religion should be lowered and
give place to a standard of "righteousness and true holiness." Jesus said, "except your righteousness exceed the
righteousness of the Scribes and Pharisees ye cannot enter
the Divine government." Herein is the Father glorified.

     Now we need, specially in this day, to be bringing
forth good works, and to have our faith firm. We need a
faith that shall remove mountains, far more than we need a
faith in mysteries and in miracles. And this we have seen
brought about in our day. Is it not a marvellous work that,
by crying aloud and sparing not, God who has seen the af-
flictions of His people has come down to deliver them, letting them see that they were verily guilty concerning their
brother? Apart from the battle field which, lamentable to
be said, is still the ultimate appeal of nations, we have
seen how this Northern people demanded the abolition of
slavery. And your servant in Washington issued his proclamation—a wonderful proclamation it was. And what has been
the result? Did the most sanguine Abolitionist anticipate
such a result? Nay, it was by the almighty power of God,
and yet it is marvellous in our eyes. The instrumentality
seemed so simple—yet such was the influence of the power of
truth over error, of justice over injustice and cruelty!
Here is the great law—the power of justice and mercy and
truth over injustice and cruelty and falsehood. It is mighty
through God. One does chase a thousand and two put ten thousand to flight. We have seen it in our day, and we are
called upon to rejoice at the condition of our country in
that we are now better prepared to carry out true Republicanism—true Republican-Democratic principles.

     Have the oldest among you ever seen the time when the
heart and the hand have been so wonderfully opened to the

degraded and the poor as it is today, where there are thousands who are gathered every year to educate, to lift up
this large class of our emancipated fellow-beings? When
again the attempt which is being made to give them equality
before the law, in every sense—to put the ballot in their
hands—why, it is among the most wonderful works of our day!
What next? What other reformation is needed? Why, I ask
you, are you going to permit barbarism of war to go on generation after generation, when you all acknowledge it to be
the greatest of evils that afflict mankind? "He that taketh
the sword shall perish by the sword." War being evil, its
results are evil. They must be evil and that continually.
Well, now, this is no isolated Quaker doctrine against war,
because for two hundred years we have settled our differences peacefully, without even going to law one with another,
by reference, by arbitration. And thus we have interested
the serious, thinking public to advocate peace; and it is
beginning now to be advocated beyond the pale of our religious society or of any other. Why, my friends, you ought
to be ashamed that you did not honor Worcester more when he
devoted himself to enlightening his fellow-beings by circu-
lating statements for peace and against war. Channing followed. How beautifully he wrote in favor of peace and
against war. And yet not taking the ground that war was inconsistent in self-defence. Still, as far as he did go, how
valuable are his writings. They were printed in England and
reprinted in 1840. (Are they out of print now?) I love Dr.
Channing. I love his prophetic words, and believe they are
equal to and more easily understood than the prophecies of
Daniel. I never read in any Quaker book a clearer testimony
in their works than in your own Dr. Channing to this principle in the human mind: I refer to the inward principle, to
the power of discerning and doing right, to the voice of God
to man. This is the greatest gift of God to man. "All the
mysteries of science and of theology fade away before the

simple perception of duty which draws upon the mind of a
little child. From that moment he stands before a tribunal
on the decision of which his whole happiness rests. He
hears a voice which if faithfully followed will lead him to
happiness, and refusing to attend to which will lead him to
inevitable misery."

I love to think of such words as these, so that when
they are asking, Show us the way of truth and of life—you
let them know that it is He who is thus reasoning with them.
Believe me, that as you bow to it, as you yield to it; as
you faithfully follow the intimation of duty (and each must
find his own mission), as you believe that it is He—His
Divine Spirit, His Words, His Power that shall come up from
thee, His holiness that dwelleth in thee, then shalt thou
know the commandment of the Lord to be pure, enlightening
the eye, the [statutes] of the Lord to be right, rejoicing
the heart. Then shall we see that while we are satisfying
ourselves with the enjoyments of this life, apart from His
Divine teaching, that we are strangers to "the peace of God
which passeth all understanding." Believe, then, my friends,
that God giveth us richly all things to enjoy. But it is a
day of extravagance, and retrenchment is needed. There
needs that you should look to your adornings, and see whether the meek and quiet spirit, the "pearl of great price,"
is not of far more value than that in which you may be
decked for a time and enjoy "the pleasures of sin for a season." I pray to God, the apostle said, that ye do no evil.
Not that ye should appear as prudes, but that ye should do
that which is honest. This is what is wanted: that you
should do that which is honest in society. The gospel understood, is "glad tidings of great joy" to all people. Are you
making it so? Are you doing your part to make it so? Here
is the eight-hour labor demand. Do you consider that these
eight-hour laborers have as good right to make that demand,
and to reap the fruits of their labor, as your school

teachers would have, as your minister has? I know that we
have splendid gifts in these days, far better than a mere
devotion to the building of almshouses. We have the munifi-
cence of a Peabody, and of your own Stewart, if it may be;
and of Vassar, who has founded a college for the education
of women.

Oh, that I had another hour to speak to the young women! But I want these great subjects to be taken hold of
and acted out. I am glad that there is a stir about these
tenement houses. Let this be a country, as it ought to be,
the tendency in which is to equalize society—but no great
agrarian movement, no infringement upon the rights of individuals. And then, Free Trade. Why, there is a principle
in that far more than in the protective system. Women, to
be sure, have no right to meddle with political economy.
The law has made the husband and wife one person, and that
person the husband—Blackstone says. But while woman is
thus bridged over in every way—if this is the case—if we
are not expected to enter into the difficult question of fi-
nance and of political economy, believe me—and I speak as
to wise men!—believe me, if you are worthy the name you
bear you will take up some of these great questions; you
will bring your religion right into your politics, right
into your commerce. And why should you not? Why should we
be satisfied to let the State be corrupt in its doing? Why
should we be satisfied to let your votes go for the wrong
rather than for the right? Believe me, if your works are
pleasing to God, they will after all be acceptable to man;
for, after all, everybody loves truth better than error,
everybody loves goodness better than wrong-doing.

I want you to think of these things; and if we know
them, happy are we if we do them. I feel that an apology
is necessary for the time I have spent, I feel grateful for
the kind and attentive audience you have given me and I wish
to thank you, and in separating from you, to add, in a

spirit of gratitude to the Lord who has put it into the
hearts of so many to love the right better than the wrong
—that the Lord is good: His mercy is everlasting, and His
truth endureth to all generations.

[*The Friend*, January 1868.]

GOING TO THE ROOT OF THE MATTER

*REMARKS, DELIVERED AT THE PENNSYLVANIA PEACE SOCIETY
AT ITS SECOND ANNIVERSARY, NOVEMBER 19-20, 1868*

I think it is very important that we should have just
such speeches as we have listened to. While we have the
Government based upon war; and the paraphernalia of war is
so attractive, it must be that there are some among us who
shall go great lengths and speak as we have heard this evening, and present the crime in its true light; and it is
well that there is daring enough among us to speak the whole
truth on this subject. Everything depends upon going to the
root of the matter and speaking of radical principles. Long
enough have we been accustomed to apologize for the slaveholder, to be reconciled to the system because it was connected with the government, because iniquity was protected
by law. The fact that there were those who came forward and
held up this great crime in its true light, roused the people, and they did not love to have it so.

I regard the abolition of slavery as being much more
the result of this moral warfare which was waged against the
great crime of our nation: than as coming from the battle
field, and I always look upon it as the result of the great
moral warfare. It is true that Government had not risen to
the high moral point which was required to accomplish this
great object, and it must use the weapons it was accustomed
to employ, and in it[s] extremity it was compelled to do this
great work. So in regard to war, it must be held in its true

311

light and the enormity of the crime be laid where it belongs.

Such arguments as we have heard this evening and others that can be presented should be given and I doubt not that
there will be persons who will go forth imbued with peace
principles who will be able to go on farther and farther.

The progress that has already been made is encouraging.

I remember when Joshua Blanchard and other friends entered upon the subject some were afraid to go too far and
too fast, they thought that war in self-defense must be permitted, and they were looking forward for some millennial
day when peace would take the place of war.

We know there has been progress since that time, and
from that time the peace principles have spread considerably,
and as far as we have gone we have become more nearly sound
in the principles of peace, and now we look at war in its
true light, and it is well to do all we can to enlighten the
people on this great subject, so that they shall come to
look at the possibilities of peace.

We have to look for a change in public sentiment and
in the government before we shall have attained to the state
that the advocates of peace desire.

We must be able to speak of things which we have known,
what our hands have handled of this good word of life.

When we thus present to the people the sound policy of
the peaceful state, the reasonableness of arbitration and
reference among nations for the settlement of International
difficulties as we have been accustomed to settle individual
difficulties.

When all the troubles that are connected with man's relations, that are now made the causes of war, have been presented to the people in the light which they can readily perceive to be true, they will readily accept them for there is
a love of peace in the heart of every one. They will come to
see that there is a reasonable principle that will lead us to

abandon the barbarism of war.

It will not be long before the whole nation may be
brought to see that peace is possible and desirable in a
christian state.

Another result, that we may look forward to with hope,
is the removal of the death penalty and when this is the
case we can present this to the people as something that
can be carried out now.

It will be just as it was with Slavery, just as the
rights of man are coming to be considered all over the
world in a far better light than they ever have been before.

These things may be brought about long before all mankind have come to acknowledge the great principles of right,
the love of liberty and the hatred of oppression, so will it
be with the barbarism of war, it will be so presented to the
people that they will be aroused to a sense of its enormity.
Thus placing the crime where it belongs, and then showing
that governments can be maintained without resort to deadly
force. I believe the governments can be brought to be like
the kingdom of our Lord and his Christ, without waiting till
all shall be converted to the principles of peace. This is
my idea of this work, that it is much nearer at hand than
many suppose, and I am sure our faith should be firm now,
that prayers were manifestly answered in regard to the great
crime of Slavery.

So it seems to me that war should be presented to the
people in a way that shall lead them to examine it carefully.
Why we know how it was with the practice of duelling only a
short time ago and this has been held up to view in such a
light that it is no longer considered admissible—so we have
had the barbarism of Slavery presented, and we must do the
same on the question of war and we may hope to influence the
public mind and present the great principles of christianity,
of right, of justice, of peace and love.

We may hope to influence the public mind and also the

nations, that they may be lead to appeal less to the force
of arms, and look for the reasonable mode——of arbitration.
We have long been accustomed to settle our individual differences in this way. We should look at human beings as
accessible to the truth, as easily prevailed upon to accept
the truth if we only go to work in the right way.

We see that all the societies for moral reform which
have marked our age so emphatically, are doing great good
among the people, and the churches are moving in these directions, and the people can bear to hear of these things
and by speaking of these evils in their true light and at
the same time being hopeful, we shall find our efforts
blessed.

Notwithstanding all the apparent love of war and fighting there is an innate love of peace, an innate love of justice. The hearts of the people are right. Let us therefore
respect those and keep on in our work, do that which our
hands find to do, and though our meetings may be small, not
many of us, not many learned, not many great ones, we must
be satisfied to work on. We can do much better than we did
in the early days of the women's Anti-slavery Society [when] we di
not know how to take a vote——we had to call in a colored man
and ask him.

But in this Peace movement we understand better what
to do, there will be stronger men and stronger women and
they will all aid us and I doubt not the time is far nearer
than many of us anticipate, when this barbarous custom will
be abandoned, and I always mean to have hope that the good
will ever prevail.

[*Bonds of Peace*, February 1869.]

RELIGIOUS ASPECTS OF THE AGE

*SERMON, DELIVERED AT FRIENDS MEETING, RACE
STREET, PHILADELPHIA, JANUARY 3, 1869*

I read a few days ago, in an article by some radical
writer, the belief that christendom had not yet begun to
understand the force of the declaration, that God should
teach his people himself, that it would be no longer necessary for man to teach his neighbor or his brother, saying
"know the Lord, for they shall all know me from the least of
them unto the greatest of them."

It impressed me that there was great truth in the remark.

When we look over christendom and see the position of
the Priesthood, not to say Priestcraft, when we see in the
more enlightened parts, as we deem them, of christendom, the
dependence upon pastors or teachers upon authorities; how
few there are who are prepared to take truth for authority;
rather than authority for truth; we can but feel the force
of this sentiment in the slow movement of christendom. We
say christendom because we have a right to look for more enlightened advancement with those who make the high profession of christianity.

It is a high profession as compared with the religions
of the preceding ages and of many, very many generations
since that time. And yet how little have we advanced. How
slow are we to believe that we have this great inward teacher—this Divine Monitor within? How much is it entangled

315

with an educated conscience? How little is the distinction
made between the conscience of sect and the conscience which
is created by the divine power operating in the soul of the
recipient of these inward teachings? How little do we understand that it was expedient that Jesus should pass away
so that the spirit of truth might more fully come unto men.
How clearly he stated this, and in after times the Apostles
saw and felt that though they had known Christ Jesus after
the flesh, yet now henceforth should they know him no more,
but by his inward presence, by the life of God in the soul,
by the spirit of truth which Jesus declared unto them
"should teach them all things, and show them things to
come."

We have had, it is true, seers and prophets, tellers
of things to come, from the time to the present, but these
messiahs of their generation have been few and far between.

When the disciples went forth and enquired of their
fellow believers, "have ye received the holy spirit since ye
believed the holy ghost?" their answer was "we have not so
much as heard whether there be any holy ghost." So it is
down to the present day. It becomes a controverted question, when the sufficiency of "the light" is dwelt upon—
when the teachings of the divine spirit are held up as being
all sufficient for us as to what are these teachings? How
are we to distinguish them? How are we to decide what they
are? It is easy enough if we look at the authorities to see
when these differences of creeds and opinions arise, we may,
readily understand why this controversy, why these differ so
much. When we look at the conscience of sect, the conscience
of education in any way, we shall clearly understand all
this. But we shall find that despite these, there is no difference of opinion among men when it comes to great principles—the attributes of God, by which he reveals himself to
his children. There is not found any controversy as to what
constitutes justice and love, mercy and charity and all those

great divine gifts to man which constitute him god-like, or
of divine creation—the breath of divine life which was
breathed into his soul. So when we come to the tender affections of his nature we do not find any dispute as to
what pity is, sympathy one for another in their weakness is,
or that charity is which is pouring out of it abundance and
riches in giving to the poor and the needy.

There is no difference of opinion in regard to all
these; they have been found to be the same in all ages. How
beautiful it has been. How tender the sentiment poured into the breast of the mourner! That he ever will comfort
them that mourn, that he ever will be with them that are
sorrowful—the true-hearted. He will not suffer the waves
of affliction nor the floods to overflow them. We find
these sentiments to be universal.

He causeth his sun to shine on the just and the unjust.
His judgments are not as erring man's; we see how abundantly
his favors are bestowed upon all.

When affliction does come, when any great accident occurs, when fatality is among the people, when there are
mourners abundant upon the earth, as have been peculiarly so
of latter years, it is not needful to assume an angry God
whose just judgments are visited upon the people.

We need not view them in that light, for they are as
much the natural results of causes as any thing in outward
nature, as all the great movements of the universe are in
accordance with divine laws.

The reference is coming to be placed with greater fullness of faith in the operation of these laws than in the assumption of special and partial Providences. "I do assert
eternal Providence and justify the ways of God to man." This
saying of the Poet impressed me when I was very young and I
have no doubt there are many now who have ceased to pray or
put up petitions for special favors in relation to outward
gifts, or outward things. They know there are means by

which these shall be acquired, and if these means are followed even in acquiring great wealth by improper means they
will succeed and they may have all the heart desires, yet
"leanness will be sent into their souls" as was said of old.
"They lusted after the flesh and I gave them the desire of
their hearts but I sent leanness into their souls."

I remember many years ago reciting the lines of Cowper,
a Poet whom the world has not appreciated.

> Perhaps she[the world] owes her sunshine and her rain
> Her blooming spring and plenteous harvest,
> To the prayer he[the good man] makes.

I was stopped by Edward Stabler, who said "no, I would
not repeat it for I do not like the blooming spring and
plenteous harvest to be attributed to the prayers of the
good man. We must look to natural causes for natural effects."

I was young then but it impressed me so that I have
never forgotten it. The more we seek truth——the more we
look at this subject with an eye and heart to "God teaching
his people himself" the more we shall discover our prejudices and traditions. We need to be shocked, christendom
needs to be shocked. While there are those who still adhere
to the doctrine of human depravity, and all the speculations
concerning rewards and punishments hereafter, it needs that
we be shocked, as well as for some of the past generations
to be shocked by the utterances of Elias Hicks. Well was it
for that generation that we had a John Woolman, and many
others. Well was it for the age in which George Fox and his
contemporaries lived——those sons of thunder at that time.
Well was it that they roused the people of their day on the
subjects of unconditional election, and reprobation, predestination, the old trinitarian ideas, and many other dogmas
of the sects which were regarded as sacred. Well was it
that they had those teachers who could go before them and
utter the truth. They did their work and great has been the

result of that work. We are profiting by it today, even
though we, as a body, may be small compared with other denominations. Although the more liberal sects may be small
compared with those who retain more of their old forms,
their old traditions and creeds, yet such is the power of
truth over error that it modifies and regulates it, and it
cannot be resisted. It was said of those who opposed the
believers formerly that they could not withstand the power
of truth.

The thirty nine articles may remain and the Pope may
be in power, yet after all there is a new philosophy in the
world, they do not admit what would seem to be the meaning
of their verbal creed, they laugh at us if we suppose they
believe so. They do not so read it and interpret it.

My friends, among ourselves there are some clauses in
our discipline which we have outgrown, which are gradually
becoming a dead letter, so every denomination and every age
has its growth.

I was impressed with a prophecy of the past generation,
"Mighty powers are at work in the world, and who shall stay
them? God's word has gone forth and it shall not return unto him void: a new comprehension of the christian spirit, a
new reverence for humanity, a new feeling of brotherhood,
and of all man's relations to a common Father, these are
among the signs of our times." Do you not like, my friends,
to hear anything like these prophetic utterances and to perceive that in a generation's time there is a recognition of
their fulfillment. Certainly there are evidences that there
is a new feeling of the brotherhood of man in this generation. There is a more enlarged toleration, shall I use that
selfish word, there is a more enlarged recognition of the
right to worship and believe as circumstances may lead the
believer and worshiper.

There is a better understanding of these things and it
has been brought about in a great measure by a union for

great and good purposes. People have learned that their
neighbors are better than they thought them, that their
dissenting friends were better than they had been taught to
believe. With all the adoration for the name of Jesus and
the fear of a denial of his divinity, many seem to forget
that men should be judged by their fruits—by their works,
by their love one unto another. They seem not to understand that he said, "an evil tree cannot bring forth good
fruit," therefore "by their fruits ye shall know them."
But after all men do judge one another more by their fruits,
by their everyday life than by their professions, a life
of righteousness and true holiness, goodness is ever held
in high estimation, not mere sectarian piety. It speaks
well for the general judgment of the children of men, aye
of the children of God, for I recognize all as children of
God—of one common Father, instinctive of love of goodness
and all that belongs to him, intuitive in the highest sense
and understanding of truth, of allegiance to the Father. As
this comes to be better understood, as people learn that
"he is teaching his people himself," there will be richer
fruits still. We see it now in the great benevolent acts
of the age, we may call this mere morality, but let us not
disparage this disposition to give before death, rather
than leave to be distributed after death.

Thousands upon thousands are now devoted to the building of better tenements for the poor, for education, and
the bettering of the condition of society. All this goes
to show that there is a new comprehension of the christian
spirit, a new reverence for humanity, a new feeling of
brotherhood and of all men's relations to a common Father.

We Quakers Friends, as we love better to call ourselves, if we had adhered strictly to this great inward
light doctrine, if we had not been so desirous to please
men as to have abandoned our simple creed so as to embody
some of the orthodox faith of the age, we should have done

still more in spreading a knowledge of this great doctrine
of the inward light. Depend upon it, it is not an ignis
fatuus, it is no vain chimera. It was declared when our
fore-fathers came forth, aye long before——when Jesus gave
forth the declaration——the kingdom, the government of God
is within you.

When he compared it to "a little leaven that was hid
in the three measures of meal" to "a grain of musterd seed"
and all those beautiful parables by which he illustrated it
to his blind hearers. Long before George Fox, he declared
the same doctrine, yet how little was it received? How he
mourned over their darkness "ye are slow of understanding"
"ye fools and blind." He was asked what new doctrine whereof thou speakest is? He assures them it was "that which was
from the beginning; it was with God and it was God." This
was his idea   if not his words. We find among the prophets
of olden time there was a recognition of the same divine
teachings, else would not the prophet have been prepared to
say the time will come when man "shall no more need to teach
his neighbor or his brother saying, 'know the Lord for all
shall know him from the least unto the greatest.' They
would not have known how to speak so beautifully of this inward diving light" declaring that "the law of the Lord is
perfect converting the soul."

The law on tables of stone was not perfect, as was declared "I gave them laws which were not good and commandments
by which they could not live but the time shall come when I
will write my law in their hearts." "The statutes of the
Lord are right——the commandments of the Lord are pure," "the
testimonies of the Lord are sure." "The reproofs of instruction are the way of Life." "Thou gave us also thy good spirit to instruct us" and Job who is considered still older
said, "There is a spirit in man and the inspiration of the
Almighty giveth them an understanding."

I know the veneration there is for the scriptures.

Taken as a whole it is far too high. Many are shocked at
the idea of not believing in the plenary inspiration of the
book from beginning to end.

But my friends we must learn to read this as we should
all books with discrimination and care, and place that which
belongs to the history of a more barbarous age where it belongs, and never take the wars of the ancients as any authority for war in this enlightened age. It has good and evil
in it and because men take this as authority is one reason
that truth has made such slow progress. Mark how it has upheld the great crime of human slavery. Mark how the subject
of temperance has been retarded by quotations from this book
on the subject of wine. Friends have had to suffer because
they dared to assert that war was wrong in every age of the
world. Many thought it conflicted with some of the testimonies of the bible. But we are learning to read the bible
with more profit, because we read it with more discriminating
minds, we are learning to understand that which is inspiration that which is only only historical, for the righteous judgment that comes of the reception of the right spirit dares
to judge all things—"ye shall judge angels," how much more
the records of the ancients. It is time that we should learn
to take truth for authority and not authority for truth and
these pages from the beginning of Genesis to the end of Revelations contain truths. "If thou doest well shalt thou not
be accepted, if thou doest not well, sin lieth at the door."
That was an evidence that Cain knew what well was. From that
time through all the ages of the past down to the present not
in the records of the bible alone, but in the researches of
those capable of going into the language of other nations
even the most ignorant and barbarous nations—there are many
references to the same inward and divine teachings.

I heard George Thompson, after residing in British
India speak of an organization found there the members of
which did not believe in war, who would have nothing to do

with warlike actions. These evidences in all parts of the
world are the fullest testimony to the teaching of the divine spirit, independent of man's teachings, showing that
the same divine principles of goodness and love are to be
found wherever man is found, in whatever age or nation or
country to some extent. We grant that a great deal depends
upon the proper cultivation of the mental powers, that where
there is ignorance there is barbarism and superstition. But
all through these ages there are striking instances of
righteousness, goodness and truth and these to a far greater
extent than biblical history furnishes.

If we read the researches and examinations of those
who dare to think for themselves, who dare to publish to
the world their thoughts we shall find that truth has been
the same in all ages of the world, that it has ever been
given as far as people have been prepared to receive the
idea that "God is the teacher of his people himself." We
do not need to depend upon ministers, bibles, pulpits,
teachers of any kind. We can go directly to the fountain
head, and certainly it is time that we should be more enlightened than to look to public preaching, to authority,
time that we should do more of our own thinking, and that
when we do speak one unto another it should be for edification, for comfort, more in recognition of this inward teaching. We need not direct how, or in what particular path
one or another shall be led. The course may be a very different one as regards special individual duties, as we may
be prepared by talents, tastes, or education, but most of
all by faithful obedience to the inward monitor. Many are
particularly led to the sick and suffering. Their lives
are devoted greatly to ministering to their wants. These
give of their abundance or of whatsoever they may have. None
are to be excused though their labors may be directed in
different channels.

This is an age in which there is very much done in all

these directions, in these Christmas and New Year's times,
when it is so much the custom to give—to be blessed by
giving and by receiving. It is well that we hail this also
as a sign of the times which indicates progress. There is
progress amongst us in every way, and in nothing is it more
manifest than in the religious assemblies of the people, in
that they can bear one another's burdens, and will hear that
which they may not entirely approve, many have been taught
not to consider reasoning wicked when applied in the right
way. We are to use our reason in the examination of everything, it is our duty to do this even in the matter of faith
and of worship, we are to look at and reason in these things
properly.

It was the complaint formerly my people do not consider, and they were said to be worse than the stupid ox.

"The ox knoweth his owner and the ass his master's crib
but Israel doth not know, my people do not consider." We
need to reason and to consider and to have all our faculties
called into action, and not take upon trust that which we
hear from the "pulpit and gallery." That which is the pro-
duction of one generation may not be intended for another.
We must look for truth and love it for it is from the Eternal source of light. Then let truth ever be our guide, and
let us remember that God teaches his people himself.

Let us treat one another kindly even though we may not
receive some of the ideas which they present, let us strength-
en one another to do that which is regarded as right.

The ability is often far higher, far beyond ourselves.
Surely that which has been effected in our country in regard
to slavery has been so much higher than the most ardent abolitionists had hoped for, that there is enough to encourage
all those who went forth weeping, scattering the seeds of
truth and justice and mercy before the people. So when there
is proper reverence for truth all that comes to us in our
abundant blessings, we shall see that there is enough to in-

spire a spirit of praise and gratitude, even though it may
not be on the bended knee in the assemblies of the people,
it may be in the closet, as Jesus wisely recommended in his
day.

There will be more gratitude and praise as there is
less belief in special providences, gratitude and praise to
our Father for the bounteous gifts, for the marvellous works
which are in the world.

The Apostle said to some in his day, "ye ask and receive not because, ye ask amiss that ye may consume it on
your lusts." So how many there are that find that their
prayers are not answered. Then let us see that our faith,
our prayer, our praise are all intelligent and from the soul,
then shall we understand that "justice and judgment are the
habitations of his throne." When we look to judgment as
punishment only we do not see the whole. We know the result
of evil and wrong doing, and surely there is enough of it in
the world, yet instead of speaking to the wicked alone of
the suffering and danger of punishment hereafter we should
do as George Fox did endeavor, to call the people away from
the hell that was in themselves and bring them to a Heaven
within themselves. Search the scriptures, they testify of
truth and you will find that it is not so much a judgment in
the future as a judgment now that we must look to. There
may be a looking forward to the conditions of the hereafter
as well as a hope of a blessed reunion in heaven into which
we are to enter.

Still there will be that understanding which will lead
us not to speculate so much, or make our preaching so much
in reference to what will be hereafter, as to enable us to
come unto a Heaven now.

The wrong doer will thus be brought to see the result
of his action, and thus we may speak of that which we do
know of the results of disobedience.

Then we can speak intelligently, then we can bring to

the heaven within and away from the hell within themselves.

Let us understand this and look at it properly. I
well remember the words of our Doctor Parrish—we revere
his memory that "although justice and judgment are the ha-
bitation of God's throne yet thanks be unto him, for his
mercy endureth forever."

[Sermons. MSS. Friends Historical
Library, Swarthmore College.]

THERE IS A PRINCIPLE IN THE HUMAN MIND

*ADDRESS, DELIVERED AT FRIENDS MEETING, RACE
STREET, PHILADELPHIA, MARCH 14, 1869*

There is a principle in the human mind which renders
all men essentially equal. I refer to the *inward* principle,
to the powers of discerning and doing right, to the moral
and religious principle. This is the great gift of God to
man; I can conceive no greater. This sentiment of one of
the apostles of our times is worthy of all acceptation. But
as the veneration of the believer and worshiper among us
generally is directed more to the outward authority of the
Scriptures, I would quote: "This is the true light which
lighteth every man that cometh into the world."

This principle, or doctrine, or great tenet of the
Quakers, so called, of the Religious Society of Friends,
from its origin, is becoming more and more the accepted
creed of many of the enlightened of other professions. Many
attached to other religious organizations, and who have a
right to that attachment, have still an increasing interest
and faith in that divine inward principle.

It matters less as to the various beliefs with regard
to the doctrine of the Trinity or Unity, or predestination
or Fore Ordination of any kind. As regards many of these
religious tenets of the professors, they are held in faith
or they are not, according to the circumstances of education
and the daring, the increasing daring of men, to do their
own thinking, to reason and judge for themselves, to "try

all things, prove all things, and only hold fast to that
which is good."

    After the Apostle Paul had enlarged on the catholi-
city, if I may so speak, of the religion which he would advocate and spread, he returned to his Jewish education, and
said the question might be asked: "What advantage then hath
the Jew? or what profit is there of circumcision?" And his
answer was "Much every way." So it seemed to me reflecting
on this great interrogatory and its answer, since I took my
seat here; so it seemed to me might be said of the Quaker,
or Friend, with the general belief—the belief in the universal salvation of all sects or denominations, and equally
those of no particular sect or denomination with the universality of the light which they preach; what advantage
then hath the Quaker? or what benefit in these peculiar and
specific teachings?

    May we not answer: Much every way. And Why? Because
from the early days of this Society of the faith in this
inward principle and its teachings as the great monitor,
directing aright, turning to the right hand or to the left,
saying: this is the way; walk in it. The attention of the
people has been directed to this, and to its immediate
teachings, in every little concernment of life. The great
duty has been constantly urged of faithfulness in little
things, of obedience to every manifested duty, clearly discriminating and judging intelligently whether this manifested duty arises from mere sectarian education, from the circumstances of ignorance in which we have been placed, or the
clear indisputed teachings of the Divinity within. So
judging, so concluding, then results the great duty of
yielding to its manifestations, of making such sacrifices as
truth may require, or in other words this inward light as
truth may require. And then the philosophy of it is apparent to us that whoever has faith in the light shall be made
ruler over more, "If thine eye be single; thine whole body

shall be full of light." And the converse by experience is
found to be equally true, he who is unjust or unfaithful in
the light, will be also unfaithful or unjust in that which
is greater.

Then, again, is the righteous judgment which all may
be free, one of another, of the acts of men to judge: "By
their fruits ye shall know them. For of thorns men do not
gather figs, nor of the bramble bush gather they grapes."
Knowing and learning by experience this philosophy that they
learned, we have been taught to manifest our faith by our
works, by our fruits, by our everyday life, and that made to
appear in comparative trifles, letting the skill and power
of conscience direct in matters of business and trade, in
our intercourse every way in society, leading us to look at
the laborer and his wages, the producer and the capitalist,
as he is called. I would there were fewer capitalists. I
desire this religion of the fruits, this all pervading religion of God and of Christ and of humanity, the tendency of
which is conclusively to level, to bring all into oneness
and into equality before God and before men. "All the highways and banks of long continuance shall be cast down and
the valleys filled up, that Israel may go safely in the fear
of the Lord." This was a beautiful prophecy so many years
ago. And then we might pray the fore-runner of Jesus: Make
straight, smooth, level; make all plain. Prepare ye the way
of the Lord. The Kingdom of God is at hand.

It has always been the call of the reformer: The Kingdom of God is at hand. Because the entrance into this Kingdom is made so plain, so easy: "Thou shalt not see a fierce
people of deeper speech than thou canst perceive; of a stam-
mering tongue that thou canst not understand." The way shall
be plain. "The wayfaring men though fools shall not err
therein."

I know it is often gloomily pointed out, with all the
gloomy asceticism of Romanism. I would that we remembered

that Wisdom's ways were always ways of pleasantness, and
all her paths were paths of peace. Sacrifice though there
may be and must be, "taking up the cross," to use that sym-
bolical phrase, and the willingness to part as with the
right hand or the right eye, so as to enter this Kingdom
pure; yet clearly being brought to a willingness to make
this sacrifice, to bear this cross, then comes the peace
that is without understanding, the peace that flows as a
river, the cheerfulness that comes of a pure conscience,
the good hope that cometh of a cheerful countenance. All
this emphatically belongs to a religious life in order that
religion may be rightly understood. In order that it may
be, we have much to do in clearing away these gloomy appendages of the sects. The idea that religion, that devotion
to truth and to humanity should lead us to go mourning on
our way, making our path through life gloomy, and despon-
dent, and full of trouble; why it is all an error of education. It is all an error of religious training. It comes
not of the pure principle of life and light. When Jesus invited those who were weary and heavy laden, whether it was
with tradition, or it may be with the vices and other sins
of whatever character, by whatever means they were borne
down, weary and heavy-laden. His call was to them to come
unto the Truth; for "Me" is but a synonym for the Truth.
"Come unto Me, and ye shall find rest unto your souls."
"Take my yoke on you," What yoke? The simple plain yoke of
obedience to His Father, our Father, to His God and our God.
"Take My yoke upon you, and learn of Me; for I am meek and
lowly in heart, and ye shall find rest unto your souls. For
My yoke is easy." Mark this, my friends! Look not at religion as some cold achievement, or attainment, or profession,
but believe it belongs at once to simplicity of youth as
well as to older age. "You will find My yoke easy, and My
burden light."

        Now, we need to be made sensible of this; we need to

bear with the gloomy ideas connected with piety and devotion.
I am glad this day is coming to be better understood, and
that in the various teachings of the little children in the
Sunday Schools there is a greater opportunity to interest
them in the little common things and the little everyday
duties of life without making the teachings of the character
of old catechism, of old theories and worn-out systems. So
far as I can understand—and I am interested in hearing what
facts I can, and in noticing the results of this Sunday
School teaching—I believe that there is a great advance in
society, and we see it in the life around us, with regard
to the observance of this day of the week. I was glad to
day, and it was a great accommodation to me, to find the
passenger cars running on this day of the week.

All these things come not from a greater disinclina-
tion to religious training, not from the desire for an opportunity that shall lead into licentiousness, but from a
better understanding of what truth requires, of what this
inward light requires, this inward principle in man's soul,
to make life at liberty for just such religious entertainment as this day of the week affords; For the Jew, for the
Catholic and the Protestant, as well as those who are uncon-
nected with the religious associations, and who find their
enjoyment and their religious devotions out of and aside
from any sectarian union, who are equally good and pure and
religious in taking their pleasure and their means of piety
in the broad woods and forests of our country, or in the re-
tirement of their chamber and closets, in their reading and
all the various ways in which they may be employed in the
day of the week. I say, with all these we do see there is
a better understanding of the requirements of truth, of religion, of devotion and of worship. We are coming to understand that the quiet, retired prayer which Jesus recommended,
in the closet with the door shut, directed to the great
Source of all good, to the Father of all Spirits — that

these prayers in secret are answered openly, and are as
rich in the fruition as many of the vocal, oral utterances
in the assemblies of the people. We are learning this also,
and other denominations are beginning to have their solemn
pauses in the assemblies of the people, their silent prayers
arising with their invocations.

All these things encourage me in the belief that there
is an advance, especially when I see the influence of the
early teaching of George Fox, William Penn and their associates. When we go further back, we see throughout the teaching of Jesus this inward Divinity, this inward light likened
to a seed, to a little leaven, to all these simple comparisons, spreading its influence in His life and character, and
showing the good fruits of the God-dwelling life in its results. In His benevolence continually occupied in action,
in His mercy, His charity ever abounding, in His pity for
the afflicted, in every aspect of His character we see the
bearing of this same inward principle, this God dwelling in
man. Then when George Fox and his contemporaries came out
in the midst of a perverse and corrupt generation, in the
midst of the darkness of a benighted age, and declared this
principle and showed by their life and conversation what it
would lead unto, their good acts, their testimonies against
oppression and wrong, their testimony as in the progress of
things it came forth against iniquity, intemperance and
every wrong. How bold a stand they made with regard to the
ministry equalizing it in its operations, in its advocacy
with men and women, enlarging the pulpit, and holding their
religious meetings in such a way that every one present feeling bound to give utterance to the convictions of his soul,
to tell what had been done for his soul or her soul, should
be at liberty to do it. All this, I say, has had its influence, not only immediately around them at the time but
through their descendants others enter into this labor, which
has come down to us unto this day.

Then there is their testimony against the extravagance and luxurious indulgence of the age. Their testimony
to simplicity of life and character, even though, by being
carried out from generation to generation, it has manifested itself with too much peculiarity, perhaps, for it could
not have been borne as it has been without evidencing, to
some extent, its defect, peculiarity. Peculiarity in their
garb, their language, their address one to another. All
having been of good reason in the origin of the testimony,
may now be borne more traditionally; and the time may come
that some of these things will pass away, and a more intelligent appreciation of the principle will leave out some of
these peculiarities. A non-conformity in some of these may
be required of some of us, who would be only faithful to
our convictions of non-conformity. I wish that in all denominations those enlightened among us were true to their
highest convictions. Here, still we need faith. Faith and
Faith in theological systems? Faith in divinities and
atonements? Faith in the divinity of elections and repro-
bations? Faith in baptisms and communions, Faith in worship, obtaining salvation by merit? In all these things, I
ask: What is it? I overlook the question. What we need of
faith is in the teachings of this inward principle, letting
it bear upon our life, our conduct, and our highest conditions being brought out, now.

If there were more of non-conformity in the various
denominations, there would not be a solitary Bishop of
Colenso here, and another radical there. There would be
more rising up and protesting against all articles and
creeds and confessions of the past; there would be more acknowledging that they came to the table unworthily, that
they could no longer submit their minds to the control of
others nor their bodies to water baptism. I mourn when our
young friends, imperfectly educated as they may be in our
principles, are ready to go back to the weak and beggarly

elements from which our fathers were withdrawn, feeling
that the time was past, that they were now called with a
baptism that was not with water, with a baptism that was
"the answer of a good conscience towards God," a baptism
that pardoned all their old lives as well as the sins which
may most easily beset them. This baptism was union with
the Highest, not dependent on the bread and on the wine,
not dependent on any of the forms of the Church, but a union in the Spirit. A Sabbath of rest of which the outward
Sabbath never could do more than typify; a rest wherein we
feel we have come to that rest which is of God"; a rest
that was good, and a land that it was pleasant, and he
bowed his shoulder to bear."

Let us, then, try to understand better what these
great figures mean; what these "schoolmasters to bring to
Christ," as the Apostle said, are. Then let there be honesty enough, faith enough in the principles we profess to
come out of it and say: We can no longer worship in this,
that, or the other way: we can no longer give credence to
the Thirty-nine Articles, or accept the provisions of the
Discipline. Our own Discipline, in advance, as we may regard it, of all the other systems or principles of government that we know of, may yet contain peculiar passages and
obligations which ought to be removed. We are not to found
our veneration upon anything outward, upon any confession of
the times, or upon any arrangements or systems of our father.
We are to take truth for our authority, and not authority
for truth.

Then, again, in the influence of the teaching, the
practical teaching of the Society of Friends—I came not
here with any feeling of vain glory for the Society of
Friends. Far be it from me! If I look with any peculiar
interest, now, on any one religious movement over another,
attached as I am to the Society in which I was educated and
wherein I have been for many years, still I look with inter-

est beyond anything else to a great movement now in New
England, and in some other parts of our country; and judging from a German document offered to me a day or two ago,
spreading among this large class of people of this country,
for a free religious organization, like that which has had
it[s] existence for a year or two in New England, the basis
of which is this same inward divine light that I love to
honor, that I would [have] the veneration of all of every denomination in this community. This being the basis as I
believe, of this religious movement, it has my heartiest
sympathy. The leading journals of the day are also going
increasingly into the advocacy of this principle and its
teachings, as the essential and all sufficient for salvation, as beyond all authority, as not requiring authority
acting with it to sanctify it, or to sustain it.

The divine principle is "the light that lighteth every
man that cometh into the world." This, I say, as it is now
manifesting itself on our eastern coast and in some parts
of these middle states, has my interest, my desire for its
progress and that it may be carried out in such a practical
way as to have its direct bearing on its adherents in all
their relations in society. I look to it; I look to our
friends, if they will only be true to their principles, and
be the reformers they ought to be.

I look to this class for such changes in the commercial world, in the monetary system of the country, in all
the relations of capital and labor, in all the influences
around us—I look to these to do away with, to remove the
terrible oppression, the terrible wrongs which so large a
part of our fellow beings in this and other lands are groan-
ing under, and which can only be removed by the Divine power
opening and putting it into the hearts of the people to
plead on their behalf. I say the only means I know of appointed by God in any age of the world, is the faithfulness
of His children, the obedience of those who are sent, the

Sons of Him in every age, the Messiahs of their age, who
have gone forth proclaiming greater liberty, greater truths
to mankind, greater duty for that entire community. Yes,
though they may be few in number comparatively, though they
may be weak in force comparatively, yet it has been said,
and it may be again: "I have chosen the weak things to confound the strong and the wise."

And this is a remarkable truth. We see it in regard
to the early movements of our Friends, in the ignorance of
many of them, in their want of early culture, in their going about in all the simplicity of truth to proclaim the
principles of the divine nature and the duties of life.
Yet see their influence, and how their labors were blessed.
We have seen this remarkably in our day in the great anti-
slavery proclamation, so much more effectual than the most
ardent abolitionist could have anticipated in his time. We
see it now operating throughout the country in the increased
respect for the freedman of the land. Why, it is marvelous
in our eyes! There was nothing so enlarged my spirit, my
devotional feeling if I may so speak, as the wonderful success attendant on the comparatively small labors of those
who have been engaged in the reformatory movements in the
several generations past. It is wonderfully designed that
"one shall chase a thousand, and two put ten thousand to
flight," when these are under the right guidance and have
the right principles of action, and move as directed by
that wisdom which is ever profitable to truth.

I know that a large part of this audience [has] no af-
finity particularly with the Quakers, with the Friends, so
called. Some of us are very tenacious of our words. I believe if the words be enumerated, then the phenomena to
which they refer will be comprehended. If it be better
understood to use the term "Quaker," let it be used, although the term "Friend" is better, is our choice, and shows
our nature precisely. We take a catholic ground and acknowl-

edge this universal light to be in all. And I wish all held
out faithfully to the testimony; acknowledging as I do how
limited may our practice compare with this inward light I
still feel there is great advantage in our Friends' principles, much to be gained from it in every way. I therefore
desire greatly that our young people may so acquaint themselves with our distinctive principles, and with the details
wherein they differ from those held by other denominations,
and with those practices which are indulged in the world. I
desire that you all should so make yourselves well acquainted with these testimonies and principles as to be ready to
come out and acknowledge yourselves on the side of the
right. I desire that no one should be any longer inquiring:
"Who is the Lord, that I may believe Him?" But "if any man
shall say to you, Lo, here is Christ; or: Lo He is there;
believe him not."

In the multiplicity of these calls, I wonder not that
many of the young should be saying: "Who shall show us the
Lord?" I wonder not that many theories and opinions are expressed after the meeting as to what this, that, or the
other means. And I want the young to understand the answer:
"Thou hast both seen Him, and it is He that talketh with
thee." Yes, this is the light which we preach, and this is
the great truth which brings salvation. No outward atonement there, no outward divinity there, but the pure divinity
of Christ within; if I may use that term which is so often
misunderstood that I would rather use its synonym Truth, its
synonym, Light, its synonym, Light Divine "which lighteth
every man that cometh into the world."

Then though we have not seen Him, let us believe in
Him. Very soon, in very early life this truth has been
claiming access into the heart. Has it not been thy reprover for wrong doing, and thy approver for doing right,
filling the soul with love of Christ Jesus and allegiance
to God? Has not this been the cause of every divine prompt-

ing? Well then, "believe in this and thou shalt see greater
things than these." "To those who received Him, power was
given to become the sons of God." Then to thy advantage believe in this Name, in this principle, in this power.

  Believe it then, and follow. Let not the mere pleasures of life, allowable as these may be with the proper
limitation, allow not these pleasures so to take this place
and to fill the heart that there shall be no room for this
Beloved of the souls who stands at the heart waiting for
entrance until, to use the figurative expression, His "head
is filled with dew and His locks with the drops of the
night." I know how truly the religious people love the
Scriptures, and I love to quote them. I have been accustomed from very early life to examine and test the tenets
endeavored to be forced upon us by such esteemed ones as
these earnest friends. I have never been accustomed to
look at the Bible as a plenary inspiration, but I love
these Scriptures, and love to find their testimonies to the
truth in every age of which they treat. I love to find also among other ages and other people the same testimonies
to the truth and to righteousness. They all tend to
strengthen, to give force, to prove that they claimed and
observed these teachings in every condition and operation
of the mind as able to act, to convert, to adjust to the
level of all these attributes of the Deity. For these instinctive principles of our higher nature are all by which
we can claim to touch the Almighty. We cannot find them
out other than as He reveals Himself by His Spirit and by
His goodness manifested towards us or in the corroborative
testimony of the ancients, either in or out of the Bible,
to the great truths of all humanity.

  Let, then, the belief and faith in this principle
lead us more and more to humanity, to the divinity of humanity, to the divinity of Christ. Is it his divinity to place
a halo of glory over Him and regard Him as the second person

of the Deity? Is it not rather to recognize that divine humanity which we may find in all God's creatures everywhere,
if we will look aright? Let this divinity be acknowledged.
We shall not receive less the divinity of Christ in the rational understanding of it, in the unsectarian understanding of it. We shall not less admire the beautiful life and
character that we have unfolded in these Gospels, as they
are called. We shall come to understand the power of the
Gospel, that power of God unto salvation, if we come to receive it in the simple way I have described, carrying our
religion out into society, in all the duties of life; leading us to look not merely on the influenced will but also
on the influence diffused; leading the right to rejoice in
being brought low so that the poor may be exalted.

These are the proofs of this divinity, and it is this
I would endeavor to urge upon the consideration of my hearers. I speak as to the wise; judge ye what I say. I am
not afraid of any of these words that may be appropriated
to those who do not hold the faith in what is regarded as
soundness of orthodoxy. I am willing even, as the Apostle
said, "to be of no reputation among men" if I can hold
forth the truth, so that any may be brought to accept the
truth. This divine power is in every human being to lead
forth into correct principles, into correct actions, out of
all impurity, out of the excessive indulgence of the propensities, to lead to a regard of life and our great duties
in the spiritual, true, inward light.

Believe me, if this was the case there would be fewer
deaths in childhood, in youth, in early manhood, than we
now find them to be. We are not born, as one said the other
day, to live, to suffer, to die; but to live, to enjoy, and
to die when our time shall be fulfilled. I believe as the
laws of physiology and of life come to be better understood
—and I rejoice in their introduction into the early education of youth—when these come to be better understood,

there will be a responsibility attached to us to preserve
that life and keep it in its proper state, so that we may
live to old age. It will then become almost a sin to be
sick. It is wrong. There are more suicides than generally
appear. There is more lying at our door, now, of wrong
bringing on premature death than many are aware of. We are
invited to learn this.

I would that the great principle of war was so held
up—that first principle that we are so apt to neglect—
that we might look with the same eye of faith towards the
horizon of that time when the people shall indeed learn war
no more. I lament more than I can express that a military
education and training is being introduced into our public
schools. It has no business there. With such a profession
as we are making, a Christian profession, we have no right
to be instructing children in the art of war, in the art of
murdering their fellow being.

My friends, this is a subject in which our faith is
so wanting, that it seems entirely utopian to many to speak
of the days when war and a recourse to arms for settling
national grievances shall be brought to a close. But believe me, as in the other great revolutions of the times so
is this doomed to come to an end. War to come to an end!
War no longer to have advantages and success attached to it
with glories and honors thrown around it! War no longer to
continue! There is coming to be an understanding of a better means of settling wrongs and difficulties than a resort
to arms.

I came here to day purposely to attend a little meeting —I know it will be a small one—in the northern part
of our city, in Spring Garden Street; to consider with a
little handful there, how we may best advocate and support
the principle of hostility to a war, and to urge upon nations to hold a Congress of Nations to argue in peace how
they may settle all differences other than by a recourse

to war.

We are not to wait until all are converted to pure
non-resistants, any more than we had to wait for all to be
made anti-slavery in heart. We are not to wait until there
shall be no disposition to take revenge, but to declare
that revenge shall not be acted out in the barbarous ways
of the present.

I know I am speaking long, perhaps entirely too long;
but these subjects, as they occasionally come before me I
cannot leave without endeavoring to impress them in a way
that shall lead others to take up the subject and consider
it, and be prepared to act.

You middle-aged men and women of this Society of
Friends to whom I have been speaking, what are you doing
that you are not advancing our principles more earnestly
and more effectively? We are asked quarterly and yearly
whether we maintain a public testimony against bearing arms,
against all war in any form, and against military preparation. How are we to answer this inquiry if we are sitting
quietly down satisfied with the conviction that we ourselves will not consent to it? But how are we bearing our
testimony before the world? What influence are we exerting
in our day to remove this greatest of evils that now afflict
humanity? The evils of slavery and of religious persecution
have been now, to a great extent, brought to a close. War,
the leading evil, has yet to come before the people. Be ye
prepared. The Kingdom of God is at hand. "The light which
lighteth every man that cometh into the world" has shone
into the hearts of the people, to give them a knowledge of
the glory of God, in the faith of the divinity of this
principle.

[Sermons. MSS. Friends Historical
Library, Swarthmore College.]

THE SUBJECT OF PEACE IS TAKING A DEEP HOLD

REMARKS, DELIVERED AT THE ABINGTON PEACE MEETING,
ABINGTON, PENNSYLVANIA, SEPTEMBER 19, 1869

I feel greatly comforted in seeing such a large gathering here. There has been evidence ever since our late
war, that the subject of peace is taking a deep hold on the
minds of many persons, especially those who were engaged in
that contest, many of these came home more opposed to war
than ever before, and those in our society who enlisted in
the war because they felt that it was necessary to overthrow the great evil of slavery which threatened the destruction of the government. These friends have been willing to go as far as they could in acknowledging the evils
of war, and the great regret that the country was thus involved. I rejoice that there is this evidence of interest
in the cause of Peace.

The treatment of the Indians may seem, by some, not
to be strictly relevant to the subject of peace, and one
for the Peace Society to take up, but we know as in the
great crime of human slavery, that it never could have gone
to the extent it has, but for war, so with the Indians they
never could have arrived at the state of revenge and cruelty towards the white inhabitants of this land, if they had
not set the example by taking the sword.

Our friend mentioned that one great object of this
society, was the education of the people of this country.
I knew not what branch of this subject would be considered
at this meeting.

343

Greatly interested as I am in this question of Peace,
it occurred to me as I was coming to this meeting, that what
ought to be considered was the condition of our country and
our State. I know there is an effort to have a portion of
the education in the Public Schools of the country of a
military character.

I do not know how far military tactics, training, and
preparations have been introduced among the little children
in our public schools. It seems to me that it is a duty
that we owe to ourselves and to our children, to our State
and to the world, as a Peace Society, if this practice is
still continued, to bear our testimony against it —to center some protest against it, and urge that States shall not
introduce anything of this kind. I met a few days ago a
Roman Catholic father, and in speaking of the education of
that society, he said the Catholics never have given attention to the education of their people, said he, how could
that be carried on in our country, when the popular education was not in accordance with their most conscientious belief—they could not send their children to Public schools.

I believe there never was more willingness and openness in the minds of the people, to hear appeals made for
peace in a way that can be carried out, than at present. I
know that we cannot availingly advocate peace principles,
until we are prepared to carry out the spirit of peace —
that spirit which delights not in anything like revenge,
and indulging in any feeling towards the wrong doer, but a
spirit of forgiveness. That this is attainable the testimonies on record go to show, and very desirable is it that
there should be a sufficient number of the advocates of
peace, so grounded and settled in the principles of peace,
they they may know of what they speak, and thus be enabled
to labor to prepare the minds of the people, for a better
way of settling their disputes.

It may not be necessary to hold up the idea that all

must attain to this state before Peace can be established.
I believe as it was in the past, ten righteous on the subject of slavery redeemed the country.

It was by the means of the moral warfare that was carried on that slavery was brought to an end, long before the
slave holding spirit was put an end to.

It was the great moral warfare that made our Congress
anti-slavery, that made our Country ready to plead for, and
hold up the great duty of abolishing slavery. So I fully
believe with regard to war, and those who are grounded in
the principles of peace, and have the subject near and dear
to their hearts.

First I believe that those who are interested in this
Peace Society, will be blessed in their labors, and be able
to induce many, even though they may not have attained to
the full spirit of Peace within themselves, to see how barbarous the spirit of war is, and how comparatively easy it
would be for nations to settle their difficulties by the
same means that individuals do, and that would do away
with the barbarism of the sword and of war.

Some of the best writers of the age have pronounced
war to be a barbarism, second only to the great evil of religious persecution. It seems to me that the continual
holding up to the people, of the evil consequences which
result to all who are engaged in warfare, the great expense
to the country, the evils which result from exciting the
passions of men, will tend to the instruction of the people, and that war may be presented to the intelligent minds
of the country in such a manner as to induce the Government
to abandon it. If the council of the political men (and
women I trust too) will ere long be induced to look at this
subject in all its aspects, we will be able to show how
greatly to be desired is peace, and other means of settling
all difficulties, and bringing to an end the evils which result from war.

Our friend has spoken of the barbarities which have
been practiced toward the Indians, and of their present condition of degradation in contrast with their condition when
William Penn landed on this continent. It occurred to me
to ask if Friends were truly alive to their situation, and
to the fact of the treatment they have received from the
agents that have been employed by the Government, and who
have wronged them so shamefully, whether there would not
have been more frequent and more earnest protest and appeals
to the Government on their behalf. I know there have been
individuals who have been willing to sacrifice their time
and leave their families, to devote themselves to the ameli-
oration of the condition of the Indians. I remember Adin T.
Corey, Griffith M. Cooper, Halliday Jackson and more recently our friend Joseph Walton and many others who were disposed to do what they could in their limited way.

We have never considered the wrongs of the Indian as
our own. We have aided in driving them further and further
west, until as the poor Indian has said, "You will drive us
away, until we go beyond the setting sun." I would ask if,
with the profession that we as Friends have made, of care
for the Indians, we have been active enough in our labors.
I believe they were saved by the Indian Committees appointed
among Friends, from being driven entirely away from the Cat-
taraugus and other reservations in New York. So far as we
have labored by means of Committees, we have in various ways
done great good to the Indians.

So also on the subject of Peace, it is a question that
has often been with me whether as a religious body we have
borne our testimony faithfully enough; whether it would not
have prevented so many of our "young men and strong" from
being induced to enter the army. I know it is a very delicate subject, and many most conscientiously entered into
the strife with the hope of doing what they might to bring
peace in the right way, without slavery in the land, for

they knew that the war which had been waged was against the
colored people, was far greater than any war we could
have where there was an equal conflict. Considerations of
this kind were apologies, as they deemed, for entering upon
this. But all that has passed, and there certainly has been
a leniency on the part of the meetings where they have
brought these members under dealings, and there has been a
disposition to pass all by; but I trust not with anything
like a compromise of the principle. I do hope we are all
as a body, more desirous to promote "peace on earth and
good-will among men" than ever before, for now that slavery
is done away, we may see how in many ways the spirit of war
may be opposed, and appeals made for peace that would not
have been while we were engaged in such a barbarous warfare
as slavery. I want we should all be willing to look at this
subject of war in its true light, and not feel because it is
sanctioned as yet by all the nations of the earth, and there
is so much glory given to those who are the leaders in warfare, that therefore we should not seek to expose its barbarities. It seems to me that it should be the especial
duty of those who love and honor the name of Jesus to be opposed to war. I marvel when I see so much in his life and
character in favor of Peace, that in his testimonies he so
clearly pointed out these things, when he declared: "Ye have
heard it said an eye for an eye and a tooth for a tooth, but
I say unto you resist not evil—love thine enemy." How he
taught that they should do good for evil, that they should
put up the sword, for he that taketh the sword shall perish
by the sword—which means if they indulge in this spirit it
will return to them, and one of the apostles asks: From
whence come wars and fightings; come they not from the lusts
that war in the members?

I want to hold up the highest principles for our consideration and see how far we can act them out. Even in the
Old Testament we find many prophecies in regard to the

coming of a better era, when there should be no more war and
bloodshed upon the earth. I know there are those who have
quoted these Scriptures as authority for war. It was so in
regard to slavery. It is so now in reference to the Temperance movement. It has been retarded doubtless by the appeals that have been made to the Scriptures placing them as
authority for the wrong, rather than to present the many
beautiful examples that are in favor of the right. Although
it is true that we have done wrong, that nations have not
obeyed the Lord, and they have been given over to their own
destruction, as was said formerly, I proclaim that I leave
you to your wars, to famine, to pestilence, but this was
never uttered by the Highest Powers, the principles of Divine Love have never led any to war. We must go so far as
not to be afraid to speak of war or any other evil that has
ever existed in the world.

      With God there is neither variableness nor shadow of
turning. Let us have faith in this, and we shall find it
is much easier to carry out every principle of right.

      I was glad to hear how this peace principle was pro-
gressing. If we can once do away with the practice of taking life, it will be a great advance in the world. I have
been glad that in the Peace Society a strong protest has
been made against capital punishment. That we have peti-
tioned to remove the death penalty on the ground of right.
Let us never be afraid to take hold of the right, however
error and wrong may be sanctioned by usage, and by some quotations from Scripture. We know that the general run of
these is for the right, else they would not be so valuable,
if it were not that we found the testimonies of eternal
truth in them. We must not take the examples of semi-barbarous nations as authority for our action.

      [*Voice of Peace,* October 1869.]

THIS INTERNAL LIGHT OF THE SOUL

ADDRESS, DELIVERED AT RACE STREET MEETING,
PHILADELPHIA, JANUARY 23, 1870

"Thine eyes shall see thy teachers; and thine ears
shall hear a word behind thee, saying, This is the way,
walk ye in it."

The intelligent mind is often ready to inquire, What
distinction do you make between the dictates of conscience
and the teachings of this internal light of the soul—this
engrafted word which is able to save the soul; this grace
of God which bringeth salvation, and which hath appeared
unto all men? And again, the earnest inquirer who perhaps
is asked, Have you received the Holy Ghost since you believed? would be ready to answer, We have not so much as
heard whether there be any Holy Ghost, only having been
baptized with John's baptism, having only the educated conscience, we have been endeavoring to live in all good conscience before God.

They were yet old fashioned in many respects, tinc-
tured still greatly with the Judaism of their education.
And indeed the apostle Paul, when he could declare that he
had lived in all good conscience before God unto this day—
this being certainly the educated conscience of which he
spoke—he had, at the same time to acknowledge that he
formerly thought, sincerely thought doubtless, that he
ought to do many things contrary to the name of Jesus of
Nazareth.

We sometimes hear it asserted that he formerly thought

349

he was doing God's service. That, however, is not the correct rendering—it is not an exact quotation although Jesus said, the time may come when he that killeth you may think he doeth God service. But the apostle formerly thought he ought to do these many things contrary to the name of Jesus of Nazareth, because Jesus of Nazareth was held up to their view by their church and the Jewish conclave or Sanhedrin, as a great disturber of their peace—as a turner of their religious world upside down—and hence they sought in many ways to stop his progress. And when the apostle said this, he added, Which things also I did, and many of the saints shut I up in prison, and was exceedingly zealous and mad against those which thus preached, and so on. But he had to follow a higher light than an educated conscience, the internal light of truth which lightens every man that cometh into the world. The evangelist John testifies, this is the true light which lighteth every man that cometh into the world.

The people who were with him on his journey, it is said, saw a light: that is, they saw the condition in which he was placed, so stricken and smitten with the vision he had that he was going contrary to the truth; even although he thought he ought to do many things contrary to the name of Jesus of Nazarth, yet he felt that it was hard work for him, that it was to use his own expression, hard to kick against the pricks. It is said they saw a light, but heard no man; but a voice unto him, internally doubtless, said, Arise and stand upright on thy feet. It is related he was smitten to the ground with this vision—for, for this cause have I raised thee up, that thou shouldst be a minister and a witness both of the thing which thou hast seen—thou shall be a minister to the gentile world both of the things which thou hast seen and of those things in which I shall hereafter appear unto thee. Thou shalt be a light to enlighten the gentiles, to turn them from evil to good, from

doing wrong to doing right; for this is the mission, this
is the wonderful work of the Divine Master.

In this it may be distinguished by the searcher after
truth from the conscience which is held to things, of whatever nature they may be; from the conventional arrangements
of their chosen sect of denomination, whatever these arrangements may be. Thus it may bd distinguished from the conscience which might lead to the observance of days and times,
and seasons, and a reverence for churches, for pulpits, for
ministers. Through a misdirected veneration, conscience
often is led in this way; hence it is needful that the intelligent, reasonable, rational mind should examine and try
all things, prove all things, so as only to hold fast to
that which is good.

We find this language was uttered by one of the prophets of old: Thine eyes shall see thy teachers and thine
ears shall hear a word behind thee, saying, This is the way,
walk ye in it. Up to that very time, the sincere seeker
after truth was asking, How shall I appear before the Lord?
How shall I bow myself before the high God? Shall it be by
humbling myself, by bowing down in sackcloth and ashes?
Shall I give my first born for my transgressions? and so on,
alluding to the customs, to the offerings, to the sacrifices
required in that day. And mark the intelligent answer coming from him who would speak in the name of the Highest!
Say, it is shown unto thee, O man, what is good and what
doth the Lord thy God require of thee, but to do justly, to
love mercy, and to walk humbly with thy God!

Now is there any teaching, is there any claim of Divinity, is there any claim of an immediate command of the
Highest to the children of men that would lead to preaching
any other doctrine than this? Has not this been the word
of the Lord to the children of men in all ages of the
world? Has not this been that which the prophet of old
meant when he said, Thine eyes shall see thy teachers and

thine ears shall hear a word behind thee, saying, This is
the way, walk ye in it.

I do not like to dwell on the past. I am not interested in reading sermons applying especially to the times
of the past. The profitable use which we may make of these
Scriptures is to see how far we may be found in practices,
in devotions, in worships, in beliefs, and in faithfulness,
answerable to that which they were found in when the language was inspired by these things. I commanded you, your
burnt offerings and sacrifices, when I led you out of the
land of Egypt, out of the house of bondage.   Know
that this is required of thee: obey my voice—not the voice of your church—and I will be your God, and ye shall
be my people; and walk in all the ways that I commanded
you, that it may be well with thee.

May not we now with equal profit and liable to an
equal answer, say, Shall I appear before the Lord in frequent prayer meetings, in every seventh day observance in
a peculiar way? Shall I appear before the Lord by the acknowledgment of the divinity in mysteries and miracles?
Shall I appear before the Lord in a faith in thirty-nine
articles, or in a creed of any of the dissenting denominations or in the discipline of any Society of Friends? Shall
I appear before the Lord in baptism and communions, in
sitting still and saying nothing, and doing nothing, and
thinking nothing, possibly? Nay, but it is shown unto thee
Oh man, what is good.

Now here the same answer may apply, and we ought to
be ready to receive this answer so that we may not be mere
believers in this faith which is, and which we claim to be,
the fundamental part of our profession; it is the faith
which one of our people once—I remember it was when I was
young—claimed to be the *alpha* and the *omega* of religion,
the beginning and the end of the soul, the *urim* and the
hummim of our profession. So I say, while we hold this as

our almost only creed, or certainly the great principle of
our profession, the obligation and duties resting upon us
are increased because of our claiming that this is the sufficient teacher unto man—the responsibility to be found so
living, so walking, so watching, so ever faithful to the
teachings, and the inspirings of this word, to the revelations of this gospel truth, as to be found doing our everyday duty. We ought always to be going beyond our education,
leaving the things which are behind and pressing forward towards those which are before.

What was the language of Abraham when this same voice
of God internally appeared unto him. "Leave now thy kindred and thy father's house, and come unto the place which I
shall show thee." How many are there of us, were we all
true to our professions, who would be carried beyond our
education, beyond our traditions, beyond the religion of
our childhood! We find that when we were young this might
have been suited to us—this word as a schoolmaster to
bring us to Christ, to bring us to the truth; but now have
ye any longer need of the schoolmaster, when for the time,
ye ought to be teachers? Paul complained of some of his
brethren, I think of the Galatians, "Ye have need now that
one teach you which be the first principles of the oracles
of Christ, or the truths of God. Ye have need to be fed
with milk as babes, rather than with strong meat, by which
your senses might be exercised."

This is the kind of use which it seems to me we should
make of these assertions, these teachings, these great declarations of the ancients. This is the value that the Bible
may be to us. We are not to go to any authority of books,
or men, that shall supercede this divine teaching. We are
to hold fast to this internal principle as the all sufficient teacher. We shall not value the corroborative testimony
of the Scriptures the less; but we shall come to read these
more intelligently. We shall not go to them for examples,

strength and authority for the wrong; but rather to find of
the abundance that may be found there, corroborative testimony to the right. We are also to read these Scriptures as
belonging to the past in great measure, rather than to us
now. It is a book valuable enough, leaving off its sacred
titles, with everything that is superstitious and merely
traditional, taking this volume—many parts of it so highly
inspired—if it is read, as it ought to be read, we shall
never find it, if we feel rightly above the internal teachings of our own plain common-sense, and adapted to the enlightened age in which we live. Enlightened, do we say—
Do we claim to be so high in civilization, in spiritual understanding, and yet found so full of tradition, so full of
prejudice, so full of intolerance, if I may use that proud,
self-sufficient word, as someone calls it?

        Why do we meet here on this day of the week? Why are
all the congregations gathered together? Doubtless, in
great part, from the apprehension of duty, in great measure,
for the pursuit of right, of good, of truth. I have no
doubt that all the denominations, jew and gentile, catholic
and protestant, dissenter, radical and spiritualist or whatever they may be; I have no doubt at all that all these are
ministering to a great extent to the benefit of man, to his
improvement and to his instruction. At the same time, how
many keep themselves back from the instruction which they
might receive were they faithful to this internal light
they have, to their inward convictions? How many are there
who are going to the table unworthily! How many keeping
the appearance of the worship of the day so unworthily! How
many submitting to the rites of their several churches without the slightest faith in them! It is all unworthily,
when this is the case.

        What is most needed in such is the principle of light
and truth, faithfulness to it, following the light. If
thine eye be single, thy whole body shall be full of light,

as when the bright shining of the candle doth give thee
light. If thine eye be single, that is kept single to the
truth, as manifested by this superior light to the educated
conscience. By this light; by the intelligence of the age;
by the reading, perhaps, that has fallen to your lot; by
the instruction you have received; by the study of universal nature and science; by observing how this universal law
affects all, everything in every part of the physical creation. And if followed out with a mind capable of receiving it,
[it is] found tc apply equally to the moral sense, to the moral
convictions, and to the results of our actions, doing away
with the idea, in a great measure, of special providences,
of partial providences, and enlightening our minds so that
we can have more and more faith in the universal, eternal
law of God as applicable to our moral and religious sense
equally with the application to all the movements in the
physical world and in the universe.

     We are fearfully, wonderfully framed. Marvelous are
thy works, said the Psalmist; and that my soul knoweth
right well. And the more we come to feel the importance of
bowing before the eternal God, asserting the eternal providences, and vindicating the light that is eternally given
of God to man, the greater we shall find our duties to be
for ourselves and towards one another. For ourselves, towards the great Source of All, the great Giver of every
good and perfect gift (because we hold to God our Lord).
But greater will be our faith intelligently brought to bear
on the everyday acts of life, be these ever so simple, ever
so little; for a great truth of philosophy is found in the
declaration of Jesus. He that is faithful in the little,
shall be made master over more, and will be disposed to be
faithful in that which is greater; while the counter proposition is equally true: he that is unjust in the little, is
unjust in that also which is great. For if the light which
is in thee become darkness, how great is that darkness. And

this was no new doctrine as preached by that blessed Messiah to the Jews. It had been proclaimed long before. To
be sure, it was so overshadowed with ceremonies, with forms,
with ignorance and superstition, that it needed just such a
non-conformist as was Jesus to make such declaration of the
truth as that which he made, that the words which He spake
unto them they were spirit and they were life. And how remarkably satisfactory it is to know that where he simply
declared the truth before the people, the people heard him
gladly. Though the sects may be wounded, though the Jewish
Sanhedrin might seek to destroy him, yet the common people
heard Him gladly, and their declaration was, "Never man
spake like this man." Their declaration was, He speaks as
one having authority, and not as the scribes. And so it
will ever be. It has been so since His day; it was so before His day. Those who are sent as the messengers of the
highest to bear witness of this internal light and of the
everyday fruits of righteousness which obedience to it would
bring forth, have ever had their gatherings. The people
gathered with Jesus, as we read, till they trod one upon another, anxious to hear the gracious words which proceeded
out of His mouth.

     Have you not evidence of these who, since His time,
have been as the anointed of the Lord, who have been as the
watchmen on Mount Zion, who have been willing even as He
was, to give up their lives for the brethren, to lay down,
as the apostle said, lives for this truth? Have not these
ever found the people to hear them gladly? And because
there is such a sense of right, such an inherent and intuitive sense, an intuitive sense of right and of the truth,
that it needs no teachers. "Thine eyes shall see thy
teachers; and thine ears shall hear a word behind thee,
saying, This is the way, walk ye in it."

     Let the beautiful sayings in the Sermon on the Mount
be translated into any language, and there will be a re-

sponse of the people, apart from the common tenets of sectarianism; for theology has its abundant commentators. And
here is where we are to distinguish between the conscience
and the spiritual light of truth. The truth will ever find
those who will receive it with gladness. Though disobedient
they may be for the time, they cannot resist the wisdom and
power with which truth speaks to the understanding.

There is, then, less need than we imagine for long
expositions of the truth. Let us be satisfied, and especially ought we to be in our meetings, with shorter appeals
than we are wont to make, and I am sure I may take this to
myself. For, if the people know these things, where is the
novelty of religion to them? All that we can do is to stir
up the mind by way of remembrance. All that we can do is
to endeavor to lead the people to an inward rather than an
outward salvation, and away from the letter that killeth to
the spirit that giveth light.

And will there be less true devotion, then? Will
there be less true spiritual prayer, then? I fully believe
there may be less of the oral supplication in the assemblies of the people. The wise recommendation of Jesus is
when thou prayest enter into thy closet, and when thou hast
shut the door, then pray in secret to Him that seeth in
secret. While prayers are now perhaps increasing, as the
custom for the time being of the day, I rejoice in believing that we are learning more and more the efficacy of spiritual prayer; and I trust by our lives we may show that we
are accustomed to this inward approach to Him who seeth in
secret: for the spirit itself maketh intercession, even in
moanings which may not be uttered.

The apostle complained of his brethren, Ye ask and
receive not, because ye ask amiss that ye may consume it on
your lusts. Why how many are the prayers now put up for
temporal blessings, for the removal of the evils that belong
to the outward nature, and which it would be folly to pray

for to be removed! This is all superstitious, my friends,
it all comes from the want of a proper knowledge of the
overruling power of Omnipotence. When we shall come to the
knowledge of this, and thus put up our prayers, there will
be no lack, my friends, of the praises in secret, and also
of the solemn vows which belong unto Him who liveth forever and ever.

        [Sermons. MSS. Friends Historical
        Library, Swarthmore College.]

THE FREE RELIGIOUS ASSOCIATION
AND THE ADVANCE IT HAS MADE

*EXTRACTS FROM REPORTS OF ADDRESSES, DELIVERED AT THE
ANNUAL MEETINGS OF THE FREE RELIGIOUS ASSOCIATION,
BOSTON, 1870, 1871, 1872, 1873, 1875*

May 26, 1980

I wish to congratulate the Free Religious Association on the advance it has made, and the work
it has done since its formation, three years ago, when I
was also present. I am especially glad to find it taking
up such important practical subjects as that under consideration at this session.* The Association can accomplish
great good in these directions of practical reform and progress. Something has been said by some of the speakers of
the danger of a conflict of arms in this country on religious questions, and that the conflict may come on this
question which the Convention is now considering; but I can
hardly believe there is such a danger. If there be, let us
all try to avert it. We must trust to free discussion like
this, and seek to inculcate right principles. Begin in
time, and the truth will prevail without war, to the pulling down of all strongholds of injustice and wrong. As to
the Bible, I would make a discrimination there, as in other
writings, between truth and error. I cannot accept its inspiration as a whole, and cannot see why it should be read
as a book of worship in the schools or in the churches.
Ministers should dare take their texts from other books,
modern or ancient, as well as from the Hebrew or Christian
Scriptures. Let us recognize revelation and truth wherever

---

*The Relation of Religion to the Public Schools of
this Country.

we find it. If the question were, to what doctrine does the
Bible give authority, I should say the Bible would overturn
nearly all the theology in the various churches of the land.
But let the motto ever be, Truth for Authority, and not Authority for Truth.

[June 2, 1871]

I have no doubt that great good is resulting from the
free discussion of the character of Jesus, and other religious topics. Natural religion is revealed religion, inspired, as I think, in the same way as were the great utterances of Christianity. Men are too superstitious, too prone
to believe what is presented to them by their church and
creed; they ought to follow Jesus more in his non-conformity.
Those who most delight to honor the name of Jesus, have yet
to learn the nobleness of the character which led him to
live up to and act out his highest convictions, though so
opposed to the traditions of his time. The observance of
the Sabbath springs more from a superstitious than a rational motive, and certainly does not rest on the command or example of Jesus. He claimed very little for himself, but was
ever ready to bring in the name of the truth, saying that it
was the truth that made men free: I hold that skepticism is
a religious duty; men should question their theology, and
doubt more, in order that they might believe more. I would
ask those who are so satisfied to rest in the name of Jesus,
why they put so much faith in the name, without following
him in his works, and even in the greater works which he
predicted? Paul, I admit, was too much of a theologian for
me; but I know of no warrant that requires me to take him as
an authority. I think, however, there has been of late
great advance in liberality even among the strictest sects.

[May 31, 1872]

I want first to defend the apostle Paul a little. I
do not think there was any prohibition of woman's preaching
in his words. So far from it, he gave express directions

how woman should appear when she preached or prophesied,
and spoke of her repeatedly in his Epistles as a helper
with him, a "minister" in the gospel, although the transla-
tors had changed the word "minister" to "servant," in speaking of woman. Then, when he says, "I suffer no woman to
speak," it is plain to see that he was speaking to the Corinthian Church of their quarrels, their difficulties, and
their disagreements, and he recommended that women should
not mingle in the controversy; but he had not the least reference to their preaching. As regarded the relation of husband and wife, I think the Apostle was not perhaps so well
qualified to speak on the subject as some others, from the
fact that he was a bachelor, glorying in his celibacy, and
preferring that all should be such as he was. Still, reading the writings of Paul rationally, not as infallible authority, but as the record of earnest religious thought and
life, I feel there is great help and strength to be derived
from them....

The kingdom of God is always nigh at hand. It was
nigh at hand when Jesus declared it eighteen hundred years
ago, and it has been entered many and many a time since
then. I believe that it is very near us; that it is *with*
us —although some have an idea that we are not to look for
the entrance until after death, and pulpits mostly declare
what shall be *hereafter,* forgetting what the Apostle says,
that "*now* are we the sons of God, and it doth not yet appear what we shall be." It is wrong to represent religion
as a gloomy experience, opposed to true pleasure in this
life. I want to say to those who have much to say about
following Jesus, that they should remember to follow him
in his non-conformity, in his obedience to the right, however much it might conflict with the popular beliefs and
ceremonies of the day. I desire the full use of the intellectual and reasoning powers, while remembering that there
are other faculties of human nature to be considered. True

religion and freedom of thought seem to me so inseparable,
that I cannot make the comparison that it is better to be
free than to be religious. Religion and freedom must go
together. If the truth were obeyed, then should we be free
indeed.

[May 30, 1873]

As this is probably the last opportunity that I shall
have of meeting with this Association, which has endeared
itself to me from its beginning, I feel, late as the hour
is, that I want to express the great delight and satisfaction that I have had in this session, and in the meetings
of these two days, in the evidence they have afforded that
the prayers of many for this Association have been heard,
that their faith shall not fail them, and that they shall
give evidence of a deep sense of religion which will put an
end to all the vain and false theologies and useless forms
in Christendom and in Heathendom.

I have not many words to utter, but it is a great
satisfaction to me to know that instead of the science of
theology being made a study, that it will come to be, as
has been expressed to-day, the science of religion in liberty and truth, and of liberty and truth in religion; the
science —as was expressed in our first meeting by our beloved friends, John Weiss and Francis Abbott—the science
of the inspiration of the human mind; the science of truth,
as manifested in the inmost soul. This must come to be the
only science of theology which it shall be necessary to
study, or necessary to be taught. And, as regards the subject upon which so much has been written of late, the importance of faith in a personal God, we shall be content to
let our limited knowledge remain where it is, while we have
all that science can reveal, both that which is self-evident, which is natural, which is spiritual, and that which
belongs to outward nature —which it needs not that I enlarge upon, ignorant as I am, after all that has been

said. But I think that this will be found to suffice, and,
as has just been expressed, that it will pervade the universe of God, and bring us into the kingdom, which is nigh
even at the doors; and that we need not enter into any
speculations as regards the future, as regards immortality,
but that we all shall learn to rest content with the limited knowledge we have, and be confident, by fullness of
faith, that that which is best for us shall and will be ours,
while we do not endeavor by our speculations to make out or
build up a heaven. I remember when Dr. Channing, years ago,
at our house, attempted to advocate his views, and to show
what everlasting progress there would be in the hereafter,
I told him it was as interesting to me as any speculation
on the subject to which I had ever listened, but he must
allow me to say, that it was speculation still. I want we
should tread under foot our speculations, and everything
that will mingle aught that is uncertain with the religion
which we have heard presented to us to-day —which is certain, which is sure; for that which is self-evident needs
no argument. And so we come near to the beautiful truths
and testimonies that rise out of this pure religion and undefiled, that need no scholastic learning, that need no pulpit explanations. They are clear truth, justice, love —
the highest, noblest, finest instincts of the human heart
and mind, which we are to apply to all that we can imagine
of the unseen and unknown. That divine power will be ours,
if we seek it; and when these principles are stated they
are self-evident, they need no learned oratory, and it is
not employed in regard to them. You do not hear, in any
of the pulpits, a definition of what love, and justice, and
mercy, and right are. You know, and all know, that they
are innate, self-defined. Therefore, I say, preach your
truth; let it go forth, and you will find, without any
notable miracle, as of old, that every man will speak in
his own tongue in which he was born. And I will say, that

if these pure principles have their place in us, and are
brought forth by faithfulness, by obedience, into practice,
the difficulties and doubts that we may have to surmount
will be easily conquered. There will be a power higher
than these. Let it be called the Great Spirit of the Indian, the Quaker "inward light" of George Fox, the "Blessed
Mary, mother of Jesus," of the Catholics, or Brahma, the
Hindoo's God —they will all be one, and there will come to
be such faith and such liberty as shall redeem the world.

[May 28, 1875]

It seems to me very kind [of] an audience to be willing to stay and listen to the humble words of an Old Quaker
woman, after feeling how forcible are ripe words, as we
have heard them expressed this morning. When the beautiful
bouquet was brought in, I thought perhaps it was meant to
be a symbol of the words fitly spoken, to which we have
listened, which in the old Scripture were compared to "apples
of gold in pictures of silver." I have listened with the
greatest interest to the essay that has been read, and to
all your proceedings. Indeed, since my first attendance
at this Free Religious meeting, I have been a constant
reader of the productions of those interested in the promotion of its objects, and very often have entirely responded
to what has there been presented.....

When in England, in 1840, I saw one of the Egyptian
idols in the British Museum. Some one of our company said,
"Well, they don't admit that they worship such ugly images
as this; they look through and beyond this to one great Supreme Power." "They were scarcely more idolatrous," I answered, "than our Quaker friends when they read their Bible
with such reverence last evening." They brought it out
with great solemnity, and laid it on the lap of the one who
was to read it, and he bowed before it, and then opened it
and read it in what we Friends call the preaching tone. The
passages read were those that had no particular bearing

upon the lives and conduct of those then present, nor upon
the special occasion which had brought us together; but it
was "the Bible" and "Scripture," and a chapter of it must
be read in order, and in a solemn tone. I said to the
friend who was pointing out this idol to me in the Museum,
that the worship of that image was like the worship of the
Bible as we had observed it the evening before. To me *that*
was the worship of an idol.

So, too, in regard to many of the prayers that have
been offered in many of the meetings I have attended, since
I dared go without the limited inclosure of the Friends to
attend reformatory meetings. They have been so superstitious and childish, and so at variance with the idea that
Jesus inculcated with regard to prayer, that I have rejoiced
since these meetings of yours were organized, that there
has not been felt the necessity of calling on any one to
offer prayer. It is years since I have felt free to rise
in time of prayer —as is the custom in our meetings —so
entirely have I concurred with the recommendation of Jesus,
who said, "When thou prayest, enter into thy closet, and
shut the door, and there pray to thy Father in secret; and
thy Father, which seeth in secret, shall reward thee openly." This kind of prayer is as natural to man as the air
he breathes —the aspiration for divine aid, for strength
to do right, the inward desire after truth and holiness,
the yearning to be led to the rock that is higher than he.
But when it comes to praying for rain in dry weather, or
for the removal of evils that have been brought upon us by
our own violations of the laws of health and nature, then
it is most absurd and superstitious.

[Reprinted in *Life and Letters of James and
Lucretia Mott,* ed. Anna Davis Hallowell,
Boston: Houghton, Mifflin and Co., 1884.]

DOCTRINE CONCERNING DEATH

REMARKS, DELIVERED AT THE FUNERAL

OF MRS. JOHNSON, 1872

I think nothing more need be added. What the other speakers have said has been so true, so full, and so just, that to continue would only be to repeat. Cordially and emphatically I do approve the beautiful doctrine concerning death which has been enunciated here to-day—a view of this life and the other, of this world and the next, which I know was held by our dear friend whose earthly career has just closed in peace. Too many of us indulge in heathenish views of death. The dissolution of the body, the passage of the spirit, the exchange of worlds—all this, which is in itself beautiful and sacred, and which is part of the benignant ordering of a kind Providence, and which we ought to look forward to with joy and not with fear; all this, I say, has been taken up by the old and severe theologies, and turned into a bugbear, and been held over the human soul like a rod of terror. But we have had no such inculcation in the remarks made to-day. Death is here, and we are met to celebrate it, and wherever there is death there is sorrow; but we sorrow not as they that have no hope; neither do we complain against God because of His chastisement. This event is no chastisement. It is the order of nature. It is natural and right. We look at it with solemnity and tenderness, but we do not shudder at it; nor do we think it a strange and ungentle thing. It is an occasion of much joyfulness—the inward peace of the soul.

Our sister and friend at whose face we are now looking for the last time before the earth shall hide it, was
a true and noble woman. Although I was never on terms of
the most intimate friendship with her, yet I was no stranger to her devotion to the sick and afflicted; and when I
was last in her company, which was in Roxbury, Mass., one
of my own family connection shared her kindly care. My interest in her and her husband was enlisted many years
since, not only in the anti-Slavery struggle but from the
fact that, when a young man, he took thorough ground on the
subject of war and peace. His appeals were then most
searching. I watched his course with interest during the
recent years of our civil war—remembering a conversation
I had with him, and a comparison of views concerning the
bloody methods which the North and the South had adopted
for the settlement of their differences. Now that an opportunity has been presented for the settlement of international disputes without resort to force, I hope our friend's
early testimony against war will be borne anew—and not
without fruits, for are not the fields almost white unto
the harvest!

If these exercises—which to me have seemed so fit
and proper—had not already been filled so full of tribute
to our dear departed friend, and if the time had not already been so profitably spent, I would say more. But
there has been enough.

      [In Memoriam, Mary Ann W. Johnson,
      New York, 1872.]

THE SUBJECT OF CAPITAL PUNISHMENT

REMARKS, DELIVERED TO THE EXECUTIVE COMMITTEE OF
THE PENNSYLVANIA PEACE SOCIETY, DECEMBER, 1874

[I]n the year 1840, I listened to a sermon by George Harris, a Unitarian minister, in Glasgow, Scotland, on the subject of capital punishment, in which he showed the progress that had been made, and that offences had diminished very much since the law of capital punishment had been restricted to a very few cases, and he argued that if it was entirely abolished, we should have less crime, and I believe the statistics, in various countries, go to prove this.

If you will read an article at the close of one of George Combe's works, you will find some valuable suggestion[s] in regard to Penitentiaries. He proposes to make them really such, by having a committee of suitable persons to examine those who have been confined, and when by proper restraint and education, it [is] found that the end was answered, they should be discharged.

We hear the Old Testament, and even Paul quoted in favor of war. I find in the former, "If thine enemy hunger give him food, if he thirsts, give him drink"; and Saul was very much moved when he found David was not disposed to take revenge upon him.

I met a slaveholder once, who said, that we had put back emancipation fifty years; he spoke of the slaves being providentially brought here to be educated for freedom. I asked him if there were any among them who defended

slavery? Oh no, he said, every man in his inmost heart
knows that slavery is wrong. So with war, every man in
his inmost heart knows that war in itself is wrong. It was
so in the olden time; war was always pronounced as a judgment——"Because ye have not obeyed my voice, therefore will
I send war upon you. Therefore I proclaim unto you famine,
pestilence, and the sword."

[*Voice of Peace*, January, 1875.]

THE SPIRIT OF PEACE MUST BE
CULTIVATED IN OUR OWN HEARTS

REMARKS, DELIVERED AT THE THIRD ANNUAL MEETING
OF THE WOMEN'S PEACE FESTIVAL, JUNE 2, 1875

It is true, as our friend has well remarked, that the spirit of Peace must be cultivated in our own hearts, and the spirit of war eradicated before we can expect to make much progress. I have often resisted the impression that woman differs so widely from man, and I think we have not the facts to substantiate it. I cannot believe that if woman had her just rights, which I desire she should have, that all these evils will cease. The efforts which have been made in the cause of Peace have been mostly from the pens and labors of men. Very few women have actively embarked on this question until very recently. We know that women have very generally encouraged war, and in the late strife in our country the women on both sides took an active part and encouraged the men. Some of us are old enough to remember when the rod was used in the school and in the family to keep children in order. Horace Mann thought it would not do to abolish it in the schools of Massachusetts, but after a visit to England, where he saw how cruelly this was used in the factories to compel little children to perform their hard tasks, he returned home and urged the banishment of this barbarous custom.

There is a great deal to encourage us at the present time. Those of us who have been engaged in these labors for many years can look back to the time when but a few earnest men endeavored to awaken an interest in this sub-

371

ject—John Woolman, Jonathan Dymond, Elihu Burritt, and
others. The Society of Friends have always required their
members to settle their difficulties by arbitration; they
do not allow them to sue one another. We are too much in
the habit of erecting partition walls between ourselves
and others; have not associated with others as much as the
early Friends did, but wherever there has been a mingling
with them, there has been an advance of our testimonies.
Within thirty or forty years, there has been more remarkable success than ever before in all reforms. The people
are learning that the weapons of our warfare are not carnal,
to the pulling down of the strongholds. I was much interested in reading the account of the celebration of William
Cullen Bryant's 80th birthday, in which he reviewed some of
the events that had transpired during his life, and at the
close of his remarks he referred to the subject of Peace.
He hoped that the time was not far distant when standing
armies would be disbanded, and the men would be returned
to their farms and their workshops, from whence they should
never have been taken, and that through international arbitration wars would cease.

I remember as long ago as 1817 assisting my husband's
brother in stitching small Peace pamphlets to the almanacs
of that year. Everybody loves Peace better than war; everybody knows that war is wrong —indeed it has to be decked
out in all its paraphernalia to make it at all acceptable.
It is a very encouraging fact that the working people of
England and of this country are resolving that they will
not be forced into fighting any more; some of them have
gone so far as to say that they will have Peace if they
have to fight for it. I am glad to know that they are resolving that they will have no more wars; this has had its
effect. We know that all oppressors are cowards more or
less.

I believe there is a better feeling on the part of

many of the rich. We see that many individuals are now
distributing their property in their lifetime in a manner
that must tend to lift up humanity far beyond anything of
former times. Public education and the many opportunities
that the people have to rise to higher conditions are removing many of the obstacles that have been in the way of
the poor. It will be in vain that there shall be any demands for anything agrarian; the people are gradually
rising to higher conditions, and I think we may all rejoice
in these things.

I attended the Unitarian Convention in Boston last
week, in which many subjects of a reformatory character
were brought forward, and among them that of Peace. Reference was made to Noah Worcester, who was one of the pioneers. Many have been ready enough to cry, "Glory to God
in the highest," but when they came to the words, "Peace
on earth and good will to man," they were slower. I am
much encouraged when I see from the fashionable circles in
our country that many are ready to advocate the cause of
Peace. Julia Ward Howe acknowledges that it would have
been better if she had listened to the purifying angel in
her breast earlier in life; she would have come forward in
this labor instead of devoting so much time to fashionable
circles. She is now devoting herself nobly to this great
work, and I am glad to know that these meetings are being
held, as she suggested, in various parts of the world.

[*Voice of Peace,* July 1875.]

A FAITHFUL TESTIMONY AGAINST BEARING ARMS

REMARKS, DELIVERED AT THE MEETING OF THE PENNSYLVANIA
PEACE SOCIETY, ABINGTON, PENNSYLVANIA, SEPTEMBER 19, 1875

[Lucretia Mott said she was glad that Friends had
granted the use of their Meeting-house; the subject of
Peace was not new to them, but it was not so old a story;
there is always something that leads upward and onward in
its progress.] I have been instructed in this subject as
our Queries are read in regard to a faithful testimony
against bearing arms, and I sometimes think our Friends
are too apt to be satisfied that we have this testimony,
and have endeavored to carry it out practically as far as
we are personally concerned. During the late war some of
our young men, who were birthright members, were tempted to
join the army; many of these whom I have conversed with
since their return say they are more opposed to war since
they have seen its terrible evils; and I do not wonder at
this, because there is an innate feeling of love of Peace—
we all love Peace in our best moments, it is a part of the
divine nature implanted in us. I believe little children
have this feeling, but parents and care-takers often commit
the great mistake of teaching them that they must not bear
insults; then, too, they are taught by their surroundings,
by the pomp and parade of the military, they are attracted
by the music, and in many ways the terrible nature of war,
which is so revolting to every refined feeling, is con-
cealed and they are made to see it as something to glory in.

There are many things involved in bearing a faithful

375

testimony against war besides actual taking up arms; we
should have a concern not to contribute towards the support
of war in any way.

There are organizations in this country and in Europe
to advocate the cause of Peace, and since the Geneva Arbitration especially there have been most interesting meetings, and preparations have been made to continue these an-
nually. One is now in session at the Hague, and it is expected that it will meet in Philadelphia next year.

There are some among the Friends who are laboring
earnestly in this cause——Gideon Frost, of Long Island, and
I understand that Zebulon P. White, of Pawtucket, and some
others have made a liberal proposition towards raising one
thousand dollars as a permanent fund to be invested and
the interest to be used in the promotion of this righteous
cause.

It is time for all to be in earnest, the fields are
already white unto the harvest. I think there has been a
great advance since the Joint Commission met at Washington.
I remember that on that occasion some of the Peace advocates in Philadelphia asked them to take the general subject of international arbitration into consideration. These
were ridiculed by the Press at first, but when the Commission immediately responded in a favorable and friendly way,
then the papers were ready to commend it.

Many years ago I was holding a meeting in Boston, I
referred to the subject of Peace, and they told me they
had a Chamber of Commerce in that city to which all disputes between merchants and maritime men had been referred,
and so satisfactory had its labors been that there had
never been any appeal taken from their decisions, though
they had been in existence many years.

In the Society of Friends for two hundred years there
has always been a standing obligation that they must settle
their difficulties among themselves, and there has never

been an instance of a Friend being allowed to go to law to
settle any of the differences among themselves; they must
do it either by reference to the meetings or by arbitration.

There has been a disposition to look for the millenium in the future, but we are learning better, and realizing
that the kingdom is now at hand, if we will only work for it
in the right way.

The overthrow of the horrid system of human slavery
was unexpected to us all. We had been laboriing in the
Anti-Slavery cause for thirty years, but when the rebellion
came the government found it could not put it down except
by emancipating the slaves, and so it was done.

When we see that the great mountain of slavery is
cast down, we have great reason to believe that war also
will be removed for there are none but have a natural love
of Peace. It only needs an earnest desire and prayer on
the part of all the people. You know how prominent was the
blessing pronounced upon the peace-makers, "for they shall
be called the children of God."

In all the places of worship how often do we hear the
proclamation of "Peace on earth and good-will to man." I
wish more notice was taken of these old sayings, now that
there is an increasing effort to deify the man; why that is
nothing compared to the bringing up of these old sayings.
"My doctrines," he said, "are not new," and it would be
well if we were made more familiar with them. He prayed
for his enemies even to the last. How much might be done
by showing up the Peace doctrines in various ways wherever
we have opportunity. It is only by persevering in season
and out of season, that we can expect to awaken the people
to this great subject. I don't mean that there is any dislike, or any opposition to the organization, or to the efforts that are being made. There may be some that may seem
to be too radical, but I have such great confidence in the
divinity of human nature that I can trust it. I am some-

times asked if I do not believe in the divinity of Christ.
I say, yes, not only in the divinity of Christ, but of all
men. It is because I am so hopeful of the divine nature in
man that I look forward with so much confidence to the
reign of Peace and to the coming of all kinds of goodness
among mankind. It is not the church going people alone, it
is not the Sabbath-day observers, but all mankind are being
brought together in their intercourse, in their commercial
relations. I am glad to see that there are organized measures being taken in various countries to promote this good
work. The more the people are brought together, the better
they will understand this subject. Let us then be humble
enough in trying to promote this work to lose no good opportunity.

In coming from Boston, not long since, the Hutchinsons were on board the steamboat, and as they had not begun
their regular music on the boat it was proposed by some one
that they should sing. They sang several pieces, and one
of their songs was on the subject of Peace. It seemed to
open the way for me too, as [they] mentioned my name and said
I was present. I rose and said it was quite unexpected to
me, but I had just been reading an account of the celebration of William Cullen Bryant's 80th birthday, and I referred to his interesting review of this century. I spoke
at considerable length, and they listened to me with great
patience, and there seemed to be general satisfaction with
this meeting. Let me say again that I want us to be faithful, and whenever an opportunity offers give our testimony
in favor of Peace.

[*Voice of Peace,* November 1875.]

A WARLIKE SPIRIT

*REMARKS, DELIVERED AT THE WOMAN'S PEACE
FESTIVAL, PHILADELPHIA, JUNE 2, 1876*

I can but hope that the language of such a hymn put in
the mouths of little children in the Sabbath-schools, will
be carried out by the conductors of these schools as well
as by the children.

I fear very much that even now while there is this
desire for the promotion of Peace and good will among men,
by the intermingling of all nations, that many of these
conservators of these sacred songs are really creating a
warlike spirit in the community among the class of people
that Jesus most acknowledged, in the effort to close the
gates of the Centennial on the First-day of the week, and
thus prevent the laboring classes of this city, and the
country around from entering it on that day, not as a place
of amusement, not as a place forbidden by any law, as has
been shown by many of our ablest lawyers, but as a place of
profitable entertainment, a place in which they and their
families may have rational enjoyment, and such instruction
as will be a lasting benefit to them. There is a spirit
excited among these people that they have a right to go in
there on the only day in which they can do it. The attempt
of the Commission to keep the gates closed, it seems to me
is a lamentable sign of the times; a warlike sign, and
there are rumors that some of the people will demand their
rights by force. I hope as lovers of Peace, for there is
no true Peace that is not founded in justice and right, we

shall show our love for the whole people without any distinction, by using all proper means to have this opened and
by a free and open recognition of the rights of all.

There is much to encourage us in the prospect of
Peace, in the prospect of a disposition to settle all national differences by arbitration instead of a resort to
arms. In going through these Centennial grounds we see
many of the trophies of war exhibited, so that some feel
almost forbidden to enter, but this we must expect in the
present state of mankind. I want that there should be a
fulness of faith in the possibility of removing all these
things before long. The fields are now white unto harvest,
if we will only have faith enough. I don't mean a mere
sectarian faith, that will keep Sundays and do wrong on
other days. I want that there should be a belief, a faith
in the possibility of removing mountains on the side of
right. If we believe that war is wrong, and every one must,
then we ought to believe that by proper efforts on our part
it may be done away with.

When we consider what has been done in the last century, and especially within fifty years, I think we have
great reason to hope that the time is drawing near much
faster than many doubtful ones can believe.

I want that we should look back and see what a great
evil war has been in every age of the world. When it was
visited upon the Israelites it was considered as a judgment.
The texts, "If thine enemy hunger, feed him; if he thirst,
give him drink," were a quotation from the Old Testament.
There are many beautiful testimonies scattered throughout
the old Jewish history; to be sure they are not in such
measure, not in the fulness with which Jesus uttered them,
and for which he is properly called the Prince of Peace. I
want to see his beautiful example carried out in our lives.
There has been a great cry about coming to Jesus, but it
will not amount to anything unless we get into his Spirit.

It is in vain that we cry Peace while this great wrong is
done to our fellow beings. I have been much encouraged in
seeing the determination of those that are called the workingmen to resist being drawn into war. They say that they
are not willing to enter into wars that they have nothing
to do in bringing on. Some have gone so far as to say that
they would have Peace if they had to fight for it—they
have been so much accustomed to fight for everything that
this seems to them to be the only way to obtain it. Now it
seems to me that our Peace principles require of us that we
should take a firm stand against this priestly assumption
of power that would close the Centennial on the first day
of the week. It is altogether inconsistent with their own
acts. Why, their ministers are paid for their labors on
the first day of the week, and these have no difficulty in
going through the week to the Exhibition, whilst they would
keep out those who are obliged to labor every day, it is an
assumption that I hope will be overcome by a strong public
sentiment. I hope there will be more public meetings. I
have great faith in the strength of a righteous public
sentiment, the weapons of whose warfare are not carnal but
mighty through God to the pulling down of strongholds. The
public voice in this [illegible], resulting from the intelligence and morality of the people is a power that must be
felt and recognized. I claim to be religious, I have my
view of the great Eternal Source of all things, I do not
want to show my faith by my words, or by my Quaker bonnet,
I want that we may all show our faith by our works, by our
honesty and justice and mercy and love; I want love to begin with little children; they should all be governed by
love, and love only. I am glad the rod is so far banished
in the family circle and in the schools. We should never
teach children that they have wicked hearts, or try to give
them an idea of total depravity, or that it is easier to do
wrong than right, they will soon learn that it is easier to

do right than wrong. Children love Peace. The little
child knows when it says, mother, I love everybody. There
is a Divine instinct in them which prompts to this feeling.
It is very natural for those advanced in years as I am to
note with interest the progress of events within our times.
I was much gratified in reading an account of the celebration of William Cullen Bryant's eightieth birthday. They
had a banquet, and he made an address, referring to the
changes that had occurred in his time, the progress of the
temperance cause, of education, of the abolition of slavery,
he said the next thing that I look for and hope for more
than any other is success in the efforts to do away with
war. I believe the time has come when arbitration shall
supplant the spirit of warfare. This is already beginning,
and many of us have been watching with deeper interest
since the abolition of slavery, the spread of the principles of Peace. Since the Geneva arbitration there have
been three international conventions; and we regret that
Dr. Miles, who was a delegate from this country, and who
intended to give a report of these meetings in this city,
was prevented from doing this, for soon after his return
home his work was shortened by his death.

        I think the signs of the times are encouraging to us,
and I am glad that we have so many of the, so called, heathen nations amongst us. I remember hearing one of these
express that he was surprised on coming to this Christian
country to find so much warlike preparations. We read in
the Bible about Abraham when he returned from the wars, being met by Melchisedec, King of Salem, or *Peace,* and there
is no mention of his going to war any more. You may remember it humbled Saul, when he said, "I know that while I
have requited thee evil, thou hast requited me good." It
is an ancient proverb that "wickedness proceedeth from the
wicked, and righteousness from the righteous." Then it was
prophesied that the time would come when the horse should

be driven from Ephraim, and the battle bow from the gates,
and Peace should reign, it should come in as a flowing
river. I am religious enough to believe all these things;
Jesus said if ye discerned the signs of the times, ye would
see these things. I want that we should have faith, and
know that if we make the sacrifice for Peace principles, we
shall in our measure realize the day when "violence shall
no more be heard in our land, wasting and destruction in
her borders."

> [Other speakers intervene;
> Mott continues.]

While I am in favor of Peace, I am also very favorable to war, I mean the firmness and combativeness that
marked us in the anti-slavery warfare. We all remember
how earnest and determined William Lloyd Garrison was, no
man stood more firm for Peace, and yet he was constantly
fighting with his tongue and his pen.

[*Voice of Peace,* July 1876.]

TO CARRY OUT OUR CONVICTIONS FOR PEACE

REMARKS, DELIVERED AT THE FOURTH MEETING OF
THE PENNSYLVANIA PEACE SOCIETY, WARMINSTER,
BUCKS COUNTY, PENNSYLVANIA, MAY 6, 1877

[Lucretia Mott opened the meeting. She referred to
Abraham being met by Melchisedec, King of Salem, who must
have been a spiritual being from the record. She said we
have no account of Abraham being engaged in war, afterwards.

She quoted numerous texts from the Old Testament,
showing that while they were a warlike people they had
beautiful ideals of Peace that [were] to come in the future. She referred to the so-called heathens who had expressed their surprise, and rebuked the professed Christians for their wars and fightings. Christians should be
peaceable, for if any one thing is marked more than another
in regard to Jesus, it is His advocacy of Peace.

His advent was announced by the anthem: "Glory to God
in the highest; on earth Peace and good will to men." He
frequently held out the testimony of doing good for evil.
He desired His immediate disciples "not to be troubled
when they heard of wars and rumors of wars, for the end is
not yet."

Not until lately has there been anything like a general diffusion of Peace principles.]

When the Joint High Commission met in Washington,
the Executive Committee of the Universal Peace Union wrote
to them, asking whether they could not recommend Arbitration, generally. Some of our papers sneered at this, but
when the Commission returned a courteous answer to our

385

appeal, saying they hoped something could be done, then our
[illegible] were quite prepared for it and hoped they would
do it.

To carry out our convictions for Peace there needs to
be great firmness. We cannot look for war and all its preparations to be done away with, without great efforts on
our part, and very frequent appeals, taking advantage of
every opportunity. In order to do this we must be grounded
on Peace principles ourselves—we must know how far we have
overcome the disposition to return evil for evil. If we
have faith enough we may say to this greatest of evils be
thou removed.

The great moral warfare that was carried on against
Slavery, brought so large a portion of the North to Anti-
Slavery principles, that the National Legislature became a
great Anti-Slavery meeting.

In all our resolves we never encouraged the slaves to
endeavor to secure their freedom by any acts of violence or
war, and we were gratified to see how patiently the colored
people waited and suffered unto the end, and so have continued.

[*Voice of Peace,* June 1877.]

THERE WAS NO MAN THAT DID NOT KNOW WAR WAS WRONG

REMARKS, DELIVERED AT THE PENNSYLVANIA PEACE SOCIETY
MEETING, ABINGTON, PENNSYLVANIA, MAY 20, 1877

I am sure you will find that it has been with great
difficulty that war has been made as popular as it is.
Some of the greatest warriors have declared that there was
no man that did not know war was wrong. I believe little
children are sometimes taught by their mothers to whip a
table or anything that they have hurt themselves against,
and in this way the idea of war has a beginning in their
minds. Many of the professed followers of Jesus are ready
and willing to fight, but if any one thing was more prominent in his life it was his testimony in favor of Peace;
his mission was ushered in with the anthem, "Glory to God
in the highest," which was enough, but there was added
"peace on earth and good will to man."

This was no new doctrine. The old prophets denounced
war as an evil which was sent upon the people, because of
their wickedness—a judgment of God for their disobedience.
They were given over to the evils of war, and they were
constantly looking forward to the time when the sword
should be beaten into the plowshare, and the reign of Peace
shall extend even from sea to sea, and from the rivers to
the ends of the earth. When David had the advantage over
his enemies, and acted kindly to them, how it moved Saul.
Thus we shall find evidence throughout the Scriptures of
the love of Peace and kindness. If we maintain our testimonies faithfully, war must come to an end. What has been

done by the working-people abroad has alarmed the governments. We must not give up, but must continue to bear a
faithful testimony against all wars.

[*Voice of Peace,* August 1877.]

THE NATURAL INSTINCTS OF MAN ARE FOR PEACE

REMARKS, DELIVERED TO A SPECIAL MEETING
OF THE UNIVERSAL PEACE UNION, CAMDEN,
NEW JERSEY, SEPTEMBER 16, 1877

While it is true that we need education to advance
the cause of Peace, it seems to me most of the education
has been bestowed upon war. We have schools in which war
is taught as a system.

The natural instincts of man are for Peace, and this
has ever been the case. It seems strange that in all
Christendom there should be any war, considering that He
whom they all have delighted to honor as the Prince of
Peace, and rightly so, because His advocacy of Peace was
beyond almost any other subject which He treated. Yet we
find it necessary to bring this subject up among these
professed Christians.

As in anti-slavery times we found men in the church
who thought it a greater sin to break the Sabbath, as they
called it, than to steal a man. To-day there is so much
effort made to educate men in the principles of war, that
they may learn to murder one another, that it seems necessary that we should have these special associations.

There are some who believe there is a middle ground,
and that war under some circumstances is justifiable. We
do not believe that war is justifiable under any circumstances. We are sometimes asked what we should do if we
were attacked by a highwayman. I remember an answer that
was given by Lindley Coates; he said, "I cannot tell what

389

I might do, but I know what I ought to do; but whether I
could carry it out or not I cannot say."

It seems to me there is not so much need of instruction in favor of Peace, for I believe the instinctive
principle and common sense of mankind is coming to be more
and more in favor of settling difficulties by peaceable
means, so that it only needs that we should stir up one
another by way of encouragement. Griffith M. Cooper told
me that with all his acquaintances among warlike men,
there was not one who would advocate war.

I do not know that it can be said that the advent of
the blessed Jesus was the foundation of Peace, though His
aim was to carry this out. I frequently refer to the accounts in the Old Testament in which war is spoken of as
a judgment, and Peace as the highest and best condition.

I believe Peace is the natural condition, and war the
unnatural. Even with the little children, when they are
accidentally hurt, the mother will sometimes tell them they
will whip the table or chair, or whatever it may be, that
has hurt them, thus sowing the seeds of war. We often refer to the toys that are given to children, that in many
instances are calculated to awaken a love of military trap-
pings.

I am glad to know that the workingmen are taking hold
of this subject almost everywhere. Some years ago we had a
delegation of these at one of our meetings. Some of them
are so earnest as to declare that "they will have peace, if
they have to fight for it." But we do not believe there is
any necessity for this, if we determine to act in the right
way we shall have it, and the right time is ever with us;
when we are disposed to do right, the power will be given
us.

[*Voice of Peace,* November 1877.]

LABORING TO OBTAIN THE DIVINE KINGDOM

REMARKS, DELIVERED TO THE EXECUTIVE COMMITTEE OF THE
PENNSYLVANIA PEACE SOCIETY, NOVEMBER 27, 1877

I presume there will be no dissenting voice to the
adoption of the report. It speaks of laboring to obtain
the Divine kingdom. I want that kingdom to be realized, to
be entered into and recognized while we are here. When in
the beautiful memorial of Elias Hicks Corson she [the eulo-
gist] alludes to having entered into this higher kingdom,
had he not long since entered therein? His works, his life,
his pure spirit have shown that he entered the blessed kingdom of heaven long, long ago, and that his pure spirit labored in this work of love and of peace. In our earlier
life we have known him in the advocacy of the cause of the
oppressed, the suffering, the dumb, the poor slave; and
then in the great work of temperance how earnestly has he
labored.

When I look over the religious world and see how
many are professing to follow Him who was called the
"Prince of Peace," and rightly so, for if His kingdom
comes we shall have "Peace on earth and good-will to all
mankind." I mourn that there is not more zeal, that the
people are not more interested to do away with the horrid
practice of war.

We come among you to day, my friends, feeling that
in the now passing events in the European world, there is
much to discourage us, while in our own State there are so

391

many instances of capital punishment, that we have need to
blush and hang down our heads, even as one of old said:
"Our iniquities have taken hold of us and we are not able
to look up, they are more than the hairs of our heads,
therefore our hearts fail us." Yet I cannot but believe in
the good there is in the hearts of the people, I have great
faith in the divinity in man, and I cannot but be hopeful
that there is evidence of a greater desire for harmony, for
the settlement by peaceable means—by arbitration, of all
the difficulties between nations; we have so many instances
since the Geneva Arbitration; there have been so many many
meetings in this country and in Europe, one recently at
Antwerp, of which I understand we are to have a report. I
hear that there is a prospect of one in France next year,
in connection with, or at the time of the great International Exposition, unless a war should prevent it, and I
hope it will not; I always hope for the best. I know there
is a love of peace in every heart, and I want it to be encouraged.

   [*Voice of Peace,* January 1878.]

PLACE WOMAN IN EQUAL POWER

REMARKS, DELIVERED AT THE THIRTIETH ANNIVERSARY
OF THE SENECA FALLS CONVENTION, JULY 1878

Place woman in equal power, and you will find her capable of not abusing it: give her the elective franchise, and there will be an unseen, yet a deep and universal movement of the people to elect into office only those who are pure in intention and honest in sentiment! Give her the privilege to cooperate in making the laws she submits to, and there will be harmony without severity and justice without oppression. Make her, if married, a living being in the eye of the law—she will not assume beyond duty; give her rights of property and you may justly tax her patrimony as the result of her wages. Open to her your colleges—your legislative, your municipal, your domestic laws will be purified and ennobled. Forbid her not, and she will use moderation.

[*Woman's Journal,* July 27, 1878.]

ANNOTATED INDEX OF PROPER NAMES

ABBOTT, FRANCIS. 1836-1903. An avowed non-sectarian who helped create the Free Religious Association. He believed even Unitarian orthodoxy was too restrictive.

BERNARD, HANNAH. 1754-1825. Quaker minister and champion of free thought who early in the nineteenth century came into conflict with the Society of Friends because of her beliefs.

BEECHER, CATHARINE. 1800-1878. An educator and writer who supported liberal education for women but opposed woman suffrage.

BEECHER, HENRY WARD. 1813-1887. Son of Lyman Beecher and brother of Harriet Beecher Stowe. A Congregational preacher, supporter of anti-slavery activities, and defender of the Union cause. He advocated woman suffrage and supported the theory of evolution. He was editor of the *Independent* and later the *Christian Union*.

BENEZET, ANTHONY. 1713-1784. Philadelphia Quaker, philanthropist and author who worked on behalf of the Negro. A close friend of John Woolman.

BLACKSTONE, SIR WILLIAM. 1723-1780. English jurist and lecturer. Wrote *Commentaries on the Laws of England*.

BLANCHARD, JOSHUA. 1782-1868. One of the oldest advocates of peace in the United States. He maintained that Christianity forbids war.

BONHEUR, ROSA. 1822-1899. French painter of animals whose work was popular in England and the United States.

BOWRING, SIR JOHN. 1792-1872. British diplomat, linguist, writer and first editor of the *Westminster Review*.

BRONTE, CHARLOTTE. 1816-1855. Famous English novelist.

BROOKS, PHILLIPS. 1835-1893. Episcopal bishop, influential in Boston.

BROUGHAM, LORD HENRY PETER. 1778-1868. British statesman and liberal leader in the House of Commons who lead the fight against the slave trade.

BROWN, ANTIONETTE. 1825-1921. Minister and pastor of an
    orthodox Congregational Church who ultimately espoused
    Unitarianism. Graduate of Oberlin College, author and
    woman's rights advocate.

BROWN, JOHN. 1800-1859. Abolitionist and supporter of
    liberation of slaves through armed intervention. Captur-
    ed at Harpers Ferry, W. Va. in 1859 and was hanged.
    Regarded as a martyr among many northern abolitionists.

BRYANT, WILLIAM CULLEN. 1794-1878. Poet, newspaper editor
    and critic. Associate editor of the *New York Evening
    Post*. Supported the abolition of slavery.

BUCKLE, HENRY THOMAS. 1821-1862. English historian who
    emphasized the history of civilization and the idea
    of progress. He attempted to make history a science.

BURLEIGH, CHARLES. 1810-1878. Abolitionist and anti-sab-
    batarian. Editor of the *Pennsylvania Freeman*.

BURRITT, ELIHU. 1810-1879. Reformer, founder of an anti-
    slavery journal and organizer of the American Peace
    Society.

CHAMBERS, JOHN. Independent Presbyterian clergyman in
    Philadelphia.

CHANNING, WILLIAM ELLERY. 1780-1842. Unitarian minister
    and author. Emphasized humanitarianism and tolerance
    rather than credal orthodoxy. Although he wrote on
    slavery he was never directly allied with abolitionists.
    He denounced war as evil.

CHAPIN, EDWIN. 1814-1880. Clergyman, supported universal-
    ism. Delegate to peace conferences and editor of an
    abolitionist magazine.

CLARKSON, THOMAS. 1760-1846. English Quaker abolitionist.
    An influential force in the abolition of British slave
    trade.

COATES, LINDLEY. Quaker abolitionist who was active in the
    underground railroad in Lancaster County.

COBBE, FRANCIS POWER. 1822-1904. British philanthropist
    and writer on religious and social subjects including
    the condition of women. Edited the works of Theodore
    Parker.

COLENSO, BISHOP JOHN WILLIAM. 1814-1883. Bishop of Natal
    and author. Wrote *Commentary on St. Paul's Epistle to
    the Romans*. He was deposed by the Anglican Church be-
    cause of his attacks on the sacramental system.

COMBE, GEORGE. 1788-1858. Scottish phrenologist. Wrote
    *Constitution of Man Considered in Relation to External
    Objects*. Sympathetic to abolition and other reforms.
    Lectured in the United States.

COOPER, GRIFFITH M. Hicksite Quaker who opened a school for
    the Seneca Indians in Cattaraugus, N.Y. in 1833.

COREY, ADIN T. New York Quaker who worked among the
    Onondaga Indians.

DARLING, GRACE. 1815-1842. Rescuer, who with her father
    saved five persons from a sinking ship.

DAVIS, EDWARD M. Abolitionist and son-in-law of James and
    Lucretia Mott.

DAVIES, RICHARD. 1635-1708. An early Welsh Quaker.

DIX, DOROTHEA. 1802-1887. Reformer and advocate of humane
    treatment for the insane. Influential in founding
    hospitals for the insane.

DYER, MARY. d. 1660. Quaker who was executed in Massa-
    chusetts.

DYMOND, JONATHAN. 1796-1828. Quaker author who believed
    that war contradicted the tenets of Christianity. He
    argued for equal educational opportunity for women as
    well.

EDGEWORTH, MARIA. 1767-1849. Irish novelist. Supporter
    of education for women.

EDWARDS, JUSTIN. 1787-1853. Clergyman, advocate of tem-
    perance. Secretary of the American and Foreign Sabbath
    Union.

FOSTER, STEPHEN S. 1809-1881. Abolitionist who was hos-
    tile toward both church and state. Husband of Abby
    Kelly.

FOX, GEORGE. 1624-1691. Founder of the Society of Friends
    and author of many tracts.

FROST, GIDEON. Long Island Hicksite Quaker and peace advo-
    cate who suggested that Friends boycott the 1876

Centennial celebration because of its warlike character.

FRY, ELIZABETH. 1780-1845. British Quaker prison reformer
     who worked to improve conditions among female inmates
     in Newgate prison.

FURNESS, WILLIAM. 1802-1896. Unitarian minister in Phila-
     delphia. Author and supporter of abolition.

GAGE, FRANCES D. 1808-1884. Reformer and author. Sup-
     ported temperance, anti-slavery activities and women's
     rights.

GARRISON, WILLIAM LLOYD. 1805-1879. Abolitionist and edi-
     tor of the *Liberator*. Supported immediate and uncondi-
     tional liberation of the slave.

HARRIS, GEORGE. Minister of the Unitarian Chapel, Glasgow,
     Scotland.

HERSCHELL, CAROLINE. 1750-1848. English astronomer who
     discovered eight comets and three nebulas.

HICKS, ELIAS. 1748-1830. Long Island Quaker preacher who
     opposed slavery. Important force in Hicksite branch
     of the Society of Friends.

HOWARD, JOHN. 1726-1790. English prison reformer who ad-
     vocated humane and sanitary conditions for prisoners.
     Influential in convincing the House of Commons to sup-
     port penal reform in 1774.

HOWE, JULIA WARD. 1819-1910. Social reformer who support-
     ed woman suffrage, abolition and world peace. She was
     the author of the Battle Hymn of the Republic.

HOWITT, WILLIAM. 1792-1879. Liberal English writer born
     of Quaker parents.

HURLBUT, ELISHA. Author of *Essay on Human Rights and Their
     Political Guarantees* (1845) in which he defended the
     rights of women.

HUTCHINSONS. A family singing group who often included
     abolitionist songs in their repertoire.

JACKSON, HALLIDAY. A Hicksite Friend who worked among the
     Seneca Indians in Cattaraugus County, N.Y.

JONES, ELIZABETH. 1813-1896. Anti-Slavery and woman's
     rights lecturer. Co-editor of the *Anti-Slavery Bugle*.

LAY, BENJAMIN. 1677-1759. English born Quaker who lived in
the United States and was one of the earliest opponents
of slavery.

LUNDY, BENJAMIN. 1789-1839. Pioneer abolitionist of Quaker
parentage. Publisher of *The Genius of Universal Emancipation*. Supported the formation of colonies abroad for
freed slaves.

MANN, HORACE. 1796-1859. Educator, secretary of the Massachusetts state board of education and first president of
Antioch College.

MARRIOTT, CHARLES. New York City Quaker abolitionist. Disowned by Friends for allegedly promoting disunity within the Society.

MARTINEAU, HARRIET. 1802-1876. English journalist and
author. Supported the abolition of slavery.

MILL, JOHN STUART. 1806-1873. British philosopher and
economist who supported the emancipation of women and
other liberal reforms.

MITCHELL, MARIA. 1818-1889. Astronomer and discoverer of
a comet in 1847. She was the first woman to be elected
to the American Academy of Arts and Sciences.

MORGAN, LADY. Sydney née Owenson, 1883 (?)-1859. An Irish
woman of letters.

O'CONNELL, DANIEL. 1775-1847. Irish Catholic political
leader who supported the Irish fight for Catholic
emancipation.

PARKER, THEODORE. 1810-1860. Theologian and social reformer. A Unitarian who by his liberal views alienated
many Unitarians. Advocated transcendentalism and supported abolitionism and other reforms.

PEABODY, GEORGE, 1795-1869. Financier and philanthropist
whose educational fund promoted education in the
southern United States.

PENN, WILLIAM. 1644-1714. English Quaker, author and
founder of the colony of Pennsylvania.

PHILLIPS, WENDELL. 1811-1884. Reformer and orator who
advocated the abolition of slavery and woman's rights.
He broke with Garrison over the latter's desire to dissolve the American Anti-Slavery Society after the Civil
War. After throwing his support behind the fifteenth

Amendment, he worked to secure woman suffrage as well.

POTTER, ALONZO. 1800-1865. Influential in the development
of public education in Pennsylvania, but opposed to efforts to raise female teacher's salaries.

POTTER, RAY. Baptist minister in Pawtucket, R.I. Active
in organizing the R.I. anti-slavery society.

PULSKY, MADAME THERESE. The sister of Louis Kossuth, the
Hungarian Patriot. While her brother refused to visit
the Mott's during his American tour lest it ally him
with abolitionists, she did so.

PURVIS, ROBERT. 1810-1898. Negro Philadelphia abolitionist and close friend of the Motts. One of the founders
of the American Anti-slavery society and an organizer
of the Underground Railroad.

SANDIFORD, RALPH. 1693(?)-1733. Philadelphia Quaker merchant and author. A radical abolitionist who appealed
to fellow Quakers on behalf of the slave. Expelled
from Society of Friends.

SOMMERVILLE, MARY. 1780-1872. English astronomer, mathe-
matician and geographer.

SPENCER, HERBERT. 1820-1903. English philosopher and author who supported the principle of evolutionary
progress.

STANTON, ELIZABETH CADY. 1815-1902. Leader of the woman's
rights movement and long-time friend of Lucretia Mott.

STONE, LUCY. 1818-1893. A leader in the woman's rights
movement and supporter of abolition. She broke with
Stanton and Anthony to found the American Woman   Suffrage Association and in 1870 she founded the *Woman's
Journal*.

STOWE, HARRIET BEECHER. 1811-1896. Novelist and humani-
tarian. Author of *Uncle Tom's Cabin*. She supported
temperance and woman   suffrage.

THOMPSON, GEORGE. 1804-1878. Scottish born abolitionist
who travelled to the United States and worked with the
American Anti-Slavery Society.

TILTON, THEODORE. 1835-1907. Journalist and editor of
the *Independent* and later the *Golden Age*. He was a
supporter of woman   suffrage.

TUCKERMAN, JOSEPH. 1778-1840. Unitarian minister who
studied pauperism and the administration of charity.

VASSAR, MATTHEW. 1792-1862. Philanthropist and founder of
Vassar college.

WALKER, TIMOTHY. 1806-1856. Jurist and author of *Introduction to American Law*.

WALTON, JOSEPH. Quaker who worked among Seneca Indians in
New York state.

WEISS, JOHN. 1818-1879. Unitarian minister, abolitionist,
advocate of woman's rights, transcendentalist and
author of *American Religion*.

WHITE, JOSEPH BLANCO. 1775-1841. Irish-Spanish priest who
was excommunicated from the Catholic church because of
his unorthodox views on Scripture and doubts about the
Trinity and Atonement. He became an Anglican and subsequently a Unitarian. His *Autobiography* was one of
Mott's favorite books.

WILBERFORCE, WILLIAM. 1759-1833. British statesman and
member of Parliament. Influenced by evangelicalism.
Supported abolition of the slave trade.

WOLLSTONECRAFT, MARY. 1759-1797. English author and early
supporter of educational equality for women. Author of
the *Vindication of the Rights of Women*.

WOOLMAN, JOHN. 1720-1772. Quaker minister and powerful
advocate of the abolition of slavery.

WORCESTER, NOAH. 1758-1837. Congregational minister and
peace advocate.